If Taxes Were People

Abbas Sadak

If Taxes Were People
Written by Abbas Sadak

For permissions or inquiries, contact:
Abbas Sadak
Email: info@coolbehaviourfoundation.org

Published By Abbas Sadak
First Edition: August 2025

ISBN: 978-1-0683208-5-9 (Paperback)
ISBN: 978-1-0683208-6-6 (E-Book)

CONTENTS

Preface

A Taxing Mystery Awaits

If you've ever wondered where your money disappears every payday, you're not alone. Sam Harper certainly did—until the day taxes walked right into his life. Literally.

It started with a knock at the door and a briefcase-toting stranger who introduced himself as Income Tax. Before Sam could process what was happening, Sales Tax slipped in behind, grinning like he'd just found loose change in your sofa. And that was only the beginning.

In Sam's world, taxes aren't just numbers on a page—they're characters with quirks, grudges, and a knack for showing up at the worst possible moment. There's Sin Tax, who never misses a party, and Audit Tax, who can spot a suspicious receipt from a mile away. Even Loophole lurks in the shadows, promising shortcuts that are almost too good to be true.

As Sam stumbles through this bizarre landscape, he discovers that taxes are more than just a yearly headache. They're woven into every coffee, every pay cheque, every late-night impulse buy. They fund the roads he drives, the schools he passed as a kid, and the hospital that patched up his sprained ankle after a run-in with a rogue shopping cart.

This is a story about the world's oldest love-hate relationship. It's about the rules we live by the loopholes we chase, and the strange, sometimes hilarious ways we try to outsmart the system. Along the way, you'll meet a cast of unforgettable characters, learn a few secrets, and maybe—just maybe—see taxes in a new light.

So, settle in, grab your favourite snack (don't worry, we won't tax it), and join Sam on a journey through the wild, weird, and occasionally wonderful world of taxes.

Welcome to the adventure.

Abbas Sadak

PART I

The Basics of Taxation

CHAPTER 1

The Taxing Beginnings

Sam Harper had always considered himself a simple man. He liked his coffee black, his weekends quiet, and his finances... well, he didn't really think about his finances. As far as Sam was concerned, money came in, bills went out, and whatever was left was his to spend on life's essentials: pizza, streaming subscriptions, and the occasional impulse purchase of a gadget he didn't need but absolutely had to have. Life was good—or at least, it was until the day Income Tax showed up.

It started like any other Monday morning. Sam was sitting at his desk, sipping his coffee and staring at the mountain of unopened mail that had been silently judging him for weeks. He had just convinced himself that none of it was urgent when there was a loud knock at the door.

"Mr. Harper?" a voice called out, deep and authoritative, like a judge about to sentence someone to life without parole. Before Sam could answer, the door swung open, and in walked a man in a pinstripe suit, carrying a briefcase that looked like it contained the secrets of the universe—or at least a very large calculator.

"Who... who are you?" Sam stammered, clutching his coffee like it was a life preserver.

The man adjusted his tie and gave Sam a look that could curdle milk. "I'm Income Tax," he said, as if that explained everything. "And we need to talk."

Sam blinked. "Income Tax? Like... the tax? You're a person?"

Income Tax sighed, the kind of sigh that suggested he had been asked this question far too many times. "Yes, I'm a person. Do you think taxes just collect themselves? Someone has to do the dirty work, and that someone is me."

Sam stared at him, trying to process what was happening. "Okay, but why are you here? I mean, I already pay my taxes. I think. Don't I?"

Income Tax opened his briefcase and pulled out a stack of papers that looked like they had been printed in the 1800s. "Let's see," he said, flipping through the pages. "Ah, yes. You filed your taxes last year, but there's a slight issue. It seems you forgot to report your freelance income from that... what was it? Dog-sitting app?"

Sam's face turned red. "That was one weekend! And the dog ate my shoes!"

Income Tax raised an eyebrow. "Be that as it may, you earned income, and I'm here to collect my share. You know the saying: nothing is certain except death and me."

Sam groaned. "I thought it was death and taxes."

"Same thing," Income Tax said with a smirk. "Now, let's talk deductions. Did you really claim your Netflix subscription as a 'business expense'?"

Sam fidgeted. "I was... researching documentaries?"

Income Tax didn't even blink. "And the pizza delivery?"

"Fuel for the research."

Income Tax scribbled something on his notepad. "Right. We'll be revisiting that during the audit."

Just as Sam was about to argue, there was another knock at the door. This one was lighter, almost cheerful, like the person on the other side was trying to sell him cookies. Before Sam could say anything, the door opened, and in walked a wiry man in a bright yellow suit, jingling a pocketful of coins.

"Hey there!" the man said, grinning like he'd just won the lottery. "I'm Sales Tax, and I couldn't help but overhear that you're having a little chat with my buddy here."

"Your buddy?" Sam asked, looking from Income Tax to Sales Tax and back again.

"Oh, we go way back," Sales Tax said, slapping Income Tax on the back. "He takes your income; I take your spending. It's a beautiful partnership."

Sam groaned. "You've got to be kidding me."

"Not at all!" Sales Tax said, pulling a receipt out of his pocket. "Let's see… last week, you bought a coffee, a bagel, and a pack of gum. That's, what, a few Pennies for me? It adds up, you know."

Sam buried his face in his hands. "Why are you both here? Can't you just… take your money and leave me alone?"

Income Tax and Sales Tax exchanged a look, then burst out laughing.

"Oh, Sam," Income Tax said, wiping a tear from his eye. "We're not here to take your money. We're here to make sure you understand how much we've already taken."

"And to remind you," Sales Tax added, "that we're not going anywhere. Ever."

As the two taxes bickered over who was more important, Sam felt his sanity slipping away. He tried to tune them out, but their voices grew louder and louder, like a pair of auctioneers fighting over a microphone.

"Without me, the government wouldn't have any money!" Income Tax declared.

"Oh, please," Sales Tax shot back. "You're just a once-a-year headache. I'm the one who's there every day, making sure people pay their fair share."

"Fair share? You tax gum!"

"And you tax dog-sitting!"

Sam finally snapped. "Enough! Both of you, out of my office!"

The room fell silent. Income Tax and Sales Tax stared at him, then at each other, then back at him.

"Out?" Income Tax said, his voice dripping with disbelief. "You can't just kick us out. We're taxes. We're inevitable."

"Yeah," Sales Tax said, crossing his arms. "We're like gravity. Or bad Wi-Fi. You can't escape us."

Sam groaned. "Fine. Just... can you at least explain what you want from me?"

Income Tax smiled. "Oh, we'll explain. But first, you might want to clear your schedule. Things are about to get... complicated."

And with that, the door burst open again, and in walked a third figure, wearing a trench coat and carrying a magnifying glass.

"Sam Harper?" the figure said, his voice low and menacing. "I'm Audit Tax, and I think we need to have a little chat."

Sam's coffee cup slipped from his hand and shattered on the floor. This was going to be a long day.

CHAPTER 2

The Audit Awakening

Sam Harper had always thought of audits as something that happened to other people—like getting struck by lightning or being asked to explain the plot of a Christopher Nolan movie. But now, as Audit Tax loomed over him with a clipboard the size of a small child, Sam realized that his time had come. And it wasn't going to be pretty.

Audit Tax was not a man to be trifled with. His trench coat billowed dramatically, even though there was no wind in the room, and his glasses glinted with the kind of cold, calculating precision that suggested he could spot a misplaced decimal from a mile away. He didn't just walk into Sam's office, he invaded it, like a storm cloud rolling in to ruin a perfectly sunny day.

"Sam Harper," Audit Tax said, his voice low and gravelly, as if he moonlighted as the narrator of true crime documentaries. "We need to talk."

"Uh... talk about what?" Sam said.

Audit Tax smirked, pulling out a magnifying glass and inspecting the coffee mug in Sam's hand. "Oh, I don't know. Maybe about the fact that you claimed this coffee as a 'business expense.'"

Sam blinked. "I... I work from home! Coffee is essential for productivity!"

Audit Tax raised an eyebrow. "Productivity? Or procrastination? Because according to your internet history, you spent three hours last Tuesday watching videos of raccoons stealing garbage".

Sam's face turned red. "That was... research."

"Research?" Audit Tax flipped open his clipboard, revealing a page covered in red ink and sticky notes. "Let's see. You also claimed a gaming chair, a subscription to a streaming service, and—oh, this is my favorite—a £50 charge for 'client entertainment' at a taco truck."

Sam perked up. "That was legitimate! I was networking!"

Audit Tax's pen hovered over the clipboard. "The client's name is listed as 'Dave.'"

"Yeah, Dave! He's, my barber. We were discussing his plans to expand his business."

Audit Tax stared at him, unblinking. "And did Dave hire you?"

Sam hesitated. "Not exactly. But he did give me a free haircut."

Audit Tax sighed, the kind of sigh that suggested he had seen the worst of humanity and was no longer surprised by it. "Mr. Harper, do you know what happens to people who try to cheat the system?"

Sam's stomach dropped. "They... get fined?"

Audit Tax leaned in close, his voice barely above a whisper. "Worse. They get audited. Again."

Audit Tax didn't just ask questions—he interrogated. Every receipt, every deduction, every questionable expense was scrutinized with the intensity of a detective solving a murder case. Sam felt like a criminal on trial, except his crimes were things like buying too many tacos and claiming his cat as a "security expense."

"Let's talk about this," Audit Tax said, pointing to a line item on his clipboard. "You claimed £200 for 'office supplies.' Care to elaborate?"

Sam scratched his head. "Uh... pens? Paper? Maybe a stapler?"

Audit Tax raised an eyebrow. "Really? Because according to your bank statement, that £200 was spent at a store called 'Gamer's Paradise.'"

Sam winced. "Okay, fine. It was a gaming chair. But in my defense, I do a lot of sitting while I work!"

Audit Tax scribbled something on his clipboard. "Noted. And what about this £75 for 'professional development'? It says here you spent it on a subscription to a streaming service."

Sam brightened. "That was totally legit! I was watching documentaries to expand my knowledge."

Audit Tax flipped through his notes. "Documentaries? Or an entire season of The Great British Bake Off?"

Sam fidgeted. "It's... inspiring?"

Audit Tax didn't even blink. "And the pizza delivery? Was that also 'professional development'?"

Sam threw up his hands. "I was hungry! Is that a crime?"

Audit Tax scribbled furiously on his clipboard. "Not a crime. But it's definitely going in the report."

Just as Sam was about to collapse under the weight of his own guilt, the door to his office creaked open. A man in a flashy suit and sunglasses strolled in, exuding the kind of confidence that only comes from being completely untrustworthy.

"Sam Harper!" the man said, grinning like a used car salesman. "You look like a man in need of a little... assistance."

Audit Tax groaned. "Oh, great. It's you."

Sam looked from Audit Tax to Loophole, thoroughly confused. "Who... who is this guy?"

Audit Tax pinched the bridge of his nose. "He's a troublemaker, that's who. Always popping up when people are desperate, offering 'solutions' that are more trouble than they're worth."

"Hey, hey, hey," Loophole said, holding up his hands. "I'm just here to help. You know, find a few creative ways to save our friend Sam some money. Maybe a little offshore account here, a little 'business expense' there. Nothing illegal. Just... flexible."

Sam's eyes lit up. "Flexible sounds good. I like flexible."

Audit Tax slammed his clipboard onto the desk. "Don't listen to him, Sam. Loophole is nothing but trouble. Sure, he might save you a few bucks in the short term, but in the long run? He'll cost you everything."

Loophole smirked. "Oh, come on, Audit. Don't be so dramatic. I'm just giving the people what they want—freedom from the tyranny of taxes!"

Audit Tax glared at him. "Freedom? Is that what you call it? Because I call it fraud."

Sam raised his hand. "Uh, quick question. If I were to, hypothetically, work with Loophole... would that mean no more audits?"

Audit Tax's eyes widened in horror. "Absolutely not! In fact, it would mean more audits. Bigger audits. The kind of audits that make grown men cry."

Loophole shrugged. "Or, you know, it could mean no audits at all. Depends on how good you are at shredding documents."

Audit Tax pointed a finger at Loophole. "You're a menace."

"And you're a buzzkill," Loophole shot back.

As the two men bickered, Sam sank into his chair, his head spinning. On the one hand, Audit Tax was terrifying, but at least he was honest. On the other hand, Loophole was offering a way out, albeit a shady, probably illegal way out.

"Okay, okay, enough!" Sam said, holding up his hands. "I can't deal with both of you at once. Can we just... I don't know, take a break?"

Audit Tax crossed his arms. "There are no breaks in auditing."

Loophole grinned. "But there are loopholes."

Sam groaned. "I hate both of you."

Audit Tax adjusted his glasses. "Get used to it, Mr. Harper. Because this is just the beginning."

And with that, he flipped to the next page of his clipboard, ready to dive even deeper into Sam's financial chaos. Meanwhile, Loophole leaned against the wall, casually flipping a coin and waiting for his moment to strike.

Sam sighed. It was going to be a long, long audit.

Chapter 3

The Price of Pleasure and Prestige

It was Friday morning and Sam had barely survived the relentless grilling from Audit Tax and the dubious charm of Loophole all week, when his office door creaked open again. He froze mid-sip of his cup of coffee, his nerves frayed to the point where even the sound of a door hinge felt like a threat.

"Please," he muttered to no one in particular, "just let it be the pizza delivery guy. Or a Girl Scout selling cookies. Or literally anyone who doesn't want to talk about my finances."

But, of course, the universe had other plans.

A tall, elegant figure sauntered into the room, wearing a crimson suit so sharp it could cut glass. She carried a cigarette holder in one hand (though the cigarette was unlit—she wasn't a monster) and a martini glass in the other. Her heels clicked against the floor with the confidence of someone who knew they were about to ruin your day and look fabulous doing it.

"Sam Harper," she purred, her voice dripping with sophistication and just a hint of menace. "We meet at last."

Sam blinked. "Uh… who are you?"

She smirked, taking a slow sip from her martini glass. "I'm Sin Tax, darling. And I'm here to talk about your… indulgences."

Sam frowned. "My indulgences? What does that even mean?"

Sin Tax raised an eyebrow, as if the answer was painfully obvious. "Oh, you know. Your little vices. Your guilty pleasures. The things you do when you think no one's watching but your bank account definitely is."

Sam's confusion deepened. "I don't have vices."

Sin Tax let out a laugh so rich and throaty it could have been bottled and sold as a luxury perfume. "Oh, sweetie. Everyone has vices. Let's see..." She reached into her designer handbag and pulled out a clipboard (because apparently, everyone in the tax world carried one). "Ah, here we are. Last month, you spent £120 on craft beer, £50 on chocolate, and—oh, this is my favourite—£75 on a karaoke night where you sang Bohemian Rhapsody six times in a row."

Sam's face turned beet red. "That was... a team-building exercise."

"Team building?" Sin Tax smirked. "Darling, the only thing you were building that night was a hangover."

Sam groaned. "Okay, fine. Maybe I have a few... habits. But why do you care?"

Sin Tax leaned in close, her perfume intoxicating and slightly overwhelming. "Because, darling, I'm the one who makes sure your bad decisions come with a price tag. Every beer you drink, every cigarette you don't smoke but think about smoking, every sugary treat you can't resist—it's my job to make sure you pay for it. Governments love me because I bring in revenue and make them look like they care about public health."

Sam stared at her, horrified. "So, you're like... a fun tax?"

"Exactly," she said, raising her martini glass in a mock toast. "I'm the price of fun."

Before Sam could respond, the door creaked open again, and in walked a man who could only be described as obnoxiously fabulous. He was tall, with perfectly coiffed hair, a tailored suit that screamed "custom-made," and a silk scarf draped around his neck like he was auditioning for a role in a 1920s murder mystery. He carried a clipboard in one hand and a glass of champagne in the other, because of course he did.

"Ah, Mr. Harper," the man said, his voice dripping with condescension. "I've heard so much about you. I'm Luxury Tax, and I must say, I'm appalled."

Luxury Tax wrinkled his nose, as if the very act of breathing the same air as Sam was offensive. "At your lifestyle, darling. It's so... pedestrian."

Sam frowned. "What's wrong with my lifestyle? I think it's pretty normal."

Luxury Tax let out a dramatic sigh, the kind that suggested he had been personally victimized by Sam's existence. "Normal? Oh, sweetie, there's nothing normal about spending £15 on a bottle of wine and calling it a 'splurge.' Where's the decadence? The extravagance? The luxury?"

Sam crossed his arms. "I don't need luxury. I'm perfectly happy with my budget-friendly lifestyle."

Luxury Tax gasped, clutching his chest as if Sam had just insulted his mother. "Budget-friendly? Darling, that's a phrase for peasants. Don't you understand? I'm here to ensure that when you do indulge in the finer things, you pay for the privilege."

Sam raised an eyebrow. "You mean, like a tax?"

"Exactly!" Luxury Tax said, swirling his champagne glass. "You see, I'm the one who makes sure that when you buy a yacht, a diamond-encrusted watch, or even a slightly overpriced handbag, you contribute to society. After all, if you can afford luxury, you can afford me."

Sam snorted. "Well, I don't have a yacht or a diamond-encrusted anything, so I guess you're out of luck."

Luxury Tax smirked, pulling out his clipboard. "Oh, really? Let's take a look, shall we? Last month, you bought a pair of noise-cancelling headphones. Luxury. You also spent £200 on a weekend getaway. Luxury. And—oh, this is my favourite—you paid extra for guacamole at a burrito place. Luxury."

Sam threw up his hands. “Guacamole is not a luxury! It’s a necessity!”

Luxury Tax raised an eyebrow. “Is it, though? Because according to my calculations, you’ve spent more on guacamole this year than on your car insurance.”

Sam opened his mouth to argue, then closed it again. He couldn’t deny it. The man had a point.

As Sin Tax and Luxury Tax began bickering over who had the bigger claim on Sam’s wallet, he sank deeper into his chair, wondering if it was possible to die from second hand embarrassment.

“Without me, the government wouldn’t have any money!” Sin Tax declared.

“Oh, please,” Luxury Tax shot back. “You’re just a guilt trip in a fancy dress. I’m the one who taxes the real indulgences—yachts, private jets, designer handbags. You’re just here to ruin dessert.”

“Ruin dessert?” Sin Tax gasped. “I’m the one who keeps people from drinking themselves into oblivion. You’re just a glorified status symbol.”

Sam finally snapped. “Enough! Both of you, out of my office!”

The room fell silent. Sin Tax and Luxury Tax stared at him, then at each other, then back at him.

“Out?” Sin Tax said, her voice dripping with disbelief. “You can’t just kick us out. We’re taxes. We’re inevitable.”

“Yeah,” Luxury Tax added, crossing his arms. “We’re like gravity. Or the endless queue at the DMV. You can’t escape us.”

Sam groaned. “Fine. Just... can you at least explain what you want from me?”

Sin Tax smiled. “Oh, we’ll explain. But first, you might want to clear your schedule. Things are about to get... indulgent.”

Chapter 4

Inheritance Tax – The Grim Collector

It was Monday morning and Sam Harper was starting to think his office door was cursed. Every time it creaked open, it brought with it another tax character determined to make his life more complicated. He stared at the tall, imposing figure who had just entered, their black suit so sharp it could probably cut through steel. They carried a clipboard shaped like a gravestone and a box of tissues under one arm.

"Sam Harper," the figure intoned, their voice low and ominous, like they moonlighted as the narrator for ghost stories. "We meet at last."

Sam blinked. "Uh... who are you? And why do you look like you just crawled out of a Charles Dickens novel?"

The figure smirked, revealing teeth that were just a little too sharp. "I am Inheritance Tax, the Grim Collector. And I'm here to discuss what happens when you die."

Sam groaned, slumping in his chair. "Oh, brilliant. Death taxes. Just what I needed. Let me guess—you're here to make sure I can't even rest in peace?"

Inheritance Tax chuckled darkly. "Rest in peace? Oh, Sam, there's no peace when I'm involved. I'm the tax that ensures even your final goodbye comes with a bill."

Inheritance Tax stepped forward, their shoes making no sound on the floor, and placed their gravestone-shaped clipboard on Sam's desk with a dramatic thud. "That's right, Sam. Even in death, you cannot escape me. I am the tax that comes for your wealth when you're no longer around to protect it."

Sam frowned. "Wait, so you're telling me that after I die, the government still gets a cut of my money? Isn't that a little... I don't know... rude?"

Inheritance Tax raised an eyebrow. "Rude? Oh, Sam, it's not rude—it's inevitable. You see, when you pass on your assets to your heirs, the government steps in to take its share. It's my job to ensure that your wealth doesn't just sit there, gathering dust. After all, why should your kids get everything for free?"

Sam raised an eyebrow. "Because it's my money? I worked for it. Shouldn't I get to decide what happens to it?"

Inheritance Tax shrugged. "Oh, you can decide. But I'll still be there, waiting. Like a vulture circling a particularly juicy carcass."

Sam shuddered. "That's... comforting."

Inheritance Tax pulled out a flowchart that looked like it had been designed by a particularly morbid accountant. "Let me break it down for you, Sam. In the UK, when you die, your estate—everything you own, from your house to your savings to that collection of novelty mugs you think no one knows about—gets valued."

Sam blinked. "Wait, how do you know about my novelty mugs?"

Inheritance Tax smirked. "I know everything, Sam. Now, if the total value of your estate exceeds £325,000, your heirs have to pay 40% tax on the amount above that threshold."

Sam's jaw dropped. "Forty percent? Are you serious? That's almost half!"

Inheritance Tax nodded solemnly. "Indeed. It's one of the highest inheritance tax rates in the world. But don't worry—there are ways to reduce it. For example, if you leave your estate to your spouse or civil partner, they won't have to pay any inheritance tax."

Sam frowned. "So basically, if I die and leave everything to my wife, she's fine. But if I leave it to my kids, they're screwed?"

"Precisely," Inheritance Tax said, grinning. "Unless, of course, you leave it to charity. Then it's tax-free."

Sam snorted. "Oh, great. So, my options are: give it to my wife, give it to charity, or let the government take a chunk of it. What a choice."

Inheritance Tax shrugged. "It's not all bad. If you leave at least 10% of your estate to charity, the inheritance tax rate drops to 36%."

Sam groaned. "Oh, fantastic. A discount for being generous. How thoughtful."

Sam leaned back in his chair, rubbing his temples. "Okay, but why does this tax even exist? Isn't it bad enough that I have to pay taxes while I'm alive? Why do I have to pay them when I'm dead, too?"

Inheritance Tax sighed, as if they'd heard this question a thousand times before. "Sam, it's not about punishing you for dying. It's about fairness. The idea is that large inheritances create inequality. By taxing them, the government can redistribute wealth and fund public services."

Sam snorted. "Redistribute wealth? More like rob my kids blind."

Inheritance Tax smirked. "Oh, come on, Sam. Do you really think your kids need all that money? What are they going to do with it? Buy a yacht? Start a tech company? Blow it all on avocado toast?"

Sam glared at them. "That's not the point. The point is, it's my money. I should get to decide what happens to it."

"And you can," Inheritance Tax said, holding up a finger. "But if you want to avoid me, you'll need to get creative. Trusts, gifts, charitable donations—there are ways to reduce your tax liability. But be warned: if you try to cheat the system, you'll have to deal with my cousin, Audit Tax."

Sam groaned. "Of course I will."

Before Sam could respond, the door burst open, and a new figure stormed in. They were dressed in a tracksuit, carrying a baseball bat, and had the kind of energy that screamed, *I'm here to cause problems.*

"Oi!" the newcomer shouted. "What's all this about taking my inheritance?"

Inheritance Tax sighed, pinching the bridge of their nose. "Ah, yes. This is Angry Heir, one of my... frequent visitors."

Angry Heir slammed the baseball bat onto Sam's desk, making the papers jump. "You're telling me that after all the years I spent putting up with my dad's terrible jokes and his obsession with model trains, I'm not even going to get the full inheritance? What kind of scam is this?"

Sam blinked. "Who... who are you?"

Angry Heir pointed a finger at Inheritance Tax. "I'm the one who has to deal with this guy every time someone in my family kicks the bucket. And let me tell you, it's a nightmare. Forty percent? Are you kidding me? That's highway robbery!"

Inheritance Tax gave a small shrug. "It's the law."

Angry Heir groaned, throwing their hands in the air. "The law? The law is a joke! My dad worked his whole life to build up that estate, and now you're just going to take a chunk of it? For what? Potholes?"

Sam leaned back in his chair, watching the chaos unfold. "I mean, they do have a point."

Inheritance Tax sighed. "Look, I don't make the rules. I just enforce them. And besides, it's not all bad. There are exemptions, reliefs, and loopholes—"

Loophole plopped down onto Sam's desk, kicking his feet up and grinning like he owned the place. "Alright, folks, let's talk strategy. Inheritance Tax here might seem scary, but trust me, there are ways around them. Trusts, gifts, offshore accounts—you name it, I've got it."

Inheritance Tax glared at Loophole. "You're not supposed to be here."

Loophole smirked. "Oh, come on. You know you love me. Without me, people would actually have to pay you."

Sam raised an eyebrow. "Wait, are you saying I can avoid Inheritance Tax?"

Loophole grinned. "Avoid? No, no, no. Mitigate. It's all perfectly legal… mostly."

Inheritance Tax groaned. "Loophole, you're the reason my job is so difficult."

Loophole shrugged. "And you're the reason I have a job. It's a symbiotic relationship, my friend."

As the argument between Inheritance Tax and Loophole escalated, Angry Heir started pacing the room, muttering about "government conspiracies" and "starting a revolution." Sam, meanwhile, sat back and watched the chaos unfold, sipping his now-cold coffee.

Finally, Inheritance Tax stood up, straightened his tie, and said, "Look, Sam, I know this is a lot to take in. But at the end of the day, I'm just here to ensure fairness."

Sam snorted. "Fairness? You're taxing people for dying."

Inheritance Tax gave him a pitying look. "It's not about death, Sam. It's about… redistribution."

Loophole smirked. "And I'm here to redistribute it back."

Angry Heir slammed their baseball bat onto the desk again. "And I'm here to make sure I get what's mine!"

Sam groaned, burying his face in his hands. "I should've just become a monk. At least then I wouldn't have to deal with this nonsense."

By the end of the meeting, Sam was thoroughly drained. Inheritance Tax handed him a pamphlet titled *"Planning Your Estate: How to Die Without Losing Everything,"* and left with a mournful sigh. Angry Heir stormed out, muttering about "starting a GoFundMe," and Loophole winked at Sam before disappearing into the shadows.

As the door closed, Sam leaned back in his chair and muttered, "I should've just stayed in bed. At least then I wouldn't have to deal with this circus."

Little did he know, his next visitor would make Inheritance Tax look downright cheerful.

Chapter 5

Bracket Creep and the Taxing Raise

Not long after his run in with Inheritance Tax, Sam's fortunes seemed to turn. But with every silver lining, there was a tax-shaped cloud...

Sam Harper had always thought a raise was supposed to be a good thing. You work hard, you get rewarded, and maybe—just maybe—you can finally afford to buy the good coffee instead of the stuff that tastes like it was filtered through a gym sock. But as he sat in his office, staring at his latest paycheck, he realized that his raise had come with an unexpected guest: Bracket Creep.

"Congratulations, Sam Harper!" he bellowed, his voice echoing off the walls. "You've officially entered a higher tax bracket! Welcome to the big leagues!"

Sam groaned, already regretting every decision that had led him to this moment. "Who the hell are you?"

Sam frowned. "What do you mean, higher tax bracket!? I worked hard for that raise!"

Bracket Creep laughed, a high-pitched cackle that made Sam want to throw his stapler at him. "Oh, I'm sure you did, buddy. But here's the thing: when you make more money, you pay more taxes. And when you pay more taxes, you get to meet me!

I'm the guy who sneaks into your paycheck and makes sure you don't actually feel richer."

Sam stared at him, horrified. "So you're telling me that the more I earn, the less I get to keep?"

"Exactly!" Bracket Creep said, clapping his hands like a game show host revealing a grand prize. "It's called progressive taxation, my friend. The government takes a bigger slice of the pie as your income grows. And let me tell you, they love pie."

Sam groaned. "This is ridiculous. I thought a raise was supposed to help me get ahead, not drag me down."

Bracket Creep smirked, pulling out his calculator and punching in some numbers. "Oh, don't worry, Sam. You're still ahead. Just... not by much. See, your raise bumped you into a higher tax bracket, which means a bigger chunk of your income goes to taxes. But hey, at least you're contributing to society, right?"

Sam glared at him. "Contributing? I'm barely surviving! How am I supposed to pay my bills when you're taking all my money?"

Bracket Creep shrugged. "Not my problem, buddy. I'm just here to make sure the system works. And by 'works,' I mean 'confuses the hell out of everyone.'"

Before Sam could respond, the door creaked open again, and in walked a man wearing a powdered wig and a colonial-era coat. He carried a quill in one hand and a scroll in the other, looking like he had just stepped, out of a history book.

"Ah, Mr. Harper," the man said, his voice dripping with old-world charm. "Allow me to introduce myself. I'm Historical Taxation, here to provide some much-needed context."

Sam blinked. "Context? For what?"

"For your suffering, of course," Historical Taxation said, unfurling his scroll with a dramatic flourish. "You see, taxation has been a thorn in humanity's side for centuries. From the Roman Empire to the Boston Tea Party, people have always hated paying taxes. But here's the kicker: they've always been necessary."

Sam groaned. "Great. Another lecture. Just what I needed."

Historical Taxation ignored him, launching into his speech with the enthusiasm of a history professor who had just discovered a captive audience. "Did you know, Mr. Harper, that in ancient Egypt, citizens were taxed on everything from their crops to their cooking oil? And if they couldn't pay, they were forced to work on the pharaoh's construction projects. Imagine being taxed into building a pyramid!"

Sam raised an eyebrow. "That sounds awful."

"Oh, it gets better," Historical Taxation said, grinning. "In medieval England, there was a tax called the 'window tax.' The more windows your house had, the more you paid. People actually bricked up their windows to avoid it. Can you imagine living in the dark just to save a few coins?"

Sam sighed. "Honestly? That doesn't sound much worse than what I'm dealing with now."

Bracket Creep snorted. "Oh, come on, Sam. At least you don't have to pay a beard tax."

Sam frowned. "A what?"

Historical Taxation nodded solemnly. "Yes, the beard tax. Introduced by Peter the Great in 17th-century Russia. If you wanted to keep your beard, you had to pay a fee. If you couldn't pay, they'd shave it off for you."

Sam stared at him, horrified. "That's insane."

"Indeed," Historical Taxation said, rolling up his scroll. "But it just goes to show that taxation has always been a creative endeavor. And you, Mr. Harper, are simply the latest victim of its ingenuity."

Sam turned back to Bracket Creep, his frustration boiling over. "So what am I supposed to do? Just accept that my raise is basically worthless?"

Bracket Creep grinned. "Oh, it's not worthless, Sam. It's just... less. But hey, look on the bright side: you're helping fund schools, roads, and hospitals. Doesn't that make you feel warm and fuzzy inside?"

Sam glared at him. "No. It makes me feel broke."

Bracket Creep shrugged. "Well, that's the beauty of the system, buddy. You can't escape me. No one can. I'm like gravity—inevitable and completely unfair."

Sam buried his face in his hands. "This is a nightmare."

Historical Taxation patted him on the shoulder. "Cheer up, Mr. Harper. At least you don't live in ancient Rome. Back then, they had a tax on urine."

Sam looked up, his face a mix of confusion and disgust. "Urine? Seriously?"

"Oh, yes," Historical Taxation said, nodding enthusiastically. "Urine was used for tanning leather and laundering clothes, so it was considered a valuable resource. The government taxed it to make a profit. Imagine being charged for your own bodily functions!"

Bracket Creep burst out laughing. "Now that's a tax I'd love to enforce."

Sam groaned. "I hate both of you."

As Bracket Creep and Historical Taxation continued to bicker about the merits of ancient taxes versus modern ones, Sam couldn't help but wonder what fresh hell awaited him next. He had already met Income Tax, Audit Tax, Sin Tax, Luxury Tax, Inheritance Tax and now Bracket Creep. How many more taxes could there possibly be?

But deep down, he knew the answer. There were always more taxes. And if the whispers he'd heard were true, the worst was yet to come. Somewhere out there, lurking in the shadows, was a figure known only as Tax Reform—a mysterious entity that promised to simplify the system but always seemed to make things worse.

Sam shuddered at the thought. If these taxes were this bad, he could only imagine what Tax Reform would be like.

CHAPTER 6

Capital Gains and Wealth Taxes - The Price of Success

Friday morning and Sam was checking the progress of his stocks while the stock market ticker scrolled across Sam's television, a parade of green and red numbers. He watched, bemused, as his modest investments danced up and down. Just as he was about to celebrate a rare gain, his phone buzzed with a notification: "Congratulations! You owe capital gains tax." Sam stared at the screen, realising that in the world of finance, every win comes with a price-tag—and a new tax friend eager to collect. He was mid-sip of his coffee—his last remaining comfort in this tax-infested nightmare—when the door to his office slammed open yet again. Sam didn't even flinch this time. He just sighed, set his mug down, and muttered, "Let me guess. Another tax?"

A tall, smug-looking man in a tailored suit strolled in, carrying a briefcase that looked more expensive than Sam's entire wardrobe. His hair was slicked back, his shoes were so shiny they could double as mirrors, and his smile was the kind of smile that made you want to punch him on principle.

"Ah, Mr. Harper," the man said, his voice oozing with condescension. "I'm Capital Gains Tax, and I'm here to talk about your... investments."

Sam groaned. "Of course you are."

Capital Gains Tax placed his briefcase on Sam's desk and opened it with a dramatic flourish, revealing a stack of papers so thick it could probably be used as a weapon. "Now, let's get down to business, shall we? I understand you've recently sold some assets."

Sam frowned. "Assets? What assets? I don't even own a house."

Capital Gains Tax smirked, pulling out a sheet of paper. "Oh, I'm not talking about real estate, Mr. Harper. I'm talking about your stocks. According to my records, you sold some shares last month and made a tidy little profit."

Sam blinked. "You mean the £200 I made from selling my one share of that tech company? That's what you're here for?"

"Precisely," Capital Gains Tax said, adjusting his tie. "You see, whenever you sell an asset for more than you paid for it, I'm entitled to a percentage of the profit. It's only fair."

Sam stared at him, incredulous. "Fair? I made £200! That's barely enough to cover my grocery bill for the week!"

Capital Gains Tax shrugged. "Ah, but profit is profit, Mr. Harper. Whether it's £200 or £2 million, I'm here to take my share. After all, the government needs its cut."

Sam groaned. "Of course it does. Let me guess—you're going to tell me this is for the greater good?"

"Exactly!" Capital Gains Tax said, beaming. "Your contributions help fund public services, infrastructure, and—"

"Yeah, yeah, I've heard this speech before," Sam interrupted. "Let me ask you something: if I lost money on my investments, would the government give me a refund?"

Capital Gains Tax's smile faltered. "Well... no. But that's not the point."

Sam threw up his hands. "Of course it's not. Why would it be? This whole system is rigged!"

Before Capital Gains Tax could respond, the door creaked open again, and in walked a woman who radiated pure disdain. She was dressed in a designer pantsuit, her hair was perfectly styled, and she carried a clipboard that looked like it had been dipped in gold.

"Ugh," she said, wrinkling her nose as she looked around the office. "What is this place? A storage closet?"

Sam glared at her. "It's my office."

She raised an eyebrow. "Well, it's depressing. I'm Wealth Tax, by the way. And I'm here to talk about your... assets."

Sam groaned. "I don't have any assets! I just told this guy—" He gestured to Capital Gains Tax, who was now polishing his briefcase. "—that I don't even own a house!"

Wealth Tax smirked. "Oh, I know. That's why I'm here. You see, I'm not interested in what you have. I'm interested in what you don't have."

Sam frowned. "What does that even mean?"

"It means," Wealth Tax said, leaning in close, "that if you ever do manage to accumulate any significant wealth, I'll be there to make sure you don't get too comfortable with it."

Sam stared at her, horrified. "So you're like a pre-emptive tax? A tax on potential?"

"Exactly," she said, smiling sweetly. "Think of me as a reminder that no matter how much you earn, you'll never truly be rich. Not as long as I'm around."

Sam buried his face in his hands. "This is a nightmare."

As Capital Gains Tax and Wealth Tax began bickering over who had the bigger claim on Sam's hypothetical fortune, he felt his sanity slipping away.

"Without me, the government wouldn't have any money!" Capital Gains Tax declared.

"Oh, please," Wealth Tax shot back. "You're just a glorified toll booth for stock traders. I'm the one who ensures the rich don't hoard all their wealth."

"Hoard?" Capital Gains Tax scoffed. "I'm the one who keeps the economy moving! Without me, people would just sit on their assets forever."

Sam finally snapped. "Enough! Both of you, out of my office!"

The room fell silent. Capital Gains Tax and Wealth Tax stared at him, then at each other, then back at him.

"Well," Wealth Tax said, adjusting her clipboard, "if that's how you feel, you might want to brace yourself."

Sam frowned. "Brace myself for what?"

As if on cue, the door creaked open again, and a new figure stepped into the room—a tall, shadowy figure wearing a hooded cloak. The room seemed to grow colder as they entered, and Sam felt a chill run down his spine.

"Sam Harper," the figure said, their voice low and menacing. "I'm Tax Reform, and I'm here to... simplify things."

Sam's coffee mug slipped from his hand and shattered on the floor. This was going to be a very, very long day.

PART II
Advanced Tax Concepts

CHAPTER 7

Tax Reform – The Simplification That Wasn't

Sam Harper had officially given up on the idea of peace. His office, once a quiet sanctuary where he could sip coffee and pretend to be productive, had turned into a revolving door for the most bizarre and infuriating characters imaginable. And now, to start another crazy week, standing in the doorway, cloaked in shadow and radiating an aura of bureaucratic menace, was the one figure he had hoped he'd never meet: Tax Reform.

"Sam Harper," the figure intoned, their voice low and gravelly, like a movie trailer narrator who had taken up a side gig in tax policy. "I am Tax Reform, and I'm here to... simplify your life."

Sam blinked. "Simplify? You? Are you serious?"

Tax Reform nodded solemnly. "Indeed. I am the harbinger of clarity, the destroyer of confusion, the—"

"Yeah, yeah," Sam interrupted, waving a hand. "Cut the dramatic intro. I've met enough of you tax people to know that 'simplify' probably means 'make everything ten times worse.'"

Tax Reform chuckled, a deep, unsettling sound that made Sam's skin crawl. "Oh, Mr. Harper. You wound me. I'm not here to make things worse. I'm here to fix the system."

Sam raised an eyebrow. "Fix it? You mean the same system that's been driving me insane for the past week? The one that's so complicated I need a PhD just to file my taxes?"

"Exactly," Tax Reform said, stepping closer. "I'm here to streamline, consolidate, and modernize. To take the chaos of the current tax code and turn it into something... beautiful."

Sam snorted. "Beautiful? It's taxes, not a sunset."

Before Tax Reform could respond, the door to Sam's office burst open (again), and in marched Income Tax, Sales Tax, and Bracket Creep, all looking thoroughly annoyed.

"Whoa, whoa, whoa," Income Tax said, pointing an accusatory finger at Tax Reform. "What the hell are you doing here?"

Tax Reform turned to face them, their voice calm but firm. "I'm here to simplify the system."

Sales Tax scoffed. "Simplify? You mean eliminate. Don't think we don't know what you're up to."

Sam frowned. "Wait, eliminate? Is that true?"

Tax Reform shrugged. "Not eliminate, per se. Just... consolidate. For example, why have separate taxes for income, sales, and property when you could have one unified tax that covers everything?"

Income Tax's face turned red. "Unified? Are you kidding me? That's my job you're talking about!"

Bracket Creep crossed his arms. "Yeah, and what about me? If you simplify the system, I'm out of a job! Who's going to sneak people into higher tax brackets if everything's straightforward?"

Sam raised a hand. "I mean, I wouldn't mind if you were out of a job."

Bracket Creep glared at him. "Rude."

Tax Reform ignored the protests and turned back to Sam. "You see, Mr. Harper, the current system is bloated and inefficient. It's full of loopholes, redundancies, and unnecessary complexities. My goal is to create a single, streamlined tax that's easy to understand and fair for everyone."

Sam tilted his head. "Fair? You're talking about taxes, right? The same taxes that make me pay extra for guacamole and punish me for getting a raise?"

"Exactly," Tax Reform said, nodding. "Under my system, there would be no more guacamole taxes, no more bracket creep, and no more confusing deductions. Just one simple tax rate for everyone."

Income Tax snorted. "Oh, please. You think people are going to like that? They hate me, but at least I'm predictable. You? You're a wildcard."

Sales Tax nodded. "Yeah, and what happens to all the little guys like me? You think people are going to be happy when they realize their morning coffee is taxed at the same rate as their paycheck?"

Sam frowned. "Wait, is that true? Would my coffee be taxed the same as my income?"

Tax Reform hesitated. "Well... yes. But think of the simplicity!"

Sam groaned. "Simplicity? That's not simplicity. That's insanity! I'd be paying the same tax rate on a £5 latte as I would on a £5,000 bonus!"

Tax Reform shrugged. "It's all about fairness, Mr. Harper. Everyone pays the same rate, no matter what."

Before the argument could escalate further, the door creaked open, and in walked Historical Taxation, still wearing his powdered wig and looking thoroughly amused.

"Ah, Tax Reform," he said, clapping his hands together. "We meet again."

Tax Reform sighed. "Oh, great. You."

Sam frowned. "Wait, you two know each other?"

"Of course," Historical Taxation said, smirking. "Tax Reform has been around for centuries, always promising to simplify things and always making them worse. Did you know, Mr. Harper, that in 1861, the United States introduced its first income tax to fund the Civil War? It was supposed to be temporary, but guess what? It's still here."

Sam groaned. "Of course it is."

"And let's not forget the Tax Reform Act of 1986," Historical Taxation continued. "It was supposed to simplify the tax code, but all it did was create new loopholes and make accountants even richer."

Tax Reform glared at him. "That's not fair. I've made progress."

"Progress?" Historical Taxation laughed. "You're like a bad haircut. Every time someone tries to fix you, they just make it worse."

As the taxes continued to argue, Sam felt his sanity slipping away once again. He had survived Income Tax, endured Audit Tax, and barely made it through Sin Tax, Luxury Tax, Bracket Creep, and Capital Gains Tax, but this? This was too much.

"Enough!" he shouted, slamming his hands on the desk. "I don't care about simplification or fairness or any of this nonsense! I just want to live my life without being taxed for every little thing!"

Then Tax Reform smiled. "Oh, Mr. Harper. You can't escape taxes. They're like death, but with more paperwork."

Sam buried his face in his hands. "This is a nightmare."

As the taxes continued to bicker, Sam couldn't shake the feeling that this was only the beginning. Somewhere out there, lurking in the shadows, there were even more taxes waiting to make his life miserable. Carbon Tax, Estate Tax, Pension Tax, the list went on and on.

And then there was the one figure he had heard whispers about, the one they all seemed to fear: Tx Evasion. A shadowy, elusive figure who promised freedom from taxes but came with a price of their own.

Sam shuddered at the thought. If these taxes were this bad, he could only imagine what Tax Evasion would be like.

Chapter 8

Meet Psyche Tax – The Mind Games of Money

It was a quiet Monday evening when Sam stumbled upon an old psychology textbook, its pages bookmarked with sticky notes about "loss aversion" and "mental accounting." As he read, he realized that taxes weren't just about numbers—they were about feelings, fears, and the strange ways our minds twist financial reality. Enter Psyche Tax, ready to play tricks not just on Sam's wallet, but on his very sense of logic.

The following day Sam ventured across town for his appointment at Psyche Tax's office. Her office was a cross between a therapist's den and a government records room. The couch was upholstered in shredded tax return forms. The walls were lined with motivational posters: "You Are More Than Your Tax Bracket!" and "Feelings Are Deductible (But Not Really)." There was a faint smell of lavender and printer ink. Sam sat down, clutching a mug that read "World's Okayest Taxpayer," and tried not to think about the Tax Office on the tissue box.

"Welcome, Sam," Psyche Tax purred, adjusting her glasses. "Let's talk about your feelings."

Sam blinked. "My... feelings? About taxes?"

Psyche Tax nodded. "Of course! Taxes aren't just about numbers. They're about guilt, anxiety, denial, and—if you're lucky—a little bit of pride. Tell me, when did you first realize you hated paying taxes?"

Sam thought back. "Probably when I was eight and my mom took half my Halloween candy for 'parental services rendered.' She called it the 'Mommy Marginal Rate.'"

Psyche Tax scribbled a note. "Classic case. You see, Sam, tax morale is a real thing. Some people feel a sense of civic duty when they pay taxes. Others feel like they're being mugged by a guy in a suit. And some—like your mother—just want a cut of the action. It's all part of the psychological rollercoaster we call 'fiscal responsibility.'"

Sam nodded. "I guess I do feel a little guilty every April. Like, maybe I should have kept better records. Or not tried to write off my Netflix subscription as 'research' for my future as a trivia champion."

Psyche Tax smiled. "That's perfectly normal. Governments know this, which is why they send you friendly reminder letters. 'Thank you for paying your taxes!' they say, as if you had a choice. It's all about behavioural nudges. Make you feel like a hero for doing what you were legally required to do anyway. It's like getting a gold star for not setting the kitchen on fire."

Sam sipped his coffee. "So it's not just me?"

"Not at all," Psyche Tax assured him. "Some people get angry. Some rebel. Some go through all five stages of grief before they even open TurboTax. But deep down, we all want to believe our taxes are making the world a better place. Or at least paying for pothole repairs. Or the mayor's new statue of himself."

Sam looked hopeful. "So, is there a cure?"

Psyche Tax leaned in. "Only acceptance, Sam. And maybe a good accountant. Or a support group for people who've tried to deduct their pets."

Just then, the door burst open and Flat Tax stormed in, waving a pamphlet. "Everyone should pay the same! It's only fair!"

Psyche Tax rolled her eyes. "Not now, Flat. Sam's working through some issues. Go practice your elevator pitch."

Flat Tax huffed and left, muttering about "participation trophies" and "the tyranny of progressive brackets."

Sam grinned. "You know, this is actually kind of fun. I haven't talked about my tax feelings since that time I tried to expense my therapy sessions."

Psyche Tax handed him a tissue. "That's the spirit. Now, let's talk about your feelings on gig work, cryptocurrency, and why you keep labelling your Amazon orders as 'business research.'"

Psyche Tax led Sam through the five stages of tax grief, complete with interpretive dance and a playlist called "Songs to Cry To While Filing":

1. *Denial:* "Maybe if I ignore the envelope from the Tax Office, it'll go away. Or at least turn into a coupon."
2. *Anger:* "How dare they tax my fantasy football winnings! That's not even real money! And what about my Monopoly earnings?"
3. *Bargaining:* "If I donate enough old socks to charity, maybe I'll get a refund. Or at least a thank-you note from Goodwill."
4. *Depression:* "I'll never understand the Tax Return Form. I'm just going to live in a van and barter with potatoes. Or maybe start a commune."
5. *Acceptance:* "Fine, take my money. Just let me keep my sanity. And maybe my collection of novelty mugs."

Sam realized he wasn't alone. Psyche Tax explained that "tax morale"—the willingness to pay taxes—varies wildly. In Scandinavia, people pay up with a smile, imagining their taxes building schools and funding healthcare. In other places, taxes are seen as a shakedown, a government-sponsored mugging with paperwork and a free pen.

"Why do some people feel proud to pay taxes, while others feel robbed?" Sam asked.

Psyche Tax grinned. "It's all about trust. If you believe your taxes are being used wisely, you're more likely to pay without grumbling. If you think they're funding the mayor's new yacht, not so much. And if you're in Italy, you just hope the paperwork comes with a free espresso."

Psyche Tax showed Sam a collection of government letters from around the world:

- *The cheerful reminder*: "Thank you for being a responsible citizen! Your taxes help build code Playgrounds and fund adorable puppies. (No, really. There's a puppy budget.)"
- *The guilt trip*: "Did you know your neighbour already filed? Don't be the last one on your block! (We're watching.)"
- *The threatening nudge*: "Failure to file may result in penalties, audits, and a lifetime supply of government cheese. (It's not even the good kind.)"
- *The existential*: "Remember, taxes are the price we pay for civilization. And also, for that new roundabout nobody wanted."

Sam laughed. "Do these actually work?"

Psyche Tax nodded. "Surprisingly, yes. Behavioural economists have found that a well-timed nudge can increase compliance by up to 20%. People want to feel good about themselves—even when they're writing a check to the government. It's like donating to charity, but with more paperwork and fewer tote bags."

Sam confessed, "I have a friend who brags about never paying taxes. He calls himself a 'sovereign citizen.' He also thinks the moon landing was faked and that you can pay your water bill in seashells."

Psyche Tax rolled her eyes. "There's always one. Some people see taxes as a challenge to their independence. Others just like the thrill of rebellion. But beware: the Tax Office has more patience than a Buddhist monk and more resources than Batman. And they never forget. Ever."

She told Sam about famous tax rebels: the Boston Tea Party, the Whiskey Rebellion, and that one guy who tried to pay his taxes in pennies as a protest. (Spoiler: it didn't work, but it did make the bank teller's day a lot more interesting.)

But it's not all doom and gloom. Psyche Tax reminded Sam that taxes pay for things we all use: roads, schools, firefighters, and the world's most expensive staplers for government offices. She even had a "Taxpayer's Bingo" card:

- "Cross off a pothole-free road!"
- "Spot a fire hydrant!"
- "See a government building that isn't under construction!"

"Think of it this way, Sam: every time you drive on a pothole-free road, you're getting your money's worth. Sort of. And if you ever see a pothole, just remember: you're helping fund job security for road crews everywhere."

Sam smiled. "I guess taxes aren't all bad. At least I get a sticker."

Psyche Tax handed him a sticker: "I Paid My Taxes and All I Got Was This Lousy Sticker." She also offered a coupon for "One Free Deep Breath During Tax Season."

As Sam left Psyche Tax's office, he felt lighter. Maybe, just maybe, he could face tax season without a panic attack. Or at least with fewer snacks. He even considered starting a support group: "Taxpayers Anonymous—First Rule: Bring Your Own Calculator."

CHAPTER 9

Tax Credit Assistance – A Helping Hand

Sam Harper was at his wit's end. After being harassed by Income Tax, guilt-tripped by Sin Tax, and nearly driven to madness by Bracket Creep, he was ready to throw in the towel. He had started fantasizing about moving to a remote island where the only tax he'd have to pay was the emotional toll of being eaten alive by mosquitoes. But just as he was about to Google "how to fake your own death to avoid taxes," the door to his office burst open (again).

This time, however, the figure that entered wasn't menacing or smug. In fact, they were practically glowing. A cheerful, bubbly individual in a bright yellow suit skipped into the room, carrying a clipboard covered in stickers that read things like "You've Got This!" and "Tax Relief FTW!" They had a cape tied around their neck that looked like it had been made from an old Tax Office pamphlet, and their smile was so wide it could probably be seen from space.

"Sam Harper!" the figure exclaimed, striking a superhero pose. "Your savior has arrived!"

Sam blinked. "Uh... who are you?"

Sam frowned. "Savior? Are you sure you're in the right place? Because unless you're here to pay my taxes for me, I don't see how you can help."

TCA gasped, clutching their chest like Sam had just insulted their mother. "Oh, Sam, you wound me! I'm not here to pay your taxes—I'm here to reduce them! I'm the hero you didn't know you needed!"

Before Sam could respond, TCA plopped down in the chair across from him and pulled out their clipboard. "Now, let's see what we're working with here. Do you have kids?"

Sam blinked. "Uh… no."

TCA scribbled something on their clipboard. "Okay, no Child Tax Credit for you. Do you own a business?"

Sam hesitated. "I mean, I'm self-employed…"

TCA's eyes lit up. "Perfect! That means you might qualify for the Earned Income Tax Credit! It's like a little pat on the back from the government for working hard and not giving up on life."

Sam raised an eyebrow. "A pat on the back? More like a slap in the face. I barely make enough to cover my rent."

TCA waved a hand dismissively. "Details, details. The important thing is that you're eligible for something. And if you're self-employed, you might also qualify for the R&D Tax Credit!"

Sam frowned. "R&D? I'm not a scientist. I don't even know what R&D stands for."

"Research and Development!" TCA said, beaming. "It's a credit for businesses that innovate and create new products. Have you invented anything recently?"

Sam snorted. "Does a new way to procrastinate count?"

TCA laughed, slapping their knee. "Oh, Sam, you're a riot! But no, procrastination doesn't count. Unless, of course, you've developed an app for it. Have you?"

Sam stared at them. "Do I look like someone who knows how to code?"

TCA shrugged. "Fair enough. But don't worry! There are plenty of other credits we can explore. For example, have you made any energy-efficient upgrades to your home?"

Sam blinked. "Energy-efficient? I can barely afford to keep the lights on."

TCA scribbled something on their clipboard. "Okay, no energy credits. What about education? Have you taken any classes recently?"

Sam sighed. "Does watching YouTube tutorials on how to unclog a sink count?"

TCA tapped their pen against their chin. "Hmm... probably not. But hey, at least you're trying! That's worth something, right?"

Sam groaned. "Is it, though?"

As TCA continued to rattle off a list of potential tax credits, Sam couldn't help but feel like a hyperactive game show host was interrogating him. Every time he said "no" to one of their questions, they'd respond with an overly enthusiastic "That's okay! We'll find something else!" It was like being stuck in a never-ending episode of Who Wants to Be a Taxpayer?—except the only prize was slightly less financial misery.

At one point, TCA pulled out a flowchart that looked like a drunk spider had designed it. "Okay, let's try this: Do you have any dependents?"

"No."

"Do you own a home?"

"No."

"Have you donated to charity?"

Sam hesitated. "Does giving my neighbor a cup of sugar count?"

TCA frowned. "Not unless you got a receipt."

Sam groaned. "Who asks for a receipt for sugar?"

"Smart taxpayers, that's who!" TCA said, wagging a finger. "Remember, Sam: every little bit helps. Even a £5 donation to a local cat shelter can make a difference."

Sam raised an eyebrow. "You're telling me I can get a tax credit for helping cats?"

"Absolutely!" TCA said, nodding vigorously. "Cats, dogs, hamsters—you name it. As long as it's a registered charity, you're golden."

Sam leaned back in his chair, rubbing his temples. "This is insane. How does anyone keep track of all this?"

TCA grinned. "That's what I'm here for! Think of me as your personal tax fairy, sprinkling credits and deductions wherever I go."

Sam snorted. "A tax fairy? More like a tax clown."

TCA gasped, looking genuinely offended. "Clown? Sam, I'll have you know that I am a professional. I've helped thousands of taxpayers just like you save money. Why, just last week, I helped a guy get a £500 credit for installing a solar-powered birdbath!"

Sam stared at them. "A solar-powered birdbath? That's a thing?"

TCA nodded. "Oh, absolutely. The government loves anything that's good for the environment. You should see the credits you can get for buying an electric car."

Sam rolled his eyes. "Yeah, because I can totally afford a Tesla on my budget."

As the conversation continued, TCA's relentless optimism started to wear on Sam. At one point, they leaned in conspiratorially and said, "You know, Sam, there's even a tax credit for… certain medical expenses."

Sam frowned. "What kind of medical expenses?"

TCA smirked. "Let's just say, if you've ever bought anything from a 'specialty' store, you might be eligible for a deduction."

Sam's eyes widened. "Are you telling me I can write off… adult toys?"

TCA shrugged. "Hey, if it's for medical purposes, who's to say? I don't make the rules—I just find the loopholes."

Sam burst out laughing, shaking his head. "This is officially the weirdest conversation I've ever had."

TCA grinned. "Welcome to the wonderful world of tax credits, my friend. It's a wild ride."

By the end of the meeting, Sam was no closer to understanding his taxes, but he had to admit that TCA's enthusiasm was infectious. As they packed up their clipboard and prepared to leave, they turned to Sam and said, "Remember, Sam: every credit counts. You just have to know where to look."

Sam sighed. "Yeah, well, if you find any credits for 'mentally scarred by taxes,' let me know."

TCA laughed, giving him a thumbs-up. "Will do! And don't forget: I'm always just a phone call away."

As they skipped out of the office, Sam leaned back in his chair and muttered, "A tax fairy. What's next? A tax genie?"

Little did he know, the next visitor would make TCA look downright normal.

Chapter 10

Tax Evasion vs. Tax Avoidance – The Great Debate

Sam Harper was starting to think his office needed a revolving door. Every time he thought he'd seen the last of the tax characters, another one would waltz in, bringing chaos, confusion, and a fresh dose of existential dread. He was halfway through a stale bagel—his first meal in what felt like days—when the door creaked open yet again.

"Let me guess," Sam muttered, not even looking up. "Another tax here to ruin my life?"

A low, slippery voice answered, "Ruin your life? Oh, Sam, I'm here to save it."

Sam looked up to see a man in a trench coat and fedora, leaning casually against the doorframe. He had the kind of face you'd expect to see on a "Wanted" poster, complete with a pencil-thin mustache and a smirk that screamed, I know a guy who knows a guy. He twirled a toothpick between his teeth and tipped his hat.

"The name's Tax Evasion," he said, sauntering into the room. "But you can call me 'Freedom.'"

Sam frowned. "Freedom? You look more like trouble."

Tax Evasion chuckled, pulling a cigar from his pocket and lighting it with a match he struck on the sole of his shoe. "Trouble? Nah. I'm the guy who helps you keep what's yours. You work hard for your money, right? Why should the government get a cut?"

Sam raised an eyebrow. "Because... taxes pay for roads and schools and stuff?"

Tax Evasion waved a hand dismissively. "Details, details. Look, Sam, I'm not saying you shouldn't pay any taxes. I'm just saying... maybe you don't have to pay all of them. You know, if you're smart about it."

Before Sam could respond, the door swung open again, and in strutted a man in a tailored suit so sharp it could probably cut glass. He carried a leather briefcase and wore a smug expression that made Sam want to punch him on principle.

"Ugh," the man said, wrinkling his nose as he looked at Tax Evasion. "I should've known you'd be here."

Tax Evasion smirked. "Well, well, well. If it isn't Tax Avoidance, the government's favorite little lapdog."

Tax Avoidance adjusted his tie and shot Tax Evasion a withering glare. "And if it isn't the poster child for criminal behavior. Honestly, Evasion, do you even own a legitimate business, or are you still running that 'offshore shell company' scam?"

"Hey, it's not a scam," Tax Evasion said, puffing on his cigar. "It's a strategy."

Sam groaned, rubbing his temples. "Okay, who the hell are you?"

Tax Avoidance turned to Sam and gave him a dazzling smile that was about as genuine as a politician's campaign promises. "I'm Tax Avoidance, the legal and ethical alternative to this... degenerate." He gestured toward Tax Evasion like he was pointing at a cockroach.

Sam frowned. "Legal and ethical? You sure about that?"

"Absolutely," Tax Avoidance said, opening his briefcase and pulling out a stack of neatly organized documents. "Unlike my shady counterpart here, I operate entirely within the bounds of the law. I help people like you minimize their tax liability through perfectly legitimate means—deductions, credits, offshore accounts, trusts—"

"Wait," Sam interrupted, holding up a hand. "Did you just say 'offshore accounts'? How is that legal?"

Tax Avoidance smirked. "Ah, Sam, it's all about the paperwork. As long as you follow the rules, you can legally reduce your tax burden. It's not about what you do—it's about how you do it."

Tax Evasion snorted. "Oh, please. You're just me with a fancy suit and a better lawyer."

What followed was the most absurd argument Sam had ever witnessed. Tax Evasion and Tax Avoidance squared off like two boxers in a ring, hurling insults and accusations at each other while Sam sat in the middle, trying to make sense of it all.

"You're nothing but a crook!" Tax Avoidance snapped, pointing an accusatory finger at Tax Evasion. "You hide income, falsify records, and cheat the system!"

"And you're a sellout!" Tax Evasion shot back. "You pretend to be all high and mighty, but you're just as shady as I am. The only difference is, you've got the government's blessing."

"I follow the law," Tax Avoidance said, his voice dripping with superiority. "I use loopholes, deductions, and exemptions that are perfectly legal. It's not my fault the system is broken."

Tax Evasion rolled his eyes. "Oh, give me a break. You're just a glorified accountant with a superiority complex."

Sam, who had been quietly eating his bagel, finally spoke up. "Okay, can someone explain the difference between you two? Because right now, you both sound like a pain in my ass."

Tax Avoidance adjusted his tie and cleared his throat. "The difference, Sam, is simple. I operate within the law. I help taxpayers like you reduce their liability by taking advantage of legal opportunities in the tax code."

"And I," Tax Evasion said, grinning, "help you keep your money by... bending the rules a little. You know, creative accounting."

Sam frowned. "Creative accounting? That sounds illegal."

Tax Evasion shrugged. "Only if you get caught."

Just as Sam was starting to wonder if he could sneak out of his own office, the door slammed open (again), and in marched Audit Tax, looking as stern and terrifying as ever. His trench coat billowed dramatically, and his clipboard was practically glowing with red ink.

"What the hell is going on here?" Audit Tax barked, glaring at Tax Evasion and Tax Avoidance. "I leave for a couple of weeks, and you two start corrupting taxpayers?"

Tax Evasion smirked. "Relax, Audit. We're just having a friendly debate."

Audit Tax narrowed his eyes. "Friendly? You're trying to drag this poor man into a world of fraud and deception."

Tax Avoidance raised a hand. "For the record, I'm not dragging anyone into anything. I'm simply offering legal advice."

Audit Tax snorted. "Legal advice? You're just a loophole salesman."

Sam groaned. "Can someone please tell me what I'm supposed to do? Because right now, I feel like I'm stuck between a rock and a hard place."

Audit Tax turned to Sam and placed a reassuring hand on his shoulder. "Sam, listen to me. Tax Avoidance may be legal, but it's a slippery slope. And Tax Evasion? Well, let's just say you don't want to end up on my audit list."

Tax Evasion rolled his eyes. "Oh, come on, Audit. Live a little."

Audit Tax glared at him. "Live a little? I'm the reason people lose sleep at night."

By the end of the debate, Sam was more confused than ever. Tax Avoidance handed him a stack of brochures titled "How to Legally Pay Less Taxes", while Tax Evasion slipped him a business card with the words "Call Me If You're Feeling Brave" scrawled across it. Audit Tax, meanwhile, stood in the corner, muttering about how he was going to "audit the hell out of both of them."

As the three of them bickered, Sam leaned back in his chair and muttered, "I should've been a bartender. At least then I'd only have to deal with drunk people."

Little did he know, his next visitor would make this debate look like a walk in the park.

Chapter 11

The Shadow Economy

Sam Harper always prided himself on being a law-abiding citizen. He paid his taxes (eventually), kept his receipts (in a shoebox labelled "Definitely Not Trash"), and only jaywalked when the crosswalk light was taking longer than a sloth on vacation. But after his deep dive into the world of pop culture taxes, Sam was ready for a break from the spotlight—and maybe a snack.

That's when he received a mysterious text:

"Meet me at the alley behind the cash-only barbershop in one hour. Come alone. Bring small bills."

It was signed, simply, *Shadow Tax.*

Sam arrived at the rendezvous point, heart pounding like a drum solo at a rock concert. The alley was dimly lit, the air thick with the scent of mystery (and possibly expired hair gel). Out of the shadows emerged a figure in a trench coat and sunglasses—at night, of course, because nothing says "I'm up to something" like sunglasses after sunset.

"Psst, Sam," Shadow Tax whispered, glancing over his shoulder like a squirrel with a secret. "Wanna buy a slightly used deduction? Cash only. No questions, no receipts, no problem."

Shadow Tax was the king of the black market, the master of under-the-table deals, and the reason your local cash-only barbershop was still in business. He moved with the stealth of a ninja and the confidence of someone who'd never seen a Tax Return Form. If there was a secret handshake for the shadow economy, he probably invented it.

Shadow Tax led Sam on a whirlwind tour of the city's hidden economy, complete with dramatic narration and the occasional jazz hands:

- *Street Vendors:* "See that guy selling hot dogs? No sales tax, no receipts, just pure, unfiltered capitalism. He's the backbone of the shadow economy—and the reason you can get a hot dog at 3 a.m. and a stomach ache at 3:15."
- *Cash-Only Businesses:* "Barbershops, nail salons, food trucks. If they don't take cards, they're probably not reporting everything. It's not illegal... unless you get caught. And if you do, just say you thought 'cash only' was a new diet."
- *Off-the-Books Labor***:** "Babysitters, handymen, dog walkers. If you pay in cash and nobody tells the Tax Office, did the work even happen? It's like the tree falling in the forest, but with more barking."
- *Black Markets:* "From fake designer bags to 'genuine' Rolexes, the shadow economy is where untaxed goods and services thrive. Just don't ask for a warranty, and definitely don't ask for a return policy."

Sam's eyes widened. "How big is this, really? Like, 'hide-and-seek champion' big?"

Shadow Tax grinned, flashing a smile that could sell ice to a penguin. "Globally? Trillions. In some countries, the shadow economy is bigger than the official one. It's the world's worst-kept secret—like your uncle's hairpiece or the fact that nobody actually likes fruitcake."

Sam asked, "But... why do people do it?"

Shadow Tax shrugged. "Sometimes it's survival. Sometimes it's greed. Sometimes it's just easier than filling out a tax form. For some, it's a protest against high taxes or red tape. For others, it's just... habit. And let's be honest, who doesn't love a good secret handshake?"

He handed Sam a counterfeit receipt. "Want to write off your lunch as a 'business meeting'? I can make it happen. I can even throw in a fake moustache for extra discretion."

Sam clutched his wallet. "I think I'll stick to the straight and narrow. My accountant already has trust issues."

Shadow Tax winked. "Suit yourself. But remember, the shadow economy isn't all bad. It keeps money flowing, helps people get by, and sometimes, it's the only option for those left out of the official system. Plus, where else can you get a haircut, a hot dog, and a knockoff superhero cape all in one block?"

But then Shadow Tax grew serious, his voice dropping to a whisper. "But there's a downside. No taxes means no funding for schools, hospitals, or pothole repairs. Workers in the shadow economy have no protections—no health insurance, no retirement, no legal recourse if things go wrong. It's a risky game, Sam. Like playing Monopoly with real money and no Get Out of Jail Free cards."

He gestured to a group of day labourers huddled in the corner. "They work hard, but they're invisible to the system. No benefits, no safety net. It's a tough gig."

Sam nodded, feeling a pang of guilt. "So, what's the solution? More rules? Fewer rules? More snacks?"

Shadow Tax shrugged. "Some say lower taxes and less red tape. Others say better enforcement. Me? I say, keep your receipts, pay your fair share, and don't ask too many questions. And maybe tip your hot dog vendor."

Just then, a spotlight swept the alley. Shadow Tax melted into the darkness, leaving Sam alone with a handful of "business expense" receipts, a fake moustache, and a newfound appreciation for the complexity of the underground economy.

A voice boomed from a nearby loudspeaker:

"This is the Tax Office! Please report all cash transactions and remember, tax evasion is a crime!"

Sam bolted, vowing to never pay for a haircut in cash again (and maybe to finally clean out that shoebox).

As Sam emerged from the shadows and into the light of day, he realized that the shadow economy was everywhere hidden in plain sight, thriving on cash, and always one step ahead of the taxman. It was a world of risk and reward, of survival and secrecy, of hot dogs and haircuts, and the occasional superhero cape.

CHAPTER 12

Carbon Tax and the Cost of Saving the Planet

Sam Harper was starting to think his office had become some kind of cosmic magnet for tax-related chaos. He was attempting to enjoy his morning coffee in a disposable cup when the door burst open with such force that a gust of wind scattered his papers across the room.

In strode a figure that looked like they'd just stepped out of a climate protest. They wore hiking boots caked with mud, cargo pants made from recycled materials, and a t-shirt that read "There Is No Planet B." Their backpack was covered in environmental badges, and they carried a clipboard made from what appeared to be compressed leaves.

"Sam Harper!" the figure announced, their voice filled with righteous indignation. "Do you have any idea how many trees died to make those papers you just scattered?"

Sam groaned, already knowing where this was heading. "Let me guess. You're another tax?"

Carbon Tax pulled out a chart that looked like it had been drawn on recycled cardboard. "Let's start with your carbon footprint, shall we? And believe me, yours is more like a carbon boot print."

Sam frowned. "My carbon what?"

"Your impact on the environment," Carbon Tax explained, rolling their eyes. "Every time you drive your car, heat your home, or buy something wrapped in plastic, you're contributing to climate change. And I'm here to make you pay for it."

"Pay for it?" Sam spluttered. "I already pay for my gas and electricity!"

Carbon Tax laughed, a sound like rustling leaves. "Oh, sweet summer child. That's just the beginning. Let me break it down for you."

They pulled out another chart, this one showing various activities and their carbon costs. "Your car? That's about 4.6 metric tons of CO2 per year. Your heating? Another 2.5 tons. That beef burger you had for lunch? That's equivalent to driving 15 miles in terms of emissions."

Sam stared at his half-eaten sandwich. "Are you saying I'm destroying the planet by eating lunch?"

"Now you're getting it!" Carbon Tax beamed. "Every action has a carbon consequence. And for each ton of CO2 you emit, you owe me money."

Before Sam could protest, Carbon Tax pulled out a calculator made from bamboo. "Let's calculate your carbon debt, shall we? And remember, every time you think about complaining, picture a sad polar bear floating on a melting ice cap."

Sam groaned. "Can't I just recycle more or something?"

"Recycling is just the beginning," Carbon Tax declared. "We need systematic change! Carbon pricing! Emission trading schemes! Green energy initiatives!"

Just then, Excise Tax burst into the room, his leather jacket creaking. "Did someone mention pricing?"

Carbon Tax glared at him. "This isn't about your kind of pricing. This is about saving the planet!"

Excise Tax smirked. "Hey, we're on the same team here. I tax gas, you tax carbon – we're both making people pay for their sins."

"They're not sins," Carbon Tax snapped. "They're environmental impacts that need to be properly priced into the market to create incentives for sustainable behavior and drive innovation in clean technologies!"

Sam watched them argue, wondering if he could sneak out without either of them noticing. But Carbon Tax caught his movement.

"Don't even think about it, Sam. We haven't even discussed your plastic consumption yet."

For the next hour, Carbon Tax explained the intricacies of carbon pricing, emission trading schemes, and environmental regulations. They showed Sam graphs of rising sea levels, charts of deforestation rates, and pictures of endangered species that made him feel guilty about every life choice he'd ever made.

"So let me get this straight," Sam said finally. "You want me to pay extra for basically everything I do?"

Carbon Tax nodded enthusiastically. "Exactly! It's called internalizing the external costs of carbon emissions into the market price of goods and services!"

Sam blinked. "Couldn't you just say 'making pollution expensive'?"

"Well, yes," Carbon Tax admitted. "But my way sounds more scientific."

As they wrapped up their meeting, Carbon Tax handed Sam a thick packet of papers.

"Wait," Sam said, "Aren't you against wasting paper?"

Carbon Tax winked. "It's made from recycled tax forms. And don't worry – for every page I gave you, I planted a tree."

As they left, Sam looked at his coffee cup, his car keys, and his lunch with new eyes. Maybe Carbon Tax had a point. Or maybe he was just developing Stockholm syndrome from all these tax visits.

Either way, he had a feeling his wallet was about to get a lot lighter in the name of saving the planet.

CHAPTER 13

Tax and the Environment (Beyond Carbon)

A local news story caught Sam's eye: "Plastic Bag Tax Raises £1 Million for City Parks." He wondered how something as small as a shopping bag could make such a big difference. As he dug deeper, Sam discovered a world of environmental taxes—on plastic, pollution, and even noise—each one shaping behavior in ways he'd never imagined.

He stumbled into the *Green Tax Seminar,* being held in the conference centre next to his offices, hosted by a woman in a hemp dress, Birkenstocks, and a clipboard so thick it could double as a solar panel. She radiated the kind of energy you only get from organic kale and a lifetime of composting.

"Welcome, Sam!" Green Tax beamed, handing him a handful of kale chips that tasted like hope and lawn clippings. "Are you ready to save the planet—one tax credit at a time? And maybe win a reusable tote bag?"

Green Tax was the undisputed champion of all things eco-friendly, from solar panels to compost bins to a water bottle that doubled as a rain gauge. She spoke fluent sustainability, sprinkled her sentences with words like "upcycle" and "carbon-neutral," and carried a reusable water bottle filled with green tea and, possibly, the tears of climate change deniers.

She led Sam on a whirlwind tour of the green tax landscape, complete with interpretive dance and a PowerPoint made entirely from recycled pixels:

- *Carbon Tax:* "The classic! Taxing carbon emissions to discourage fossil fuels. It's like a guilt trip for your gas guzzler—except this one comes with a bill."
- *Plastic Bag Tax:* "A small fee for plastic bags at the grocery store. The goal? To make you remember your reusable bags—or at least feel guilty enough to buy another one for your growing collection."
- *Congestion Charges:* "A fee for driving in crowded city centres. The message? Take the bus, ride a bike, or teleport. Just don't clog up the roads unless you're carpooling with a marching band."
- *Landfill Tax*: "A fee for dumping waste in landfills. The goal? To encourage recycling, composting, and maybe even eating your leftovers. Yes, even that mystery casserole from last week."

Sam was impressed. "So, taxes can actually save the planet? And maybe my reputation at the recycling centre?"

Green Tax nodded, her earrings made from upcycled bottle caps jingling. "Absolutely! But it's not just about taxes. It's about changing behaviour, sparking innovation, and making green choices so affordable you'll brag about them at parties."

She whipped out her clipboard like a magician pulling a rabbit from a hat. "Let's talk rebates! Solar panels, electric cars, energy-efficient appliances—the government will pay you to go green. It's like getting a gold star for adulting, and sometimes enough cash to buy a slightly smaller yacht. Or at least a kayak."

Sam's eyes lit up. "Really? How much are we talking? Enough for a solar-powered hot tub?"

Green Tax grinned. "Enough to make you feel good about yourself—and maybe enough to buy a compost bin shaped like a hedgehog. But remember: fill out the forms, keep the receipts, and don't try to claim a rebate for your hamster's solar-powered wheel. The Tax Office has no sense of humour about rodents."

She led Sam through a maze of eco-friendly deductions, each more exciting than the last:

- *Home Office Deduction:* "If you work from home, you can deduct a portion of your rent or mortgage. Bonus points if your home office is powered by solar panels and decorated with furniture made from reclaimed skateboards."
- *Charitable Donations:* "Donate to an environmental charity and deduct the value of your contribution. Just don't try to write off your old tires as 'avant-garde art.' The Tax Office is not that avant-garde."
- *Energy-Efficient Upgrades:* "Install a new furnace, insulate your attic, or buy a smart thermostat. The government will reward you for being responsible—and slightly obsessive about your utility bill."

Sam's head spun. "How do I keep track of all this? Do I need a spreadsheet, a life coach, or just a really big recycling bin?"

Green Tax handed him a color-coded spreadsheet and a coupon for organic coffee. "Start here. And remember, every little bit helps. Even if all you do is recycle your junk mail, you're making a difference. Unless it's coupons for non-organic kale. Then you're on your own."

Suddenly, a voice boomed from the back of the room:

"Green taxes are a scam! They're just a way for the government to steal our money and control our lives!"

It was *Fossil Fuel Fanatic,* a man in a gas-guzzling SUV, a t-shirt that read "I Heart Coal," and a cologne that smelled suspiciously like unleaded. He waved a plastic straw like a tiny sword.

Green Tax rolled her eyes so hard they nearly powered a wind turbine. "There's always one. Some people think green taxes are a burden on the economy. Others think they're a socialist plot to destroy capitalism. But the truth is, they're just a tool—and like any tool, they can be used for good, evil, or opening a bottle of kombucha."

As Sam left the Green Tax seminar, he realized that saving the planet wasn't just about recycling and reusable bags—it was about taxes, incentives, and the choices we make every day. It was about balancing the needs of the economy with the needs of the environment and finding a way to make green choices more appealing than the alternative. And maybe, just maybe, it was about finally remembering to bring his reusable bags to the store.

PART III

Modern Tax Challenges

Chapter 14

Crypto Tax – The Blockchain Enigma

Just when Sam thought he'd seen every kind of tax, a friend convinced him to try cryptocurrency. That night a message popped up in Sam's crypto group chat: "Anyone know how to report Dogecoin profits to the Tax Office?" The chat exploded with memes, confusion, and wild theories. Sam scrolled through, realising he wasn't alone in his bewilderment. In the digital wild west of cryptocurrency, the only certainty was that the taxman would eventually find a way to join the blockchain party. But, of course, the universe had other plans. Within days, Crypto Tax appeared, wearing a hoodie and speaking in riddles about blockchains and wallets. "Welcome to the future, Sam. Hope you kept your passwords."

"Sam Harper!" the figure shouted, pointing dramatically at him, as he barged into Sam's office. "We need to talk about your crypto portfolio!"

Sam blinked. "My what?"

Sam frowned. "I don't own any cryptocurrency."

Sam shook his head. "Nope. I don't even know how it works."

Sam raised an eyebrow. "Why? So you could tax me on it?"

Crypto Tax grinned. "Exactly."

Crypto Tax leaned forward, their sunglasses sliding down their nose. "Alright, Sam, let me explain how this works.

Cryptocurrency is digital money that operates on a decentralized network called the blockchain. It's secure, anonymous, and completely unregulated—well, it was unregulated, until people like me showed up."

Sam frowned. "So... it's like Monopoly money, but on the internet?"

Crypto Tax gasped, clutching their chest like Sam had just insulted their firstborn child. "Monopoly money? MONOPOLY MONEY?! Sam, cryptocurrency is the future of finance! It's revolutionary! It's—"

"—a scam?" Sam interrupted.

Crypto Tax glared at him. "No, it's not a scam. It's... complicated. But that's not the point. The point is, if you buy, sell, trade, or even look at cryptocurrency, I'm the one who makes sure you pay your taxes on it."

Sam groaned. "Of course you are. So how does that work?"

Crypto Tax grinned, pulling out a whiteboard from seemingly nowhere. "Let me break it down for you. Every time you sell cryptocurrency for a profit, it's considered a taxable event. That means you have to pay capital gains tax on the profit you made."

Sam frowned. "Capital gains? Isn't that the same tax I pay when I sell stocks?"

"Exactly!" Crypto Tax said, scribbling furiously on the whiteboard. "But here's where it gets fun. If you trade one cryptocurrency for another—like swapping Bitcoin for Ethereum—that's also a taxable event. And if you use cryptocurrency to buy something, like a pizza or a Tesla, guess what? Taxable event!"

Sam stared at them. "So basically, every time I do anything with crypto, you're there to take a cut?"

Crypto Tax nodded enthusiastically. "Pretty much! Oh, and don't forget about mining."

"Mining?" Sam asked, confused. "Like digging for gold?"

Crypto Tax rolled their eyes. "No, Sam. Mining is when you use a computer to solve complex mathematical problems and validate transactions on the blockchain. It's how new cryptocurrency is created. And guess what? The coins you mine are considered taxable income."

Sam groaned, rubbing his temples. "This sounds like a nightmare."

Crypto Tax grinned. "Oh, it gets worse."

Before Sam could respond, the door burst open again, and in marched Audit Tax, looking as stern and terrifying as ever. His trench coat billowed dramatically, and his clipboard was practically glowing with red ink.

"What the hell is going on here?" Audit Tax barked, glaring at Crypto Tax. "Are you confusing another taxpayer with your nonsense?"

Crypto Tax smirked. "Relax, Audit. I'm just explaining the rules."

"Rules?" Audit Tax snorted. "You don't even have proper regulations. Half the time, you don't even know what you're taxing."

Crypto Tax shrugged. "Hey, it's not my fault the government can't keep up with the blockchain."

Sam, who had been quietly sipping his coffee, finally spoke up. "Wait, are you telling me that even the government doesn't understand how crypto taxes work?"

Audit Tax sighed, pinching the bridge of his nose. "That's exactly what I'm saying. The rules are constantly changing, and most people don't even report their crypto transactions. It's a mess."

Crypto Tax grinned. "But that's what makes it fun! It's like the Wild West of taxation."

Sam groaned. "Fun? This sounds like a recipe for disaster."

Crypto Tax leaned back in their chair, crossing their arms. "Oh, you think this is bad? Let me tell you about some of the horror stories I've seen. There was this one guy who bought Bitcoin for £100 back in 2011. By the time he sold it in 2021, it was worth £10 million. Do you know how much tax he owed?"

Sam shook his head. "How much?"

Crypto Tax grinned. "Nearly £4 million. And he didn't even know he had to pay it until Audit Tax showed up at his door."

Audit Tax nodded. "It was glorious. He tried to claim he 'forgot' about the Bitcoin, but I wasn't having it."

Sam stared at them. "So you're telling me that if I accidentally make millions of pounds in crypto, you'll show up to ruin my life?"

Crypto Tax shrugged. "Pretty much. But hey, look on the bright side—you'll still have millions left over."

Sam groaned. "Unless I spend it all on taxes."

By the end of the meeting, Sam was thoroughly confused and slightly terrified. Crypto Tax handed him a pamphlet titled "Cryptocurrency and You: How to Avoid Accidentally Committing Tax Fraud," while Audit Tax muttered something about "keeping an eye on him."

As Sam watched his digital coins fluctuate wildly, he realized that even in the virtual world, taxes were never far behind. He scribbled "Find crypto receipts" on a sticky note.

Sam leaned back in his chair and muttered, "I should've just stuck to cash. At least then I wouldn't have to deal with this nonsense."

Chapter 15

The Digital Economy and Gig Work

Sam Harper had always considered himself a "traditional" taxpayer. He had a job, a cubicle, and a boss who thought "synergy" was a personality trait. But then came the layoffs, the "pivot to digital," and the realization that his most valuable asset was a half-used Starbucks gift card and a drawer full of novelty socks.

So Sam did what millions of others had done: he joined the gig economy. One day he was driving for Uber, the next he was renting out his spare room on Airbnb, and by Friday he was selling artisanal beard oil on Etsy (despite being clean-shaven). His phone buzzed with notifications, his calendar was a patchwork of side hustles, and his tax situation was... well, let's just say "complicated" is putting it mildly.

Enter *Gig Tax!*

Gig Tax was the only tax collector Sam had ever met who looked more exhausted than a barista on Black Friday. She wore a jacket covered in app logos, had a Bluetooth headset in each ear, and carried a briefcase overflowing with Tax Returns, sticky notes, and a stress ball shaped like a pound sign.

"Sam Harper?" she called, scanning a tablet with one hand and hailing a rideshare with the other. "You're up. And so is your tax bill. Also, your Uber driver is circling the block."

Sam gulped. "I thought gig work was supposed to be... simple? Like, 'set your own hours, be your own boss, and never wear pants again' simple?"

Gig Tax laughed, a sound somewhere between a cackle and a sob. "Simple? Sam, the only thing simple about the gig economy is how quickly it turns your life into a spreadsheet nightmare. You'll need a PhD in receipts and a minor in caffeine management."

Gig Tax led Sam through a dizzying tour of his own digital hustle:

- *Uber:* "You drove 47 rides last month. Did you track your mileage? Your car washes? The time you spent crying in the drive-thru after your third one-star review? And don't forget the air fresheners—those pine trees are not tax-deductible as emotional support."
- *Airbnb*: "You rented your spare room to a couple from Sweden. Did you report the income? Deduct the cost of the new shower curtain they destroyed? Declare the IKEA meatballs as a business expense? And did you ever find your missing bath towel?"
- *Etsy:* "You sold three bottles of beard oil. Did you keep receipts for the essential oils? The shipping? The therapy sessions after your first negative review? And what about the glitter explosion that's still haunting your carpet?"

Sam's head spun. "How does anyone keep track of all this? Is there an app for that, or just a support group?"

Gig Tax shrugged. "Most don't. That's why I'm here. The gig economy is a tax collector's obstacle course. Every app, every gig, every tip taxable. The rules? About as clear as a rideshare driver's directions after midnight. And don't even get me started on crypto tips."

She dumped a stack of income earned summaries on the table. "Here's your income summary from Uber, Airbnb, Etsy.

Sam stared at the pile. "Do I have to report all of this? Even the £5 tip I got in Monopoly money?"

Gig Tax nodded. "If you can Venmo it, I can tax it. And don't forget: the Tax Office gets a copy, too. They love surprises—just not the kind you're thinking of. And yes, Monopoly money is not legal tender, but nice try."

Sam tried to organize the forms by colour, then by size, then by how much they made him want to cry. He briefly considered using them as wallpaper.

"Good news, Sam," Gig Tax said, "you can deduct business expenses. Bad news: you have to prove it. And no, your 'emotional support coffee' is not a line item. Unless you can get your therapist to sign off."

Sam pulled out a shoebox full of receipts. "Is this enough?"

Gig Tax peered inside. "Let's see... gas, snacks, a rubber chicken, and a receipt for 'emergency glitter removal.' Creative, but only some of these count. The Tax Office is not known for its sense of humour, except when it comes to your expense reports."

She explained the rules: mileage, supplies, even a portion of your rent if you work from home. But woe to the gig worker who tries to write off their Netflix subscription as "market research" (Sam's face turned red). And don't even think about deducting your cat as a "business partner," unless your cat is actually running the Etsy shop.

Sam complained, "But the apps said they'd handle the taxes!"

Gig Tax snorted. "Sure, they'll send you a form. But they won't withhold taxes, track your expenses, or explain why you owe self-employment tax on £37.50 worth of dog-walking. That's on you, Sam. Welcome to the world of quarterly estimated payments! It's like a surprise party, but the only gift is a bill."

Sam's eyes widened. "Quarterly what now?"

Gig Tax handed him a calendar. "Mark your dates, or the Tax Office will mark you. And don't forget to set a reminder for 'panic' the night before."

Sam's phone buzzed. "Congrats! You just got a gig editing memes for a client in Estonia."

Gig Tax's eyes lit up. "International income! Now you get to learn about foreign tax credits, currency conversion, and why the Tax Office thinks you're running a global empire from your kitchen table. And don't forget to declare your earnings in Estonian kroon's, even though they switched to euros in 2011."

Sam whimpered. "Can I just go back to my cubicle? I miss the days when my biggest worry was running out of paper clips."

Gig Tax patted his shoulder. "Sorry, Sam. Once you go gig, you never go back. But hey, at least you're your own boss. And your own HR department. And your own IT support. And your own tax attorney. And your own janitor. And your own motivational speaker."

Gig Tax gave Sam a checklist, written in glitter pen for maximum impact:

- Track every penny, every mile, every expense (and every time you cry into your coffee).
- Save at least 25% of your income for taxes (and maybe a little extra for therapy, snacks, and glitter removal).
- File quarterly estimated payments or prepare for a "strongly worded" letter from the Tax Office (with bonus points for creative use of bold font).
- Don't trust the apps to do your taxes for you. If they could, they'd be charging you for it.
- And above all: never try to write off your cat as a "business partner." Unless your cat is actually running a YouTube channel.

Sam nodded, feeling both enlightened and exhausted. He briefly considered starting a gig as a professional receipt organizer, but then remembered he'd have to pay taxes on that, too.

As Gig Tax left Sam's office, he realized the gig economy was a wild, wonderful, and occasionally terrifying place. It offered freedom, flexibility, and the chance to be your own boss—but also the opportunity to be your own worst enemy come tax time. And if all else failed, at least he could write a memoir: "Fifty Shades of the tax return."

Chapter 16
International Tax and Post-Brexit Chaos – The Global Maze

The sound of multiple languages arguing in perfect bureaucratic harmony drifted through Sam Harper's office walls. His morning coffee had barely touched his lips when he heard what seemed to be a German VAT officer engaged in a heated debate with an American Tax Office agent about the finer points of double taxation. The cacophony of accents made his office feel less like a workspace and more like an international tax summit gone wrong. After his chaotic encounter with Gig Tax, Sam had decided to take a break. He brewed himself a fresh cup of tea, sat down, and vowed to spend the next hour doing something normal—like Googling "how to live off the grid."

But, as always, peace was not in the cards.

The door creaked open, and in walked a figure who exuded an air of worldly sophistication. They wore a tailored suit, carried a leather briefcase, and had a clipboard tucked under their arm. Their demeanour was calm, but their eyes sparkled with the kind of mischief that only comes from knowing you're about to ruin someone's day.

"Sam Harper," the figure said, their voice smooth and worldly. "It's time we talked about your global obligations."

Sam groaned. "Let me guess. You're another tax."

The figure smiled. "I'm International Tax. And I'm here to guide you through the wonderful, chaotic world of cross-border taxation."

Sam frowned. "Cross-border taxation? I don't even have a passport."

International Tax chuckled, taking a seat across from Sam. "Oh, Sam. You don't need a passport to be affected by me. In today's globalized world, I'm everywhere. Whether you're buying goods from another country, running a business with international clients, or just dreaming about moving to a tax haven, I'm the one who makes sure you pay your fair share."

Sam sighed. "Of course you are."

International Tax opened their briefcase, pulling out a map of the world that looked like it had been stolen from a spy movie. "Let's start with the basics, shall we? Imagine you're a business owner, and you're earning income in two different countries. Both countries want to tax you on that income. What do you do?"

Sam blinked. "Uh... move to a third country?"

International Tax smirked. "Clever, but not quite. That's where double tax treaties come in. These are agreements between countries to prevent you from being taxed twice on the same income. They're like peace treaties for your wallet."

Sam raised an eyebrow. "Peace treaties? So, what happens if there's no treaty?"

International Tax sighed dramatically. "Then you're at the mercy of both countries. It's like being caught in a tug-of-war between two very greedy toddlers."

Sam groaned. "Great. So how do these treaties work?"

International Tax pulled out a flowchart that looked like it had been designed by a particularly sadistic bureaucrat. "It depends on the treaty. Some countries give you a tax credit for the taxes you've already paid in another country. Others exempt the income entirely. And then there are the countries that just... don't care."

Sam frowned. "So basically, it's a mess."

International Tax nodded. "A beautiful, chaotic mess."

Before Sam could respond, the door creaked open again, and in walked a figure who looked like they'd just survived a hurricane. Their tie was askew, their hair was a mess, and they carried a stack of papers so tall it looked like it might topple over at any moment.

"Who... who are you?" Sam asked, already bracing himself for the chaos.

The figure sighed, dropping the stack of papers onto Sam's desk with a loud thud. "I'm Post-Brexit VAT. And I'm here to talk about the absolute disaster that is cross-border trade after Brexit."

Sam blinked. "Post-Brexit VAT? What does that even mean?"

Post-Brexit VAT groaned, collapsing into a chair. "It means that ever since the UK left the EU, I've been drowning in paperwork, customs declarations, and rules that no one understands. Honestly, I don't even understand them anymore."

Sam frowned. "Okay, but what exactly changed? I mean, VAT is VAT, right?"

Post-Brexit VAT let out a bitter laugh that sounded more like a sob. "Oh, Sam. Sweet, naive Sam. VAT used to be manageable. Back when the UK was part of the EU, we had this thing called the VAT Directive. It was like a big, happy family of rules that everyone followed. Sure, it wasn't perfect, but at least it made sense. Now? Now it's like a bad divorce where no one knows who gets custody of the rules."

Post-Brexit VAT pulled out a whiteboard and began drawing a diagram that quickly turned into a chaotic mess of arrows, boxes, and question marks. "Okay, let's start with goods. If you're exporting goods from the UK to the EU, you now have to deal with customs declarations, import VAT, and potentially tariffs. It's like a three-headed monster that eats your time and money."

Sam raised a hand. "Wait, what about services?"

Post-Brexit VAT groaned, rubbing their temples. "Services are even worse. For B2B transactions, the reverse charge mechanism still applies, but only if the customer is VAT-registered in the EU. If they're not, you might have to register for VAT in their country. And don't even get me started on digital services. That's a whole other can of worms."

Sam blinked. "The reverse charge mechanism? What's that?"

"It's when the customer accounts for the VAT instead of the supplier," Post-Brexit VAT explained. "It's supposed to simplify things, but in practice, it's about as simple as assembling IKEA furniture without the instructions."

As if things weren't complicated enough, Post-Brexit VAT pulled out another chart, this one labelled *The Northern Ireland Protocol: A Comedy of Errors*. "Now, let's talk about Northern Ireland."

Sam groaned. "Do we have to?"

"Oh, we must," Post-Brexit VAT said, their eyes wide with desperation. "Northern Ireland is still part of the EU's VAT system for goods, but not for services. So, if you're trading goods between Northern Ireland and the EU, you follow EU rules. But if you're trading goods between Northern Ireland and the rest of the UK, you follow UK rules. It's like trying to play two different board games at the same time."

Sam buried his face in his hands. "This is madness."

Post-Brexit VAT nodded solemnly. "Welcome to my world."

Chapter 17
Global Tax Cooperation and Competition

Sam Harper always thought taxes were a local nuisance—like potholes, parking tickets, or that one neighbour who mows his lawn at 6 a.m. every Saturday. But after his run-ins with the various taxes , Sam discovered that taxes were actually a global sport—a high-stakes game played by nations, corporations, and accountants with nerves of steel (and calculators of questionable morality).

So when Sam received a gold-embossed invitation to the *Global Tax Summit,* he expected a snooze-fest. Instead, he found himself swept into an international adventure that made "Mission: Impossible" look like a game of Candy Land.

Global Tax himself greeted Sam at the door—a suave negotiator in a pinstripe suit, sunglasses indoors, and a briefcase so stuffed with treaties it looked like it might explode into a confetti of legalese at any moment. He spoke five languages, three dialects of accountant, and one ancient form of sarcasm.

"Welcome, Sam! Ready to solve the world's tax problems?"

Sam gulped. "Honestly, I just wanted to know if I could deduct my passport fees. And maybe my emotional support calculator."

Global Tax winked. "One step at a time, Sam. First, let's take a whirlwind tour of the world's most creative tax headaches."

He whisked Sam through a dazzling expo of global tax phenomena:

- *Tax Havens*: "Countries with low or no taxes, designed to attract foreign investment. They're the Bermuda shorts of the global economy—shady, questionably fashionable, and everyone's got a pair they won't admit to."
- *Transfer Pricing*: "Multinational corporations shifting profits to low-tax jurisdictions. It's like a shell game, but the only thing under the cup is a very confused auditor."
- *Base Erosion and Profit Shifting (BEPS):* "Companies exploiting loopholes to avoid taxes. It's like finding a cheat code for the global economy, except the only prize is a stern letter from the OECD."
- *Digital Taxes*: "Taxing tech giants that operate across borders. It's like trying to catch smoke with a butterfly net, while the smoke is busy launching an IPO."

Sam's head spun. "How does anyone keep track of all this? Do you have a spreadsheet, or just a really good therapist?"

Global Tax sighed, the sigh of someone who's been to too many summits and not enough happy hours. "That's why we have summits. And treaties. And endless negotiations that make a family Christmas look like a yoga retreat."

The summit itself was a spectacle: diplomats from every corner of the globe argued, negotiated, and occasionally threw croissants at each other with the precision of Olympic athletes. The French delegation had a three-croissant lead over the Germans, but the Swiss were quietly hoarding all the butter.

Global Tax led Sam to the *Tax Haven Pavilion*, where representatives from sunny islands and mysterious principalities strutted their stuff.

"They're trying to attract foreign investment," Global Tax explained. "It's like a beauty pageant, but with tax rates instead of swimsuits. Watch for the talent portion—last year, the Cayman Islands juggled offshore accounts while singing 'Money, Money, Money.'"

Sam watched as the reps promised low taxes, minimal regulations, and secrecy so tight even your mother couldn't find your bank account.

"Is this... ethical?" Sam asked, eyeing a delegate in a sequined blazer.

Global Tax shrugged. "It's complicated. Tax havens are like that friend who always has the best party but never cleans up. They're fun, but someone else pays the bill."

Next, they entered the *Digital Tax Thunderdome,* where tech companies and governments faced off in a battle of wits, PowerPoints, and passive-aggressive tweets.

"We need to tax digital services!" the governments declared, waving pie charts and pitchforks. "They're making billions in our countries but paying almost nothing in taxes!"

"We're creating jobs and innovation!" the tech companies countered, tossing out buzzwords like confetti. "And we're already paying taxes in other countries—probably. Maybe. Ask our lawyers."

Sam watched as the debate raged on, with no clear winner—just a lot of coffee, a few broken laser pointers, and one government official who tried to Venmo a tax bill to Silicon Valley.

As the summit wound down, Global Tax gave Sam a knowing look. "Global taxation is a never-ending adventure, Sam. It's about balancing the needs of each country with the needs of the world and trying to make sure everyone pays their fair share—without anyone flipping the Monopoly board."

Chapter 18

The Tariff Tantrum – When Even Your Coffee Costs a Fortune

Sam Harper was having a rare, good day—or at least, what passed for one in his tax-riddled existence. No surprise visits from Income Tax, no passive-aggressive emails from Audit Tax, and no unexpected bills from Sales Tax. For once, he thought he could enjoy a quiet morning with his favourite imported coffee beans—a small luxury that made life just a little more bearable.

But as he opened the package, something felt off. The bag was smaller than usual, and the price tag on the receipt was significantly larger. Sam frowned, his caffeine-deprived brain struggling to process the numbers. *Did I accidentally buy coffee infused with diamonds?* he wondered.

Grabbing his phone, he called the store. "Hi, I think there's been a mistake. I bought my usual coffee, but the price is almost double what I normally pay."

The store clerk sighed. "No mistake, sir. That's the new price. Tariffs on imported goods went up last month."

Sam blinked. "Tariffs? You mean I'm paying extra because this coffee came from overseas?"

"That's right," the clerk replied. "It's part of the government's plan to promote homegrown products. They want people to buy local."

Sam stared at the phone in disbelief. "But we don't grow coffee here! What am I supposed to do, drink dandelion tea?"

The clerk chuckled nervously. "Well, you could always switch to domestic brands. But, uh, good luck with that."

Sam hung up, his blood boiling. He had barely taken a sip of his overpriced coffee when the door to his office burst open. A tall, imposing figure strode in, wearing a suit made entirely of shipping labels and carrying a clipboard the size of a small country.

"Sam Harper," the figure announced, their voice booming like a foghorn. "I am Tariff Tax, and I'm here to discuss your imported goods."

The Tariff Trap: When Even Your Groceries Are Taxed!

Sam groaned. "Of course you are. Let me guess—you're here to explain why my coffee costs more than my rent?"

Tariff Tax nodded solemnly. "Indeed. You see, Sam, tariffs are taxes imposed on imported goods. They're designed to protect domestic industries by making foreign products more expensive."

Sam threw up his hands. "Protect domestic industries? We don't even grow coffee here! What's the point of taxing something we can't produce ourselves?"

Tariff Tax adjusted their clipboard. "Ah, but that's where the government's logic comes in. By discouraging imports, they hope to encourage innovation and self-reliance. Who knows? Maybe one day, someone will figure out how to grow coffee in your backyard."

Sam snorted. "Yeah, and maybe pigs will fly. In the meantime, I'm stuck paying double for my morning caffeine fix."

Tariff Tax sat down, their clipboard resting on Sam's desk like a judge's gavel. "Sam, you have to understand. Tariffs are a balancing act. On one hand, they protect local businesses and create jobs. On the other hand, they can lead to higher prices for consumers. It's a trade-off."

Sam leaned back in his chair, his frustration mounting. "A trade-off? More like a rip-off. Look, I get the idea of supporting local businesses. But some things just can't be made here. Coffee, spices, electronics—these are things we rely on imports for. What are we supposed to do, just go without?"

Tariff Tax nodded thoughtfully. "You're not wrong, Sam. Globalization has allowed countries to specialize in what they do best. Coffee from Brazil, electronics from China, spices from India—these products are cheaper because they're made where it's most efficient. Tariffs disrupt that balance. By delocalizing production, you lose the cost savings that come from producing goods in their natural or economic sweet spots."

Sam sighed. "So, either way, the little guy gets screwed. If I buy local, I pay more because it's expensive to produce. If I buy imported, I pay more because of tariffs. How is anyone supposed to survive?"

Tariff Tax leaned forward, their expression serious. "That's the tricky part, Sam. When tariffs drive up the cost of imported goods, it doesn't just affect luxury items like coffee. It affects everything. Key ingredients, raw materials, machinery—these are all things that businesses rely on. When their costs go up, they pass those costs on to consumers."

Sam groaned. "So, let me get this straight. Tariffs make imports more expensive. Businesses raise their prices to cover the costs. And then we, the consumers, end up paying more for everything. Is that about, right?"

"Exactly," Tariff Tax said, nodding. "And when prices go up across the board, it leads to inflation. People have less disposable income, which means they spend less, which hurts the economy. It's a vicious cycle."

Sam buried his face in his hands. "Great. So not only am I paying more for coffee, but now I can't even afford to go out for dinner or buy new clothes. What's next? A tariff on happiness?"

Tariff Tax chuckled. "Not yet but give it time. Governments are always looking for new revenue streams."

Sam looked up, his frustration giving way to curiosity. "But seriously, how are countries supposed to survive without imports? I get the idea of promoting local products, but there are some things we just can't make here. What's the solution?"

Tariff Tax tapped their clipboard thoughtfully. "It's a delicate balance, Sam. Countries need to protect their industries, but they also need to recognize the importance of global trade. Some goods—like coffee, rare earth metals, and certain medicines—are essential and can only be sourced from overseas. That's why most governments use a mix of tariffs and trade agreements to manage imports."

Sam frowned. "Trade agreements? You mean like those deals where countries agree to lower tariffs on certain goods?"

"Exactly," Tariff Tax said. "Trade agreements help ensure that essential goods can flow freely between countries without driving up costs. But they're not perfect. Sometimes, they favour larger economies at the expense of smaller ones. And when tariffs are too high, they can lead to trade wars, which hurt everyone."

Sam sighed. "So, basically, it's a mess. No matter what you do, someone ends up paying the price."

Tariff Tax nodded. "That's the reality of global trade, Sam. It's complicated, messy, and often unfair. But without it, we wouldn't have access to the goods and resources we need to survive."

By the end of the conversation, Sam was exhausted. He looked at his now-cold cup of coffee and shook his head. "You know what? I give up. First, the government takes a chunk of my pay check. Then, religion wants its cut. Now, even my coffee is taxed to oblivion. What's next? A tariff on my thoughts?"

Tariff Tax smiled. "Not yet, but I wouldn't rule it out."

Sam groaned. "I'm moving to a deserted island. No tariffs, no taxes, no overpriced coffee. Just me, a hammock, and maybe a coconut or two."

As Tariff Tax stood to leave, they gave Sam a sympathetic pat on the shoulder. "Good luck with that, Sam. But just so you know, even deserted islands have import fees. Those coconuts don't ship themselves."

Sam buried his face in his hands as the door closed behind Tariff Tax. "I just wanted a cup of coffee," he muttered. "Is that too much to ask?"

CHAPTER 19
Free Trade Zones – The Tax-Free Illusion

Saturday evening and Sam was on his way to a party, while sitting in the cab he was browsing through his social media which was filled with envy-inducing photos from "tax-free" shopping paradises. But when he tried to claim his own duty-free deal, he was met with a maze of forms and hidden fees. It turned out that in the world of free trade zones, "tax-free" was often just an illusion—one that left even the savviest shoppers scratching their heads.

The ballroom was electric, buzzing with excitement and the faint scent of imported canapés. At the centre of it all was Free Trade Zone, the undeniable star of the evening. Dressed in a flashy gold suit with "TAX-FREE" emblazoned in bold letters across the back, they moved through the crowd with the confidence of someone who knew they were the main attraction. In one hand, they held a stack of business cards, and in the other, a microphone.

"Ladies and gentlemen," Free Trade Zone began, their voice smooth and persuasive, "I'm here to make your dreams come true. No taxes, no tariffs, no red tape. Just pure, unadulterated profit. Come to my zone, and watch your business thrive!"

The crowd erupted into applause. Entrepreneurs, investors, and even a few sceptical government officials leaned in, captivated by the promise of prosperity. Free Trade Zone handed out business cards like candy, each one stamped with their slogan: "No Taxes, No Worries."

Sam, clutching a glass of suspiciously cheap champagne, watched as familiar faces mingled. Small Business Tax, in a plain suit, looked on with envy. Payroll Tax nervously checked a shrinking ledger. VAT and Customs Duty exchanged worried glances by the buffet, their plates empty.

At first, the allure was irresistible. Businesses flocked to Free Trade Zone, setting up factories, warehouses, and offices. The promise of duty-free imports and exports was too good to pass up. For a while, it seemed like a utopia. Jobs were created, trade flourished, and profits soared.

But as the glitter began to fade, cracks started to show.

Small Business Tax grumbled to Sam, "How are we supposed to compete? They get all the benefits, and we're left to pick up the slack."

Nearby, VAT muttered, "I used to be busy. Now, I'm just standing around while Free Trade Zone gets all the attention."

Customs Duty nodded. "I haven't stamped a form in days. I'm starting to forget what a tariff even looks like."

Governments, too, started to take notice. Revenue streams that once flowed steadily began to dry up. "Wait a minute," said Corporate Tax, stepping into the spotlight. Dressed in a sharp black suit, they exuded authority and a no-nonsense attitude. "You're not really tax-free, are you? You're just shifting the burden elsewhere."

Income Tax, always the pragmatist, chimed in from the sidelines. "Someone has to pay for schools and hospitals. If you're not contributing, who is?"

Free Trade Zone shrugged, a sly grin spreading across their face. "I never said I was perfect," they replied, their tone unapologetic. "I'm just... strategic. Sure, I might create some imbalances but look at the jobs I've created! The trade I've stimulated! Isn't that worth something?"

The room fell silent as the crowd considered this. Corporate Tax wasn't convinced. "But at what cost?" they pressed. "Local businesses are struggling. Governments are losing revenue. And let's not forget the loopholes you create for corporations to exploit. You're not a solution—you're a Band-Aid."

From the back, Wealth Tax, who had seen it all, raised an eyebrow. "Every time we chase growth without balance, someone gets left behind."

Suddenly, Loophole appeared, sliding up to Sam with a wink. "See, Sam? Free Trade Zone is my kind of place. Lots of opportunities for... creative accounting."

Sam groaned. "Not you again."

Free Trade Zone raised their hands in mock surrender. "Hey, I never claimed to be a hero. I'm just an option. A tool. It's up to you how you use me."

The crowd murmured in agreement. Free Trade Zone wasn't a villain, but they weren't a hero either. They were a reminder that in the world of taxes, nothing is ever truly free. Every benefit came with a cost, and every solution created new problems.

As the party wound down, Free Trade Zone slipped out the back door, leaving behind a room full of people with more questions than answers. They were a paradox, a glittering promise that shone brightly but cast long shadows. And in the end, they were a reflection of the complex, messy world of taxation—a world where the line between opportunity and exploitation was often blurred.

Sam watched the crowd disperse, his head spinning. "Just once," he muttered, "I'd like to go to a party where the only thing I have to worry about is the hangover."

CHAPTER 20

Tax Havens vs. Tax Justice – The Offshore Showdown

Sam Harper was starting to suspect that his office was cursed. Every time he managed to clean up the mess from the last tax-related disaster, another one barged in, ready to wreak havoc on his sanity. He'd barely had time to skim the brochure on free trade zones when the door to his office swung open once again.

This time, it wasn't just one tax character it was two. And they looked like they were about to have a cage match.

"Sam!" Tax Haven exclaimed, diving behind Sam's desk for cover. "Hide me! They're after me!"

Before Sam could ask who "they" were, another figure stormed into the office, radiating righteous fury. This one was dressed in a crisp suit, carrying a briefcase and a banner that read "Tax Justice Now!" Their eyes blazed with the kind of moral conviction that could melt glaciers.

"There you are!" the second figure shouted, pointing a finger at Tax Haven. "You can't hide from justice, you offshore scofflaw!"

Sam groaned, sinking into his chair. "Oh, great. What is it this time?"

The second figure turned to Sam, their expression softening slightly. "I am Tax Justice, and I'm here to expose the dark underbelly of the global tax system. And this," they said, pointing at Tax Haven, "is one of the biggest offenders."

Tax Haven peeked out from behind Sam's desk, rolling their eyes. "Oh, please. I'm just providing a service. If people don't like taxes, that's not my fault."

Tax Justice glared at them. "A service? You're enabling tax evasion on a massive scale, depriving governments of the resources they need to fund public services. You're a parasite!"

Tax Haven shrugged. "Hey, I'm just giving people what they want. If governments want more money, they should make their tax systems more attractive."

Sam rubbed his temples. "Okay, can we just take a step back? What exactly is a tax haven?"

Tax Justice stepped forward, pulling out a chart that looked like it had been stolen from a political rally. "A tax haven is a jurisdiction with low or no taxes, strict bank secrecy laws, and a lack of transparency. They're used by individuals and corporations to hide their wealth and avoid paying taxes in their home countries."

Tax Haven scoffed. "That's just a fancy way of saying we're good at what we do. We offer a safe, secure, and confidential environment for people to manage their assets."

Sam frowned. "So, it's like a secret bank account?"

Tax Justice nodded. "Exactly. Except instead of just hiding your money, you're actively depriving your government of the resources it needs to fund schools, hospitals, and infrastructure."

Tax Haven rolled their eyes. "Oh, please. Governments waste money all the time. At least when people put their money in tax havens, it's being used productively."

Tax Justice glared at them. "Productively? You mean lining the pockets of the wealthy elite while the rest of the world suffers?"

Sam raised a hand. "Okay, can we just stick to the facts? What are some examples of tax havens?"

Tax Justice pointed to the chart. "The usual suspects: the Cayman Islands, Switzerland, Luxembourg, Bermuda, the British Virgin Islands. They're all notorious for their low taxes and strict secrecy laws."

Tax Haven grinned. "Hey, we're just popular. People love us."

Tax Justice stepped forward, their voice rising with passion. "Tax havens are a cancer on the global economy. They undermine democracy, exacerbate inequality, and fuel corruption. We need to shut them down."

Tax Haven scoffed. "Shut us down? Good luck with that. We're too powerful. We have friends in high places."

Tax Justice glared at them. "We're not afraid of you. We have the power of the people on our side. We're going to expose your secrets and hold you accountable."

Tax Haven rolled their eyes. "Oh, please. No one cares about taxes. They're boring."

Tax Justice smirked. "You'd be surprised. People are starting to realize that tax evasion isn't just a victimless crime. It's a theft from all of us."

Sam, caught in the middle of the showdown, raised a hand. "Okay, can we just calm down for a second? What are some of the arguments in favor of tax havens?"

Tax Haven grinned. "Finally, a good question. Tax havens promote economic growth by attracting investment and capital. They also encourage competition among tax systems, which leads to lower taxes and more efficient government."

Tax Justice snorted. "That's just a smokescreen. Tax havens are used to hide illicit wealth, launder money, and finance terrorism. They're a threat to global security."

Tax Haven rolled their eyes. "Oh, please. That's just fear-mongering. We're not responsible for what people do with their money."

Tax Justice glared at them. "You're enabling it. You're providing a safe haven for criminals and corrupt officials."

Sam leaned forward, frowning. "Okay, but how does all this affect regular people?"

Tax Justice stepped forward, their voice softening slightly. "Tax evasion deprives governments of the resources they need to fund public services. This means less money for schools, hospitals, and infrastructure. It also means higher taxes for everyone else."

Tax Haven shrugged. "Hey, I never said life was fair. Some people are just better at managing their money than others."

Tax Justice glared at them. "That's not the point. Tax evasion is a moral issue. It's about fairness and responsibility. We all have a duty to pay our fair share."

Tax Haven rolled their eyes. "Oh, please. Don't give me that moral lecture. Taxes are just a way for governments to steal our money."

Sam sighed. "So, basically, tax havens are like... a black hole that sucks up all the money and leaves everyone else struggling to make ends meet?"

Tax Justice nodded. "Exactly. They're a drain on society."

Tax Haven smirked. "Hey, we're just providing a service. If people don't like taxes, that's not our fault."

Sam rubbed his temples, feeling a headache coming on. "Why does everything in the world of taxes have to be so complicated? Can't we just have a system that works for everyone?"

Tax Haven and Tax Justice exchanged a look before bursting into laughter.

"Oh, Sam," Tax Haven said, wiping a tear from their eye. "You're adorable."

Tax Justice smirked. "A system that works for everyone? That's the dream. But in reality, it's all about power and money."

Sam sighed. "Great. So, what am I supposed to do with all this information?"

Tax Haven handed him a brochure titled "Tax Havens: Your Gateway to Financial Freedom" while Tax Justice handed him a report labeled "The Cost of Tax Evasion: A Global Crisis."

"Good luck," they said in unison before storming out of his office, still arguing.

As the door slammed shut, Sam leaned back in his chair, staring at the ceiling. "I need a vacation," he muttered. "Preferably somewhere without taxes."

Little did he know, his next visitor would make tax havens look like a walk in the park.

PART IV

Tax Scandals and Revelations

CHAPTER 21

The Panama Papers - A Leak in the System

Sam Harper had officially given up on the idea of a normal day. At this point, his office felt less like a workspace and more like the set of a bizarre reality show where taxes had personalities, egos, and a knack for ruining his life. He was still recovering from the verbal brawl between Tax Haven and Tax Justice when his phone buzzed with a news alert.

"BREAKING: Panama Papers Leak Exposes Global Tax Evasion Scandal."

Sam frowned, clicking on the headline. The article was full of words like offshore accounts, shell companies, and illicit wealth. It sounded like the plot of a spy thriller, except instead of car chases and explosions, it was all about accountants and spreadsheets.

Before he could process what he was reading, the door to his office burst open (as it always did), and in marched a new figure. They were dressed in a trench coat and fedora, carrying a briefcase that looked like it contained state secrets. Their face was partially obscured by a scarf, and they had the air of someone who had seen too much.

"Sam Harper," the figure said, their voice low and gravelly. "We need to talk."

Sam groaned. "Let me guess. You're another tax."

"Yes! They call me the leak" he said.

Sam blinked. "The Leak? That's... not ominous at all."

The Leak chuckled, tossing the folder onto Sam's desk. "I'm the one who exposes the dirty secrets of the rich and powerful. You've heard of the Panama Papers, right?"

Sam nodded slowly. "Yeah, I just read about it. Something about offshore accounts and tax evasion?"

Sam's jaw dropped. "That's... a lot of data."

"Here's how it works," The Leak said, pointing to the diagram. "A wealthy individual sets up a shell company in a tax haven like the British Virgin Islands. This company doesn't actually do anything—it's just a front. Then, they use that company to hide their assets, avoid taxes, and launder money."

Sam frowned. "And no one notices this?"

Sam leaned forward, squinting at the diagram. "Wait, are those... politicians' names?"

Sam raised an eyebrow. "Soccer players? Really?"

Sam leaned back in his chair, trying to process everything. "So, what happens now? Do these people get punished?"

Sam frowned. "That's... depressing."

Sam rubbed his temples. "So, what's the point of exposing all this if nothing changes?"

Before Sam could respond, the door burst open again, and in marched Tax Justice, looking more fired up than ever.

"The Leak!" Tax Justice exclaimed, pointing dramatically. "I've been looking for you. We need to work together."

Tax Justice shrugged. "Desperate times call for desperate measures. The Panama Papers are the perfect opportunity to expose the corruption in the system and push for reform."

Sam groaned. "Oh, great. Another team-up. This is starting to feel like a bad superhero movie."

Tax Justice ignored him, turning to The Leak. "We need to keep the pressure on. Governments are already trying to sweep this under the rug. If we don't act now, nothing will change."

Sam raised a hand. "Uh, can I just ask one thing? What am I supposed to do in all this?"

Tax Justice and The Leak exchanged a look before turning to Sam.

"You," Tax Justice said, "are going to help us spread the word."

Sam blinked. "Me? How? I'm just a regular guy."

Sam groaned. "Why do I feel like I'm being dragged into something way over my head?"

By the time Tax Justice and The Leak left his office, Sam was more confused than ever. He stared at the folder on his desk, wondering how he'd gone from a guy struggling to file his taxes to someone apparently involved in a global fight for tax justice.

"I just wanted to figure out my deductions," he muttered. "Now I'm supposed to take on the offshore finance system? How is this my life?"

As he leaned back in his chair, the phone on his desk buzzed. It was another news alert.

"BREAKING: Paradise Papers Leak Reveals More Offshore Secrets."

Sam groaned, burying his face in his hands. "I need a new job."

As the chaos of the Panama Papers continued to unfold, Sam realized that his journey through the world of taxes was far from over. The fight for tax justice was just beginning, and whether he liked it or not, he was now part of it.

Chapter 22

The Holy Collection Plate: When Even Faith Demands Its Cut

Sunday morning and sam was sitting in the church waiting for the wedding to start. The church was filled with music and laughter, but Sam's attention was drawn to the ornate collection plate making its rounds. As he watched people drop in bills and coins, he wondered: when did giving become an obligation? In the world of faith and finance, Sam was about to learn that even salvation sometimes comes with a suggested donation.

Sam Harper thought he had finally caught a break. For once, he wasn't in his office being harassed by yet another tax. No, today he was at a wedding—a joyous occasion, a celebration of love, and, most importantly, a tax-free event. Or so he thought.

The ceremony was being held in a grand old church, the kind with stained glass windows that made you feel guilty just for existing. Sam sat in the pews, trying to focus on the vows being exchanged, but his mind kept wandering. He couldn't help but notice the collection plate being passed around, even during the wedding. *Seriously?* he thought. *They're charging admission to a wedding now?*

As if that wasn't enough, the church wasn't the only religious institution cashing in. Clerics from other faiths were in attendance, each one subtly promoting their own donation schemes. A rabbi was handing out envelopes for synagogue dues, an imam was quietly distributing QR codes for mosque donations, and a Buddhist monk was selling "enlightenment packages" with tiered pricing. Sam couldn't believe his eyes. It was like a spiritual version of Shark Tank.

After the ceremony, Sam found himself cornered by a figure in flowing robes, holding a golden collection plate. Their presence radiated an air of divine authority, but their expression was that of someone who had just spotted a prime donation target.

"Sam Harper," the figure intoned, their voice calm but firm. "I am Tithe Tax, and I'm here to discuss your spiritual obligations."

Sam blinked. "My what?"

"Your spiritual obligations," Tithe Tax repeated, holding out the collection plate like a waiter presenting the dessert menu. "Faith, my dear Sam, is not free. It requires commitment, devotion, and, of course, financial contributions."

Sam stared at them, his jaw dropping. "You've got to be kidding me. Even religion demands taxes? What's next, a tax on breathing?"

Tithe Tax smiled serenely, the kind of smile that said, *Oh, sweet summer child, you have no idea.* "Oh, no, Sam. Breathing is free. But salvation? That comes with a price."

Sam groaned. "So, let me get this straight. On top of paying taxes to the government, I'm supposed to give 10% of my income to the church? That's not faith—that's extortion!"

Tithe Tax raised an eyebrow, their expression a mix of divine patience and mild annoyance. "Extortion? Hardly. It's a sacred tradition. The Bible, the Quran, the Torah—they all emphasize the importance of giving. It's not just about money, Sam. It's about showing gratitude and trust in a higher power."

Sam snorted. "Gratitude? Trust? I can barely trust my pay cheque to last the month, and now you're telling me I need to hand over a chunk of it to keep the lights on in a building I visit twice a year?"

Tithe Tax sighed, placing the collection plate on a nearby pew. "Sam, you're focusing on the exceptions, not the rule. Most religious institutions use their funds responsibly. But yes, with great wealth comes great power. And some do use that power to influence society."

Sam leaned forward, his frustration boiling over. "Influence? You mean like lobbying governments to pass laws that align with their beliefs? Or using their weight to guilt people into giving more than they can afford? Because that doesn't sound very holy to me."

Tithe Tax hesitated. "It's true that some institutions wield their influence in ways that can be... controversial. But consider this: without their advocacy, many social justice movements wouldn't exist. Religious organizations have been at the forefront of fighting poverty, promoting education, and advocating for human rights."

Sam threw up his hands. "And yet, they still demand more. More money, more loyalty, more control. It's like they're running a spiritual monopoly, and I'm just a pawn in their game."

As the wedding reception began, Sam found himself seated at a table with the rabbi, the imam, and the Buddhist monk. They were deep in conversation about the best ways to encourage donations.

"Direct debit is the way to go," the rabbi said. "It's automatic, and people barely notice it."

The imam nodded. "True, but QR codes are the future. People can donate right from their phones."

The monk chimed in, "Have you considered offering a premium membership? For £99 a month, they get front-row seats at sermons and a free tote bag."

Sam couldn't take it anymore. "Are you all seriously sitting here strategizing how to squeeze more money out of people? This is a wedding, not a board meeting!"

The rabbi shrugged. "A wedding is the perfect time to remind people of their spiritual obligations. They're already emotional—it's the ideal moment to ask for donations."

Sam groaned. "Yeah, but at what cost? Families are already struggling to make ends meet, and now they're supposed to feel guilty if they can't give? It's not just about helping others—it's about the pressure. The judgment. The sermons about how giving is a sign of faith, and if you're not giving, you're not faithful enough."

As if on cue, the door to the reception hall burst open, and in strolled Tax Haven, still wearing their Hawaiian shirt and flip-flops. They were carrying a margarita this time, looking as relaxed as ever.

"Hey, everyone!" Tax Haven said, plopping down at Sam's table. "What's the drama today?"

The rabbi frowned. "This is a serious discussion about the role of religious donations in society."

Tax Haven grinned. "Oh, I know all about that. Did you know most religious institutions are tax-exempt? They don't pay property taxes, income taxes, or even sales taxes in some cases. It's like they're the original tax havens."

Sam's eyes widened. "Wait, what? So, they're collecting money from people like me, and they don't even have to pay taxes on it?"

The imam bristled. "We're tax-exempt because we provide essential services to the community."

Tax Haven smirked. "Sure you do. And I'm just a sunny vacation spot. Let's not pretend there aren't a few loopholes being exploited here."

Sam buried his face in his hands. "I can't believe this. Even religion has a loophole. Is there anyone who isn't trying to squeeze me dry?"

By the end of the night, Sam decided he needed a drink. He wandered over to the bar, hoping to drown his frustrations in a glass of whiskey. But when the bartender handed him the bill, Sam nearly choked.

"Service charge? VAT? Imported customs duties?!" Sam exclaimed, staring at the receipt like it was a ransom note. "I just wanted a drink, not a financial audit!"

The bartender shrugged. "Welcome to the wedding industry, sir. Even your whiskey has a price."

Sam slammed the bill on the counter. "I've had enough! First, the government takes a chunk of my pay cheque. Then, every time I buy something, Sales Tax is there to grab a piece. Now, even religion wants its cut? And now my drink is taxed to oblivion? What's next? A tax on my thoughts?"

Tithe Tax appeared behind him, smiling gently. "Sam, faith is about more than money. It's about—"

Sam cut them off. "No, it's about control. You want my money, my time, my loyalty—and for what? So I can sit in a pew and feel guilty about not giving enough? Forget it. I'm done."

As Tithe Tax, the rabbi, the imam, and the monk exchanged awkward glances, Sam grabbed his coat and stormed out of the reception hall. "I'm going to find a place where no one can tax me," he muttered. "Maybe a deserted island. Or the moon."

Chapter 23

Paradise Papers – The Sequel No One Asked For

Sam Harper had officially reached the point where he was no longer surprised by anything. If a tax character burst into his office riding a unicycle and juggling flaming deductions, he'd probably just sigh and ask them to take a number. But even Sam wasn't prepared for what came next.

It started, as always, with a news alert on his phone.

"BREAKING: Paradise Papers Leak Exposes New Offshore Scandals."

Sam groaned, rubbing his temples. "Oh, great. Another leak. What is this, the Netflix series of tax scandals? Can't we just cancel the show already?"

Before he could finish his thought, the door to his office swung open (because of course it did), and in strolled The Leak, looking smug as ever. This time, they were accompanied by a new figure—a glamorous, impeccably dressed individual who looked like they'd just stepped off the cover of Forbes. They carried a designer briefcase and wore a diamond-encrusted watch that probably cost more than Sam's entire apartment.

"Sam!" The Leak said, clapping their hands together. "Meet my latest masterpiece: The Paradise Papers."

The new figure gave a dazzling smile, extending a perfectly manicured hand. "Charmed, I'm sure."

Sam stared at them, his mouth slightly open. "Wait, you're... the Paradise Papers? You're a person now?"

The Paradise Papers laughed, a sound so polished it could have been bottled and sold as luxury perfume. "Oh, darling, I'm not just a person. I'm a phenomenon. The Panama Papers were groundbreaking, sure, but I'm the sequel everyone's been waiting for. Bigger, bolder, and with even more drama."

Sam groaned. "Why does this feel like a bad movie franchise?"

Sam raised an eyebrow. "So, basically, it's the same story as the Panama Papers, but with fancier names?"

Sam sighed. "Great. So, what's the takeaway this time? That the rich are still rich and the rest of us are still paying for it? That's ... infuriating.

Before Sam could continue, the door burst open again, and in marched Tax Justice, looking more determined than ever.

"The Paradise Papers!" Tax Justice exclaimed, pointing dramatically. "I've been waiting for this moment."

Tax Justice crossed their arms. "I want accountability. The Paradise Papers are proof that the global tax system is rigged in favor of the wealthy. It's time for governments to step up and take action."

Tax Justice glared at them. "That's why we need to close those loopholes and hold people accountable. The Paradise Papers are a wake-up call."

Sam raised his hand. "Uh, can I just ask one thing? What's the difference between the Panama Papers and the Paradise Papers?"

"Ah, an excellent question," Tax Justice replies. "Think of it this way: the Panama Papers primarily exposed the offshore activities facilitated by a single law firm, Mossack Fonseca, and their use of shell companies. The Paradise Papers, on the other hand, cast a wider net, revealing the offshore dealings of multiple law firms and corporate service providers across various jurisdictions. So, Panama was a deep dive into one firm, while Paradise was a broader survey of the offshore world."

Sam sighed. "Great. So, what am I supposed to do with all this information?"

Tax Justice handed him a pamphlet titled "Demanding Tax Justice: A Citizen's Guide to Fighting Inequality", while The Paradise Papers handed him a glossy brochure labeled "Secrets of the Elite: How to Live Tax-Free (Legally)".

"Good luck," they said in unison before storming out of his office, still arguing.

As the door slammed shut, Sam leaned back in his chair, staring at the ceiling. "I just wanted to figure out my deductions," he muttered. "Now I'm stuck in the middle of a global tax revolution. How is this my life?"

His phone buzzed again with another news alert.

"BREAKING: Pandora Papers Leak Exposes Even More Offshore Secrets."

Sam groaned, burying his face in his hands. "I need a drink."

As the chaos of the Paradise Papers unfolded, Sam realized that his journey through the world of taxes was far from over. The fight for tax justice was getting bigger, and whether he liked it or not, he was now part of it.

CHAPTER 24

Paradise Papers: Secrets Unveiled

Sam Harper stared at the glossy brochure in his hand, the one handed to him by The Paradise Papers. The title, "Secrets of the Elite: How to Live Tax-Free (Legally)," glistened in gold foil, mocking him. He tossed it onto his desk with a groan.

"Why do I feel like I'm the only person in the world who actually pays taxes?" he muttered.

Before he could wallow in self-pity, the door to his office creaked open again. Sam didn't even look up this time. "Let me guess," he said, waving a hand. "You're here to tell me about another tax scandal, right? Maybe the Bermuda Briefs or the Cayman Chronicles?"

Instead of a response, he heard the sound of someone clearing their throat. He looked up to see Audit Tax, standing in the doorway with their ever-present clipboard and a look of grim determination.

"Sam," Audit Tax said, stepping into the room. "We need to talk."

Sam groaned. "Oh, come on! I've already got The Leak, Tax Justice, and The Paradise Papers breathing down my neck. What do you want?"

Audit Tax adjusted their glasses, their expression as serious as ever. "I'm here to warn you. The Paradise Papers are just the beginning. Things are about to get... messy."

Sam blinked. "Messy? Messier than this?" He gestured to the chaos in his office: stacks of brochures, charts, and pamphlets from every tax character he'd encountered so far.

Audit Tax nodded. "Much messier. The Paradise Papers have exposed some of the most powerful people in the world. Do you know what happens when you shine a light on people who are used to operating in the shadows?"

Sam frowned. "They... get mad?"

Audit Tax smirked. "Oh, they don't just get mad. They fight back. Hard."

As if on cue, the door burst open (again), and in strutted The Paradise Papers, looking as glamorous as ever. They were followed by a small entourage of equally well-dressed assistants, each carrying a stack of documents.

"Sam, darling," The Paradise Papers said, flashing their dazzling smile. "Don't listen to Audit Tax. He's just jealous because I'm stealing the spotlight."

Audit Tax glared at them. "This isn't about the spotlight. It's about accountability."

The Paradise Papers responded, "Accountability? Darling, I am accountability! I'm holding these people to account in the court of public opinion, which is far more effective than your dusty old audits."

I'm a modern day superhero!" he said.

Sam raised an eyebrow. "A hero? You're literally exposing how the rich avoid paying taxes. How does that make you a hero?"

The Paradise Papers responded,* "Because someone has to be! These people operate in secrecy, shielded by layers of lawyers and loopholes. I'm giving a voice to the voiceless, the taxpayers who are left footing the bill."

Sam groaned. "Great. So, you're the Keeping Up with the Kardashians of tax leaks."

The Paradise Papers responded, "Perhaps, but at least I'm providing valuable information! Besides, everyone loves a good scandal, darling. It's human nature."

Audit Tax smirked. "So? You're a glorified gossip column for accountants."

The Paradise Papers retorted, "And you're a glorified rule-book, darling! At least people are interested in what I have to say. When was the last time anyone threw a party to celebrate tax compliance?"

Audit Tax's face turned red. "I ensure compliance! Without me, the whole system would fall apart!"

Sam held up his hands. "Okay, okay, can we all just calm down? I'm already drowning in tax drama. I don't need you two fighting on top of it."

Before anyone could respond, the door burst open yet again (Sam was seriously considering installing a lock), and in marched Tax Haven, still wearing their Hawaiian shirt and flip-flops. They were carrying a margarita this time, looking as relaxed as ever.

"Hey, everyone!" Tax Haven said, plopping down on Sam's desk. "What's the drama today?"

Tax Haven grinned. "Miss me? I heard my name mentioned in the Paradise Papers, so I thought I'd drop by and see what all the fuss is about."

Audit Tax crossed their arms. "The fuss is about how you enable tax evasion and undermine the global economy."

Tax Haven shrugged. "Hey, I'm just a place. People come to me because I'm fun, sunny, and, oh yeah, I don't charge taxes. Is that my fault?"

Audit Tax responded, "It's about how you provide a safe harbor for illicit funds, robbing governments of much-needed revenue and creating a system where the rich get richer while everyone else suffers."

Tax Haven raised their margarita in a mock toast. "Guilty as charged."

Sam buried his face in his hands. "Why is this my life?"

As the argument between The Paradise Papers, Audit Tax, and Tax Haven escalated, Sam felt his patience slipping away. He stood up, slamming his hands on his desk.

"Enough!" he shouted. "I don't care about offshore accounts, shell companies, or tax loopholes! I just want to figure out how to file my taxes without losing my mind!"

Sam took a deep breath, running a hand through his hair. "Look, I get it. The system is broken. The rich are getting away with murder, and the rest of us are stuck footing the bill. But what am I supposed to do about it? I'm just one guy!"

Audit Tax nodded. "Knowledge is power, Sam. The more people know about how the system works, the harder it will be for the wealthy to exploit it."

Tax Haven shrugged. "Or, you know, you could just move to the Cayman Islands. I hear the beaches are lovely this time of year."

Sam glared at them. "Not helping."

As the chaos in his office finally began to settle, Sam realized that his journey through the world of taxes was far from over. The Paradise Papers had opened his eyes to the scale of the problem, but it was clear that there was still so much more to learn.

He sat back in his chair, staring at the stack of documents on his desk. "I guess I don't have a choice," he muttered. "If I'm going to survive this, I need to figure out how the system really works."

As the door closed behind them, Sam leaned back in his chair, staring at the ceiling. "I need a vacation," he muttered. "Preferably somewhere without taxes."

His phone buzzed again with another news alert.

"BREAKING: Pandora Papers Leak Exposes Even More Offshore Secrets."

Sam groaned, burying his face in his hands. "I'm never getting out of this, am I?"

Chapter 25

The Ethics of Tax Planning

Sam Harper used to think taxes were like a bad haircut: you paid for it, you didn't love it, but you moved on and hoped nobody noticed. But after his whirlwind tour through the trade zones, Sam realized taxes were also a moral minefield—a place where your conscience could trip and fall flat on its face.

So when Sam received an invitation to the "Ethics of Tax Planning Seminar," hosted by none other than Ethics Tax himself, he was both intrigued and slightly terrified. The invitation promised "light refreshments and heavy existential dread."

Ethics Tax greeted Sam at the door, looking every bit the philosopher: tweed jacket, beard, pipe, and a bookshelf groaning under the weight of books with titles like "Kant Touch This: A Guide to Moral Philosophy" and "Nietzsche and Numbers: Why the Tax Office Has No Chill." He handed Sam a cup of chamomile tea—because nothing says "let's talk about your moral failings" like a soothing herbal infusion.

"Welcome, Sam!" Ethics Tax intoned, his voice echoing with the gravitas of someone who's read too much Plato and not enough Garfield. "Are you ready to explore the moral maze of tax avoidance?"

Sam nodded, trying to look wise, but mostly just hoping there'd be snacks.

Ethics Tax led Sam through a series of exhibits, each more confusing than the last, like a museum curated by someone who'd just discovered both caffeine and moral ambiguity.

- *Tax Evasion:* "Illegally avoiding taxes. It's like robbing a bank, but with more paperwork and fewer ski masks."
- *Tax Avoidance*: "Legally minimizing taxes. It's like finding a cheat code in a video game, but the only prize is a slightly less angry accountant."
- *Tax Planning:* "Strategically managing your finances to reduce your tax burden. It's like playing chess with the Tax Office, except they are always white and always go first."
- *Tax Compliance:* "Paying your taxes honestly and accurately. It's like being a good citizen, but with less applause and more receipts."

Sam blinked. "So... where's the line between avoidance and evasion? Is it like jaywalking versus grand theft auto?"

Ethics Tax smiled, the kind of smile that said, "I know the answer, but I'm not telling."

"That's the million-pound question, Sam. And the answer depends on your conscience. Or, failing that, your lawyer."

Next came the "Ethical Dilemma Funhouse," where every mirror made your moral compass look slightly crooked.

- *The Offshore Account:* "You can move your money to a tax haven. It's legal, but is it ethical? Bonus points if you can pronounce 'Cayman Islands' without smirking."
- *The Aggressive Deduction*: "You can claim a deduction that's technically allowed, but morally questionable. Do you take the risk, or do you sleep at night?"
- *The Cash Business:* "You run a cash business and could easily underreport your income. Do you resist the

temptation, or do you buy that jet ski you've always wanted?"
- *The Charitable Donation:* "You can donate to a charity you don't really support, just to get a tax deduction. Is that ethical, or just creative accounting with a side of guilt?"

Sam scratched his head. "It depends on the situation! And maybe on how much I like jet skis."

Ethics Tax nodded sagely. "Indeed. There are no easy answers. But remember: the Tax Office has no sense of humour, and neither does karma."

Then, Ethics Tax wheeled out the "Philosophy Wheel of Misfortune," spinning through the greatest hits of moral reasoning:

- *Utilitarianism:* "The greatest good for the greatest number. Taxes should maximize happiness, or at least minimize angry tweets."
- *Libertarianism*: "Individual freedom above all. Taxes are a necessary evil, like traffic lights or pineapple on pizza."
- *Egalitarianism:* "Equality for all. Taxes should redistribute wealth, or at least make billionaires slightly less smug at dinner parties."

Sam's head spun. "Which one is right? And do any of them come with a tax deduction?"

Ethics Tax grinned. "That's for you to decide, Sam. But remember: every tax system is a reflection of our values. And our values should be guided by ethics, not just by who has the best accountant."

As Sam left the seminar, he felt a strange sense of peace. Maybe, just maybe, he could navigate the world of taxation with a clear conscience—and a good joke or two. He checked his phone. No new notifications. For the first time in weeks, he wasn't worried about audits, loopholes, or whether his moral compass needed a tune-up.

He smiled, thinking, "If taxes were people, at least they'd be interesting at parties."

Chapter 26

Tax-Free Utopia – The Dream (or Nightmare?)

Sam Harper had reached his breaking point. After surviving the Paradise Papers and Pandora Papers fiascos, he was ready to throw in the towel. The tax system was a labyrinth of loopholes, offshore accounts, and scandals, and Sam was just one guy trying to make sense of it all.

So, when a mysterious invitation arrived in his inbox with the subject line "Escape the Tax Trap – Discover Tax-Free Utopia!", Sam couldn't resist. The email promised a land where taxes didn't exist, where people lived in harmony, and where the government didn't take a single penny from its citizens. It sounded too good to be true, but at this point, Sam was desperate for a break.

"Tax-Free Utopia," Sam muttered, staring at the email. "No taxes? No audits? No paperwork? Sounds like heaven."

Little did he know, he was about to learn that paradise always comes with a price.

The next morning, Sam found himself on a private jet, courtesy of Utopia Promoter, the charismatic figure behind the email. Utopia Promoter was a slick, fast-talking individual in a white suit, with a smile so wide it could sell ice to a polar bear.

"Welcome aboard, Sam!" Utopia Promoter said, clapping him on the back. "You're about to experience the future of living. No taxes, no bureaucracy, no headaches. Just pure freedom."

Sam raised an eyebrow. "And how exactly does this place work? If there are no taxes, how does the government pay for anything?"

Utopia Promoter waved a hand dismissively. "Oh, we've got it all figured out. Tourism, voluntary contributions, and a thriving private sector. Trust me, Sam, you're going to love it."

The jet landed on a pristine island surrounded by crystal-clear waters. As Sam stepped off the plane, he was greeted by a group of smiling locals holding signs that read, "Welcome to Tax-Free Utopia!" The streets were lined with luxury shops, casinos, and five-star resorts. It looked like a postcard come to life.

"This is incredible," Sam said, taking it all in. "No taxes, and it still looks like this?"

Utopia Promoter grinned. "Told you. Now, let me show you around."

As Utopia Promoter gave Sam a tour of the island, everything seemed perfect—at first. The roads were smooth, the beaches were spotless, and the people seemed happy. But as they ventured further into the city, cracks began to show.

Sam noticed that while the tourist areas were immaculate, the residential neighborhoods were a different story. The roads were full of potholes, the schools looked run-down, and the hospitals were overcrowded.

"Uh, what's going on here?" Sam asked, pointing to a line of people waiting outside a clinic. "I thought this place was supposed to be a utopia."

Utopia Promoter hesitated. "Well, you see, without taxes, we don't have public funding for things like healthcare and education. But don't worry! The private sector has stepped in to fill the gap."

Sam frowned. "So, if someone can't afford private healthcare, what happens to them?"

Utopia Promoter's smile faltered. "They... improvise."

Sam's stomach sank. "Improvise? That doesn't sound very utopian."

As the tour continued, Sam began to notice more problems. The police force was underfunded, relying on donations from wealthy residents. Public transportation was nonexistent, and the only way to get around was by hiring expensive private drivers. Even the water supply was privatized, with residents paying exorbitant fees for clean drinking water.

Sam turned to Utopia Promoter. "So, let me get this straight. There are no taxes, but everything costs a fortune. How is this better than paying taxes?"

Utopia Promoter chuckled nervously. "Well, it's all about freedom, Sam. People here have the freedom to choose how they spend their money."

Sam raised an eyebrow. "Freedom? It sounds more like a nightmare for anyone who isn't rich."

Before Utopia Promoter could respond, a man in a tattered suit approached them, holding a sign that read, "Help! Can't Afford Rent!"

"What's his story?" Sam asked.

Utopia Promoter sighed. "Oh, he's one of the locals. You see, most of the island's revenue comes from tourism, so the locals have to work in the service industry. But with no minimum wage laws and no public housing, some of them... struggle."

Sam shook his head. "This isn't a utopia. It's a dystopia with good marketing."

Just as Sam was about to confront Utopia Promoter, a familiar voice called out behind him.

"Sam! There you are!"

Sam turned to see Income Tax, Sales Tax, Property Tax, and International Tax marching toward him. They looked furious.

"What are you guys doing here?" Sam asked, surprised.

Income Tax crossed his arms. "We're here to set the record straight. This so-called utopia is a disaster."

Sales Tax nodded. "Without us, there's no funding for public services. Sure, people complain about taxes, but at least we make sure the roads get fixed and the schools stay open."

Property Tax chimed in. "And don't even get me started on the housing crisis. Without me, there's no funding for affordable housing or urban development."

International Tax adjusted their tie. "And let's not forget the global implications. Tax-free zones like this one attract shady businesses and money launderers, which destabilizes the global economy."

Sam turned to Utopia Promoter. "Is this true?"

Utopia Promoter threw up their hands. "Okay, fine! Maybe it's not perfect. But at least people here don't have to deal with audits and paperwork!"

Audit Tax suddenly appeared, clipboard in hand. "Oh, don't worry. I'm here now."

Sam groaned. "Of course you are."

As the tax characters argued with Utopia Promoter, Sam took a moment to reflect. He had always thought of taxes as a burden, something to be avoided at all costs. But now, he was starting to see them in a new light.

"Okay, I get it," Sam said, interrupting the argument. "Taxes aren't perfect, but they're necessary. Without them, society falls apart. This place might look like paradise, but it's really just a playground for the rich."

Income Tax nodded. "Exactly. Taxes are the price we pay for a functioning society."

Sam turned to Utopia Promoter. "Thanks for the tour, but I think I'll stick with my tax-paying life. At least I know my money is going toward something useful."

Utopia Promoter sighed. "Suit yourself. But if you ever change your mind, you know where to find me."

As Sam boarded the plane back home, he felt a strange sense of relief. For the first time, he didn't dread the idea of paying taxes. Sure, they were annoying, but they were also what kept society running.

His phone buzzed with a new email. "Breaking: New Tax Simplification Bill Proposed."

Sam smiled. "Here we go again."

PART V

The Fight for Reform

CHAPTER 27

The Tax Simplification Summit – A Comedy of Errors

Sam Harper had barely unpacked his suitcase from his trip to Tax-Free Utopia when another invitation landed in his inbox. This time, it was from Tax Policy Analyst, a bespectacled, overly enthusiastic figure who had been pestering Sam ever since his name started popping up in tax-related news.

The subject line read: "You're Invited to the Global Tax Simplification Summit!"

Sam groaned. "Simplification? That's rich. The last time someone tried to 'simplify' taxes, I ended up with a 300-page instruction manual for filing deductions on my dog's chew toys."

Still, curiosity got the better of him. After all, if there was even a slim chance that this summit could make taxes less of a headache, it might be worth attending. Plus, he figured it couldn't possibly be worse than Tax-Free Utopia. Right?

The summit was being held in a massive conference center that looked like it had been designed by someone who thought "taxes" and "fun" belonged in the same sentence. The walls were decorated with banners that read, "Simplify to Amplify!" and "Flat Tax: The Future is Flat!" Sam couldn't help but notice that the coffee station was already out of creamer—a bad omen, if ever there was one.

As he wandered into the main hall, he was greeted by Tax Policy Analyst, a wiry figure with a clipboard and a permanent look of excitement, like they'd just discovered a new tax loophole.

"Sam! You made it!" Tax Policy Analyst exclaimed, shaking his hand with the enthusiasm of a used car salesman. "This is going to be life-changing! We've got experts from all over the world here to discuss how to make taxes simpler, fairer, and more efficient."

Sam raised an eyebrow. "Simpler? You mean like how a Rubik's Cube is 'simpler' after you peel off all the stickers?"

Tax Policy Analyst laughed nervously. "Oh, you're going to love this. Let me introduce you to some of the key players."

"Ah, Sam Harper," Flat Tax said, shaking his hand firmly. "I've heard a lot about you. Let me tell you, I'm the solution to all your problems. One rate for everyone. No brackets, no deductions, no nonsense."

Sam frowned. "One rate? So, a billionaire pays the same percentage as someone working minimum wage?"

Flat Tax grinned. "Exactly! It's fair because it's equal."

Sam tilted his head. "Fair? That's like saying it's fair to give everyone the same size parachute, whether they're jumping out of a plane or off a step stool."

Flat Tax's smile faltered. "Well, when you put it like that..."

Before Sam could press further, a new figure stormed into the conversation. Progressive Tax was a fiery character with a stack of charts under one arm and a megaphone in the other.

"Don't listen to this guy, Sam!" Progressive Tax shouted, pointing at Flat Tax. "He's just here to make the rich richer. I'm the real hero. The more you earn, the more you pay. It's the only way to ensure fairness."

Flat Tax rolled his eyes. "Oh, here we go. Progressive Tax loves to talk about fairness, but have you seen how complicated his system is? Brackets, deductions, credits—it's a nightmare!"

Progressive Tax smirked. "Complicated? Maybe. But at least I don't let billionaires get away with paying less than their secretaries."

Sam sighed. "Great. So, my options are 'too simple to be fair' or 'too complicated to understand.' This is going to be a long day."

"Here's the thing," Consumption Tax said, leaning back in their chair. "Why tax income at all? Just tax what people spend. It's simple, it's efficient, and it encourages saving."

Progressive Tax scoffed. "Oh, sure. Let's punish people for buying groceries while letting the rich hoard their wealth. Brilliant idea."

Consumption Tax shrugged. "Hey, I'm just saying, if you don't want to pay taxes, don't buy stuff. Problem solved."

Sam raised his hand. "But what about people who have to spend most of their income just to survive? Wouldn't a consumption tax hit them the hardest?"

Consumption Tax hesitated. "Well... yeah, but think of all the money they'd save by not buying yachts."

Sam buried his face in his hands. "This is like watching a debate between a rock and a hard place."

As the day went on, the summit descended into chaos. Flat Tax and Progressive Tax got into a shouting match over the definition of fairness, while Consumption Tax fell asleep in the middle of a presentation. Meanwhile, Tax Credit Assistance, a cheerful figure with a backpack full of pamphlets, kept interrupting to hand out brochures titled, "How to Claim Your Childcare Expenses in 47 Easy Steps."

At one point, Bracket Creep made an appearance, gleefully explaining how inflation pushes people into higher tax brackets without them actually earning more money. "It's like a stealth tax!" Bracket Creep said, laughing maniacally.

"Stealth tax?" Sam muttered. "More like a stealth headache."

The highlight of the day came when Loophole crashed the summit, wearing a trench coat and sunglasses. "Psst, Sam," Loophole whispered, pulling him aside. "You don't need to worry about any of this. Just use me, and you'll never pay a dime in taxes again."

Sam glared at him. "You're the reason I got audited last year."

Loophole grinned. "And yet, here you are, still considering it."

"Ladies and gentlemen," Tax Simplification began, "we all want the same thing: a tax system that is fair, efficient, and easy to understand. The question is, how do we get there?"

Flat Tax raised a hand. "One rate for everyone."

Progressive Tax shook their head. "Higher rates for higher incomes."

Consumption Tax yawned. "Just tax spending."

Sam stood up, exasperated. "How about we start by making the forms less confusing? I spent three hours last year trying to figure out if my dog's vet bills were deductible."

The crowd erupted into applause, and for the first time all day, Sam felt like he'd actually contributed something useful.

As Sam left the summit, he couldn't help but laugh at the absurdity of it all. Taxes might never be simple, but at least he'd learned one important lesson: no matter how complicated the system gets, there's always room for improvement—and a little humor.

His phone buzzed with a new email. "Breaking: New Tax Policy Proposal Sparks Controversy."

Sam sighed. "Here we go again."

Chapter 28

The Taxpayer's Bill of Rights – A Revolution in the Making

The next day a protest march wound its way through the city, banners waving and chants echoing off the buildings. Sam watched from the sidewalk as a group of taxpayers demanded fairness, transparency, and respect. For the first time, he realized that tax reform wasn't just about numbers—it was about people standing up for their rights.

Sam Harper had barely recovered from the chaos of the Tax Simplification Summit when his phone buzzed with yet another email. This time, it was from Tax Simplification, who had apparently decided that Sam was now their unofficial spokesperson for frustrated taxpayers everywhere.

Sam groaned. "A Bill of Rights? For taxpayers? What's next, a reality show called Tax Wars?"

Still, he couldn't deny that the idea intrigued him. After all, if anyone understood the pain of dealing with taxes, it was Sam. Maybe, just maybe, this was his chance to make a difference—or at least to stop getting surprise visits from tax characters every other day.

The meeting was held in a nondescript government building that smelled faintly of burnt coffee and despair. Sam walked into the conference room to find Tax Simplification already there, along with a few familiar faces: Income Tax, Sales Tax, Property Tax, and even Audit Tax, who was furiously scribbling notes on a clipboard.

"Sam! You made it!" Tax Simplification said, beaming. "We're drafting the first-ever Taxpayer's Bill of Rights, and we need your input."

Sam raised an eyebrow. "My input? I'm just a guy who once tried to claim a taco truck lunch as a business expense."

Audit Tax looked up from their clipboard. "And I'm still not over that."

Tax Simplification waved a hand. "Nonsense! You represent the average taxpayer, Sam. Who better to help us figure out what people really need?"

Sam sighed and took a seat. "Fine. But if this turns into another shouting match, I'm out."

The brainstorming session started off surprisingly well. Tax Simplification wrote "What Do Taxpayers Want?" on a whiteboard, and the group began throwing out ideas.

"Clarity!" Sam said immediately. "I want to know what I owe, why I owe it, and how to pay it without needing a PhD in accounting."

Income Tax nodded. "Fair enough. I'll admit, my forms could use a little… streamlining."

"Fairness!" Progressive Tax chimed in, bursting into the room uninvited. "The rich should pay their fair share, and the system should stop punishing the poor."

Flat Tax, who had also somehow found their way into the meeting, rolled their eyes. "Here we go again. Fairness is overrated. What taxpayers really want is simplicity. One rate for everyone, no exceptions."

Sales Tax raised a hand. "How about transparency? People should know where their tax pounds are going. Like, if I'm taxing gum, I want people to know it's funding schools or roads—not some politician's yacht."

Sam nodded. "That's actually a good point. I'd feel a lot better about paying taxes if I knew they were being used for something useful."

Audit Tax cleared their throat. "And accountability. If someone cheats the system, they should face consequences. But at the same time, taxpayers shouldn't feel like they're being punished for honest mistakes."

Sam smirked. "You mean like when I accidentally filed my dog as a dependent?"

Audit Tax glared at him. "Exactly."

As the group debated, the meeting quickly devolved into chaos. Flat Tax and Progressive Tax got into yet another shouting match, while Sales Tax tried to convince everyone that gum taxes were the backbone of the economy. Meanwhile, Loophole popped in through the air vent, offering "creative solutions" that everyone immediately rejected.

"Why are you even here?" Sam asked, glaring at Loophole.

Loophole grinned. "Hey, I'm just trying to help. You'd be surprised how many rights you can claim if you know where to look."

Audit Tax threw a stapler at him. "Get out."

Despite the interruptions, the group managed to come up with a rough draft of the Taxpayer's Bill of Rights. Tax Simplification wrote each point on the whiteboard, pausing occasionally to dodge flying objects.

The Draft

The Right to Clarity

Taxpayers have the right to clear, concise information about their tax obligations, including how much they owe, why they owe it, and how to pay it.

The Presentation

Once the draft was finalized, Tax Simplification announced that they would present it to the Global Tax Council, a shadowy organization that apparently oversaw tax policies worldwide. Sam wasn't sure if the council was real or just a figment of Tax Simplification's imagination, but he decided to go along with it.

The presentation was held in a grand auditorium filled with tax characters from around the world. Sam spotted Carbon Tax, Inheritance Tax, and even Luxury Tax, who was sipping champagne in the front row.

Tax Simplification took the stage, holding the finalized draft of the Taxpayer's Bill of Rights. "Ladies and gentlemen, today we stand on the brink of a revolution. For too long, taxpayers have been burdened by a system that is confusing, unfair, and opaque. But no more! With this Bill of Rights, we can create a system that works for everyone."

After the presentation, Sam was swarmed by reporters, tax characters, and even a few enthusiastic taxpayers who had somehow snuck into the event.

"You're a hero, Sam!" one reporter said. "How does it feel to be the voice of the people?"

Sam shrugged. "Honestly? I just want to file my taxes without crying."

As the crowd dispersed, Tax Simplification approached him, beaming. "You did it, Sam. You helped make history."

Sam smiled. "Yeah, but let's see if it actually changes anything. Knowing my luck, I'll still end up on hold with the Tax Office for three hours next tax season."

Tax Simplification laughed. "Baby steps, Sam. Baby steps."

As Sam left the auditorium, he felt a strange sense of accomplishment. For the first time, he wasn't just surviving the tax system—he was helping to change it. Sure, it was a small step, but it was a step in the right direction.

His phone buzzed with a new email. "Breaking: Taxpayer's Bill of Rights Faces Opposition from Lobbyists."

Sam sighed. "Of course it does."

Chapter 29

Tax and Social Justice

Sam Harper had always thought of taxes as a necessary evil—like flossing or listening to his neighbour's "experimental jazz" band (which sounded suspiciously like a blender fighting a trombone). But after a particularly heated family dinner (involving three generations, two bottles of non-alcoholic wine, and one uncle who believed billionaires were "just misunderstood"), Sam realized he didn't actually know what "fair" meant when it came to taxes.

So, he did what any confused taxpayer would do: he wandered into the grand marble halls of the *Courtroom of Fairness,* presided over by none other than Justice Tax.

Justice Tax was a sight to behold. She wore a cape made of tax brackets, a blindfold (which she peeked under to check receipts), and carried a gavel labelled "Equity." Her courtroom was packed: on one side, Flat Tax, waving a pamphlet titled "One Rate to Rule Them All!"; on the other, Regressive Tax, who looked suspiciously like a payday lender in a suit and had a wallet so thick it needed its own postal zip code. In the gallery, a group of accountants live-tweeted the proceedings, while a taxidermied moose labelled "Deductible in Canada" looked on with glassy-eyed indifference.

Sam took a seat in the "Confused but Curious" section, next to a tax professor grading papers and a protester knitting a scarf that read "TAX THE RICH" in bold, sparkly letters.

Justice Tax banged her gavel. "Order! Today, we debate: Should the rich pay more? Is a flat tax fair? Can taxes fix inequality, or do they just make accountants richer and coffee sales skyrocket?"

Flat Tax leapt to his feet. "It's simple! Everyone pays the same rate. No loopholes, no confusion, just pure, unadulterated fairness! And think of the savings on ink—no more 200-page tax returns! Even your cat could file!"

Regressive Tax sneered. "If you can't afford it, work harder! Sales taxes, payroll taxes—everyone pays, but the poor pay more. That's just the way the cookie crumbles. And by cookie, I mean yacht. And by yacht, I mean my third yacht."

Justice Tax turned to Sam. "What do you think, Sam?"

Sam stammered. "I just want to know if I can deduct my student loans… and maybe my therapy bills from doing my taxes."

Justice Tax smiled. "We'll get there. But first, let's look at the evidence."

Exhibit A: The Wealth Gap

Justice Tax projected a graph so steep it looked like a ski jump for billionaires. "The top 1% own more than the bottom 90% combined. Progressive taxes—where the rich pay a higher rate—are designed to close this gap. But every time we try, someone yells 'class warfare' and runs to their accountant, who's already hiding under the desk."

A hologram of a billionaire appeared, clutching a bag of money and a plane ticket to the nearest tax haven. "Don't mind me, just off to the Cayman Islands for a little… 'asset management.'"

Sam raised his hand. "So, do progressive taxes work?"

Justice Tax nodded. "They can. Countries with more progressive systems tend to have less inequality. But it's not just about rates—it's about loopholes, enforcement, and political will. And don't get me started on offshore accounts. Some billionaires have more money in the Bahamas than the Bahamas has sand."

A chorus of accountants in the gallery sang, "Loopholes, loopholes, everywhere! Hide your cash, if you dare!"

Exhibit B: The Wealth Tax Debate

Just then Wealth Tax burst in, wearing a monocle, a top hat, and carrying a calculator the size of a small car. "Tax the rich! One percent on every billion, and we can fund universal basic income, free college, and maybe even a national holiday for accountants! (Bring your own spreadsheets.)"

Flat Tax rolled his eyes. "That's just going to make the rich move their money to the Cayman Islands. Or under their mattress. Or into NFTs of their own yachts."

Justice Tax sighed. "It's a balancing act. Too high, and you risk capital flight. Too low, and you're just rearranging deck chairs on the Titanic. And nobody wants to be the band playing 'Tax Me Maybe' as the ship goes down."

Sam whispered to his neighbour, "Is there a middle ground?"

His neighbour, a tax professor, shrugged. "Only in theory. And maybe in Sweden. Or in a really good board game."

Exhibit C: The Regressive Reality

Regressive Tax strutted to the front. "Let's talk sales tax. Everyone pays the same, but if you're poor, it's a bigger chunk of your income. Same with payroll taxes. Fair? Maybe. But equal isn't always equitable. And don't even ask about the tax on marshmallow cereal."

Justice Tax nodded. "That's why we have credits, deductions, and exemptions. But the more complicated the system, the more it favours those who can afford good advice. Or a personal tax wizard."

Sam thought of his own tax return, a labyrinth of forms, receipts, and one very confused cat who'd been claimed as a dependent three years running.

Exhibit D: The Social Justice Tax Parade

Suddenly, the courtroom doors burst open, and a parade of new characters marched in:

- *Justice Credits*: Dressed as a superhero, handing out refundable tax credits to low-income families and high-fives to everyone else.
- *Universal Basic Income*: Wearing a sash and tossing fake money into the crowd.
- *Charitable Deduction*: Dressed as a giant check, reminding everyone that giving is good for the soul—and your tax bill.

Justice Tax smiled. "See? Taxes can be used to help level the playing field. But every new credit or deduction makes the system more complicated. It's like trying to solve a Rubik's Cube while blindfolded and being chased by an auditor."

Exhibit E: The Protesters and the Peanut Gallery

Suddenly, the courtroom erupted into chaos. Protesters waved signs: "Tax the Rich!" "Flat is Where It's At!" "Accountants Need Love Too!" Justice Tax restored order with a blast from her gavel (which doubled as a confetti cannon and played the theme from "Law & Order: Tax Unit").

A group of lobbyists in the back tried to sneak in a new loophole disguised as a pizza delivery. "It's not a bribe, it's a business lunch!" they insisted.

Justice Tax turned to Sam. "What do you think, Sam? Should taxes be used to fix inequality?"

Sam hesitated. "I think... I just want a system that makes sense. And maybe a refund. And maybe a cookie. But mostly a refund."

Justice Tax smiled. "That's all any of us want, Sam. But remember: every tax system is a reflection of what a society values. If we want fairness, we have to fight for it. And maybe bake cookies for our accountants."

Justice Tax banged her gavel. "Case adjourned! The debate continues. But one thing's for sure: taxes aren't just about money. They're about justice, opportunity, and the kind of world we want to build. And, apparently, about who can make the best protest sign."

As Sam left the courtroom, he felt a little wiser—and a lot more confused. But at least he knew one thing: fairness, like a good deduction, is always worth fighting for. And if all else fails, there's always Sweden.

Chapter 30

The Lobbyist Showdown – Taxpayer vs. The Titans

Sam Harper had barely had time to digest everything that went down in the courtroom before reality came crashing down—again. The ink on the draft Taxpayers Bill of rights wasn't even dry when his phone buzzed with a new email from Tax Simplification.

Subject: "URGENT: LOBBYISTS ARE COMING FOR US!"

Sam groaned, rubbing his temples. "Lobbyists? Great. What's next, a tax-themed supervillain team?"

He opened the email, which was filled with frantic all-caps sentences about a group of powerful lobbyists who were determined to block the Taxpayer's Bill of Rights. Apparently, these lobbyists represented "special interests" who thrived on the complexity and confusion of the current tax system. Their goal? To keep things exactly as they were—messy, unfair, and profitable for the few.

Sam sighed. "Of course. Because why make life easier for regular people when you can make billions off their misery?"

Before he could finish his coffee, the door to his office burst open (as it always did), and in marched Tax Simplification, looking more frazzled than usual.

"Sam! We're under attack!" Tax Simplification exclaimed, waving a stack of papers like a white flag. "The lobbyists are already spreading misinformation about the Bill of Rights. They're saying it's 'anti-business' and 'too taxpayer friendly.'"

Sam raised an eyebrow. "Too taxpayer-friendly? Isn't that the whole point?"

Tax Simplification nodded furiously. "Exactly! But these lobbyists don't care about fairness. They care about protecting their loopholes, deductions, and offshore accounts. We need your help, Sam. You're the only one who can stand up to them."

Sam groaned. "Why me? I'm just a guy who once tried to claim a Netflix subscription as a 'research expense.'"

Tax Simplification grabbed him by the shoulders. "Because, Sam, you're relatable. You're the man next door,. and most importantly, you're the only one who hasn't been bribed yet."

Sam blinked. "Wait, what?"

The showdown was set to take place at the National Tax Policy Forum, a grand event where lawmakers, tax experts, and lobbyists gathered to argue about the future of taxation. Sam arrived at the forum feeling like a lamb being led to the slaughter.

The lobbyists were already there, and they were a sight to behold. Each one represented a different "special interest," and they looked like they'd stepped straight out of a cartoon villain convention.

Big Loophole was a slick, oily figure in a pinstripe suit, with a grin that screamed, "I've never paid taxes in my life." He carried a briefcase labeled "Totally Legal" and had a habit of winking at everyone, which made Sam deeply uncomfortable.

Corporate Deduction, a towering figure in a power suit, had the aura of someone who could bankrupt a small country with a single spreadsheet. She carried a gold-plated calculator and spoke in a voice that could freeze a room.

Offshore Haven, a laid-back character in a Hawaiian shirt and flip-flops, sipped a piña colada while casually bragging about his "tax-free lifestyle." He smelled faintly of sunscreen and moral ambiguity.

Bracket Creep, who Sam had already met, was there too, gleefully explaining how inflation was his best friend. "I'm not a villain," Bracket Creep said, grinning. "I'm just... opportunistic."

Sam turned to Tax Simplification. "These are the people we're up against? They look like the cast of a bad heist movie."

Tax Simplification nodded grimly. "And they're very good at what they do. But don't worry, Sam. We've got the truth on our side."

Sam sighed. "Great. That and five bucks will get us a coffee."

The forum kicked off with a panel discussion, and Sam found himself seated between Tax Simplification and Income Tax, who was nervously adjusting his tie. Across the table sat the lobbyists, who looked far too confident for Sam's liking.

The moderator, a stern-looking woman with a clipboard, began the discussion. "Today, we're here to debate the Taxpayer's Bill of Rights. Let's start with opening statements. Mr. Loophole, you have the floor."

Big Loophole stood up, flashing his trademark grin. "Thank you, Madam Moderator. Ladies and gentlemen, let me be clear: the Taxpayer's Bill of Rights is a disaster waiting to happen. It's anti-business, anti-growth, and frankly, anti-fun. Do we really want to live in a world where people can't creatively interpret the tax code? I think not."

Sam raised his hand. "Wait, did you just admit to 'creatively interpreting' the tax code?"

Big Loophole winked. "I said what I said."

Next up was Corporate Deduction, who stood with the poise of someone who had never lost an argument. "The Bill of Rights is unrealistic. Simplifying the tax code would eliminate thousands of deductions that businesses rely on to stay competitive. Do you want to be the reason small businesses fail, Mr. Harper?"

Sam frowned. "Small businesses? You mean like the mom-and-pop shops that can't afford fancy accountants? Because I'm pretty sure they're not the ones benefiting from your deductions."

Corporate Deduction glared at him. "Details."

Offshore Haven was next, and he didn't even bother standing up. "Look, man, taxes are, like, optional if you know what you're doing. The Bill of Rights is just going to scare away all the cool people who keep their money in places like, oh, I don't know, the Cayman Islands. Do you really want to ruin the vibe?"

Sam stared at him. "The vibe? Are you serious?"

Offshore Haven shrugged. "Hey, I'm just here for the free snacks."

Finally, it was Sam's turn to speak. He stood up, feeling the weight of the room's attention on him. He cleared his throat, trying to ignore the smug looks from the lobbyists.

"Look, I'm not a tax expert," Sam began. "I'm just a regular guy who's tired of feeling like the system is rigged against people like me. The Taxpayer's Bill of Rights isn't about punishing businesses or scaring away 'cool people.' It's about making the system fair, transparent, and understandable."

He pointed at Big Loophole. "You talk about creativity, but what about the people who can't afford fancy accountants to find those loopholes? What about the single mom working two jobs who just wants to file her taxes without needing a lawyer or a tax advisor?"

He turned to Corporate Deduction. "And you say this will hurt small businesses, but the truth is, most small businesses don't even qualify for the deductions you're talking about. They're too busy trying to stay afloat."

Finally, he looked at Offshore Haven. "And as for you... I don't even know where to start. Maybe with a pair of shoes?"

But Sam held his ground, with help from Tax Simplification and the other tax characters. Income Tax even managed to deliver a surprisingly heartfelt speech about the importance of funding public services, which brought a tear to Sam's eye (and a groan from Big Loophole).

In the end, the debate didn't resolve everything, but it did make one thing clear: the Taxpayer's Bill of Rights wasn't going away without a fight. As the forum wrapped up, Sam felt a strange sense of hope. Maybe, just maybe, they could make a difference.

As he left the building, his phone buzzed with a new email. "Breaking: Lobbyists File Lawsuit to Block Taxpayer's Bill of Rights."

Sam sighed. "Of course they did."

Chapter 31
The Courtroom Circus - Justice vs. Loopholes

Sam Harper had officially reached the point where he was considering faking his own death to escape the madness. After surviving the Tax Simplification Summit and the Lobbyist Showdown, he thought he'd earned a break. But no—his phone buzzed with yet another email from Tax Simplification.

Subject: "URGENT: WE'RE GOING TO COURT!"

Sam groaned, staring at the email. "Court? What am I, a tax superhero now? Do I get a cape that says, 'Defender of Deductions'?"

The email explained that the lobbyists, led by Big Loophole, had filed a lawsuit to block the Taxpayer's Bill of Rights, claiming it was "unconstitutional, anti-business, and a threat to the sacred art of creative accounting." The case had been fast-tracked to the European Tax Court, and Tax Simplification wanted Sam to testify as the "voice of the people."

Sam sighed. "Great. I'm going to court. What's next, a musical number about tax brackets?"

The courtroom was packed. On one side sat the Lobbyist Dream Team: Big Loophole, Corporate Deduction, Offshore Haven, Tax Delay and their newest recruit, Tax Complexity, a shadowy figure who seemed to thrive on confusion. Tax Complexity wore a cloak made of shredded tax forms and carried a staff topped with a calculator. They looked like the villain in a low-budget fantasy movie.

On the other side sat Tax Simplification, flanked by Income Tax, Sales Tax, and Audit Tax, who was furiously flipping through a binder labelled "Evidence of Shenanigans." Sam took his seat next to them, trying not to panic.

The judge, Justice Fairshare Jnr, entered the room. He was a no-nonsense man with a gavel that looked like it could double as a weapon. "Court is now in session," he announced. "The case of Lobbyists vs. The Taxpayer's Bill of Rights will now be heard."

Sam leaned over to Tax Simplification. "Is it too late to plead insanity?"

Tax Simplification patted his shoulder. "Don't worry, Sam. We've got this."

Sam wasn't so sure.

Big Loophole was the first to speak. He stood up, flashing his trademark grin, and began pacing dramatically. "Your Honor, the Taxpayer's Bill of Rights is a dangerous, radical proposal that threatens the very fabric of our economy. It's anti-business, anti-growth, and frankly, anti-fun."

Sam raised his hand. "Can we object to the word 'fun'? Because I've never had fun doing taxes."

Justice Fairshare banged his gavel. "Mr. Harper, please refrain from interrupting."

Big Loophole continued, pulling out a pie chart that was so colourful it looked like it belonged in a kindergarten classroom. "This chart clearly shows that simplifying the tax code would lead to economic collapse, mass unemployment, and—dare I say it—fewer yachts."

Sam whispered to Tax Simplification. "Did he just say 'fewer yachts' like it's a bad thing?"

Tax Simplification nodded grimly. "He did."

Next up was Tax Simplification, who stood up with a stack of neatly organized papers. “Your Honor, the Taxpayer’s Bill of Rights is not a radical proposal. It’s a common-sense solution to a system that is overly complex, unfair, and inaccessible to the average taxpayer. Our goal is to make taxes clear, fair, and transparent.”

Big Loophole snorted. “Clear, fair, and transparent? Where’s the fun in that?”

Justice Fairshare Jnr glared at him. “Mr. Loophole, one more outburst and I’ll hold you in contempt.”

Sam leaned over to Sales Tax. “Is it bad that I’m rooting for the judge to throw him in jail?”

Sales Tax smirked. “Not at all.”

Next up was Corporate Deduction, who argued that the Bill of Rights would stifle innovation and kill unicorns.

Sam couldn’t help himself. “Unicorns? Really?”

Corporate Deduction glared at him. “Yes, Mr. Harper. Unicorns. And if you pass this Bill of Rights, you’ll be killing them.”

Sam leaned back in his chair. “Great. Now I’m the guy who kills unicorns.”

Next up was Offshore Haven, who lounged in the witness chair like it was a beach chair. “Look, man,” he said, sipping a piña colada. “Taxes are, like, optional if you know what you’re doing. The Bill of Rights is just going to harsh everyone’s vibe.”

Justice Fairshare Jnr raised an eyebrow. “Mr. Haven, are you seriously arguing that taxes are optional?”

Offshore Haven shrugged. “I mean, they are for me.”

Justice Fairshare Jnr sighed. “I’m adding ‘contempt for the court’ to your list of offenses.”

Then Tax Delay stood up and said “Your honour, I request more time to prepare for this case as I have not had enough time to review all the documents”

Finally, it was Sam's turn to testify. He took the stand, feeling like a deer in the headlights. Tax Simplification gave him a thumbs-up, which did absolutely nothing to calm his nerves.

"Mr. Harper," Big Loophole began, smirking. "You claim to represent the average taxpayer. But isn't it true that you once tried to claim a taco truck lunch as a business expense?"

Sam blinked. "Uh... yes, but—"

"And isn't it also true," Big Loophole continued, "that you once filed your dog as a dependent?"

Sam sighed. "Okay, yes, but in my defence, he eats half my groceries."

Tax Simplification stood up. "Your Honor, Mr. Harper's mistakes only prove our point. The tax system is so confusing that even honest taxpayers struggle to navigate it. The Taxpayer's Bill of Rights would make the system clearer and prevent these kinds of errors."

Sam nodded. "Yeah, what they said."

As the trial continued, the courtroom descended into chaos. Tax Complexity took the stand and began reciting the entire tax code from memory, causing several people to fall asleep. Loophole tried to bribe the judge with a "totally legal" offshore account, and Offshore Haven started handing out sunscreen to the jury.

At one point, Bracket Creep burst into the courtroom, shouting, "Inflation is my best friend!" before being escorted out by security.

Sam leaned over to Tax Simplification. "Is this normal?"

Tax Simplification sighed. "Unfortunately, yes."

After hours of arguments, Justice Fairshare finally banged his gavel. "I've heard enough. The Taxpayer's Bill of Rights is a reasonable and necessary step toward creating a fairer tax system. The court rules in favour of the Bill of Rights."

Big Loophole, however, was not pleased. "This isn't over, Harper," he hissed as he stormed out of the courtroom. "You haven't seen the last of me."

Sam smirked. "Looking forward to it."

As Sam left the courtroom, he felt a strange sense of accomplishment. Sure, the fight wasn't over, but for the first time, it felt like progress was being made.

His phone buzzed with a new email. "Breaking: Lobbyists File Appeal Against Taxpayer's Bill of Rights." Sam sighed. "Of course they did."

Chapter 32

The Taxpayer's Victory March – A Rally for the Ages

Sam Harper had barely stepped out of the courthouse when his phone buzzed again. He glanced at the screen, expecting yet another email from Tax Simplification or, worse, a smug message from Big Loophole. Instead, it was a notification from the news:

"BREAKING: Taxpayer's Bill of Rights Gains National Attention – Citizens Plan Victory March!"

Sam blinked. "A march? For taxes? What's next, a parade for parking tickets?"

Before he could process the absurdity of the situation, his phone buzzed again. This time, it was a call from Tax Simplification.

"Sam! Did you see the news?" Tax Simplification's voice was practically vibrating with excitement. "The people are rallying behind the Bill of Rights! They're organizing a march to show their support, and they want you to lead it!"

Sam froze. "Me? Lead a march? I'm not exactly a 'rally the troops' kind of guy. I'm more of a 'hide under the covers and hope the problem goes away' kind of guy."

"Nonsense!" Tax Simplification said. "You're the perfect person for this. You're relatable, you're passionate, and you're the only one who hasn't been bribed by Offshore Haven."

Sam sighed. "Fine. But if this turns into another circus, I'm out."

The march was scheduled for the following Saturday, giving Sam just a few days to prepare. Tax Simplification insisted on helping him write a speech, but their first draft was so full of tax jargon that Sam had to stop halfway through to Google what "fiscal equity" meant.

"Look," Sam said, crossing out half the speech with a red pen. "If I'm going to do this, I need to keep it simple. No one wants to hear about 'fiscal equity.' They want to hear about how they can file their taxes without crying."

Tax Simplification reluctantly agreed, and together they crafted a speech that was equal parts inspiring and relatable. Sam practiced in front of his bathroom mirror, trying to channel the energy of a motivational speaker but mostly just looking like a guy who'd had too much coffee.

Meanwhile, the news of the march spread like wildfire. Social media was flooded with hashtags like #TaxpayerRights and #SimplifyTaxes, and memes featuring Big Loophole as a cartoon villain went viral. One particularly popular meme showed Offshore Haven lounging on a beach chair with the caption: "Taxes? Never heard of her."

Sam couldn't believe it. For the first time, it felt like people actually cared about taxes—and not just in a "why do I owe so much?" kind of way.

On the morning of the march, Sam arrived at the starting point to find a massive crowd already gathered. People of all ages were holding signs with slogans like "Make Taxes Simple Again", "No More Bracket Creep!", and "Loopholes Are for Cheaters!" Someone had even brought a giant inflatable version of Audit Tax, complete with a clipboard and a stern expression.

Sam turned to Tax Simplification, who was practically glowing with pride. "This is... a lot," he said, staring at the sea of people.

"It's amazing!" Tax Simplification said. "You're about to make history, Sam. Now, go out there and inspire the masses!"

Sam took a deep breath and stepped up to the makeshift stage. The crowd erupted into cheers as he approached the microphone, and for a moment, he felt like a rock star—albeit a rock star who was about to talk about tax reform.

"Uh, hi," Sam began, his voice cracking slightly. "I'm Sam Harper, and I'm just a regular guy who's really bad at doing his taxes."

"The Taxpayer's Bill of Rights isn't about punishing businesses or making life harder for anyone. It's about fairness, transparency, and simplicity. It's about making sure that everyone—rich or poor, big business or small—pays their fair share. And it's about giving people like us the tools we need to navigate the system without losing our minds."

Sam paused, looking out at the crowd. "We're not asking for much. We're just asking for a system that works for everyone. And if the lobbyists think they can stop us, well... they've got another thing coming."

At one point, a group of protesters dressed as tax characters joined the march. Someone had dressed up as Big Loophole, complete with a fake briefcase labeled "Totally Legal", while another person wore a giant cardboard box labeled "Offshore Haven - Tax-Free Paradise." The real Offshore Haven, who was watching the march from a nearby café, looked deeply offended.

Sam couldn't help but laugh. "This is the weirdest day of my life."

By the end of the day, the march had made headlines around the world. News outlets praised the movement as a "historic moment for taxpayers," and social media was flooded with photos and videos from the event. Even Justice Fairshare released a statement supporting the march, calling it "a powerful reminder that the tax system exists to serve the people, not the other way around."

Sam, however, was just glad it was over. As he collapsed onto his couch that evening, his phone buzzed with yet another email from Tax Simplification.

Subject: "NEXT STEPS – LET'S KEEP THE MOMENTUM GOING!"

Sam groaned. "Of course there are next steps."

Chapter 33

Taxpayer Advocacy and Protest

Sam Harper always thought protests were something you watched on TV—marches, chants, and the occasional person dressed as a giant banana (or, on a slow news day, a disgruntled avocado). But after his experience at the march last Saturday, Sam found himself swept up in a sea of signs, slogans, and drummers who were suspiciously enthusiastic for 8 a.m.

At the front of the march was *Protest Tax*, waving a flag and shouting, "No taxation without representation!" Protest Tax was the spirit of every tax revolt, from the Boston Tea Party to the modern-day "Don't Tax My Snacks!" movement. He wore a tricorn hat, a Che Guevara t-shirt, and a fanny pack full of petitions, granola bars, and at least three expired coupons.

"Sam!" Protest Tax called, handing him a sign that read, "Stop Taxing My Patience!" "Join us! We're fighting for taxpayer rights! And free donuts, if we're lucky."

Sam hesitated. "I just wanted to know if I could get a refund on my parking tickets... or at least a loyalty card for repeat offenders."

Protest Tax grinned. "That's the spirit! Every great tax protest started with a small injustice. The Boston Tea Party? Overpriced tea. The California property tax revolt? Sky-high assessments. The Magna Carta? King John's weird hobbies and a suspiciously large collection of rubber ducks."

Protest Tax led Sam through a whirlwind tour of history's greatest tax uprisings, complete with interpretive dance and a PowerPoint made entirely of recycled protest signs:

- *The Boston Tea Party:* "A bunch of colonists, fed up with taxes on tea, dressed as Mohawk warriors and dumped 342 chests of tea into Boston Harbor. The message? 'We'd rather drink saltwater than pay your tax!' Also, the world's first unsweetened iced tea."
- *The French Revolution:* "The peasants were tired of paying all the taxes while the aristocrats paid none. Solution? Storm the Bastille, invent the guillotine, and make 'Let them eat cake' the world's most passive-aggressive tax slogan. Also, the only time in history when cake was considered a political weapon."
- *The Whiskey Rebellion:* "American farmers, angry about a tax on whiskey, decided to fight back. The government sent in troops. The farmers drank the whiskey anyway. Moral: Never get between a farmer and their happy hour."
- *Modern Movements:* "From anti-poll tax riots in the UK to the 'Don't Tax My Internet' rallies, people have always found creative ways to say, 'Enough!' Bonus points if your protest sign rhymes or includes a pun about deductions."

Sam was impressed. "So protests actually work? Or do they just make for great memes?"

Protest Tax winked. "Sometimes both! At the very least, they make for great stories—and even better costumes. I once saw someone protest the soda tax dressed as a giant can of cola. He was very refreshing."

Protest Tax handed Sam a megaphone. "It's not just about yelling. It's about organizing, educating, and sometimes, just being really, really annoying until someone listens. Remember: the squeaky wheel gets the tax deduction."

Sam watched as the crowd chanted, waved signs, and handed out leaflets. There were booths for every cause: "Abolish the Penny!" "Make Tax Day a National Holiday!" "Bring Back the Window Tax (for Nostalgia)!" and "Tax Credits for Cat Owners—Because Fur is Expensive."

He even spotted Flat Tax and Justice Tax in a heated debate over the merits of progressive rates, while Shadow Tax lurked in the background, selling "Tax Evasion for Dummies" pamphlets and fake moustaches (cash only, of course).

Protest Tax climbed onto a soapbox (literally—he'd brought his own, labelled "Property of Protest Tax") and addressed the crowd. "Remember, fellow taxpayers: every right you have was won by someone who stood up and said, 'No more!' The right to appeal, the right to representation, the right to not be taxed for having a beard—these didn't just happen. They were fought for! And sometimes, they were won by people with really great facial hair."

Sam felt a surge of pride. Maybe he wasn't just a confused taxpayer. Maybe he was part of something bigger. Or at least, something louder.

Protest Tax pulled out his phone. "These days, you don't even need to leave your couch to protest. Hashtags, viral videos, and memes can spark a movement. Remember the 'Tax the Rich' dress at the Met Gala? Or the time someone started a petition to make tax forms edible, so at least you'd get something out of the process? I'm still waiting for the gluten-free version."

Sam laughed. "So, what's next? Tax protests on TikTok?"

Protest Tax grinned. "Whatever you want it to be! The fight for fair taxes never ends. But with enough voices, enough signs, and enough memes, maybe—just maybe—we can make the system a little less painful. Or at least, a lot more entertaining."

As the march wound down, Sam found himself chanting along, waving his sign, and even signing a petition to abolish the penny (he'd always hated loose change—especially when it escaped in the laundry). He realized that taxes weren't just about money—they were about power, rights, and the eternal struggle between the people and the powers that be. And sometimes, they were about who could come up with the best protest pun.

Chapter 34
Taxpayer Horror Stories

Sam Harper had always thought of taxes as a necessary evil—like going to the dentist or pretending to enjoy his neighbour's slideshow of "Cats of the World." But after his wild ride through the global tax jungle, Sam was desperate for a break from all the loopholes, forms, and politicians who could dodge a question faster than they dodged a tax bill. He just wanted to hear some good, old-fashioned tax horror stories—the kind that made you laugh, cringe, and clutch your Tax Return Form a little tighter.

That's when he received a mysterious invitation:

"TAXPAYER HORROR STORY NIGHT—One Night Only! Hosted by The Taxman. Dress code: Business Casual or Business Casualty."

Sam arrived at a creaky old mansion, where the door creaked open to reveal The Taxman himself—a ghoulish figure in a pinstripe suit, monocle gleaming, handlebar moustache waxed to a point sharp enough to pierce a 1040 form. He held out a glass of something that smelled suspiciously like printer ink and regret.

"Welcome, Sam!" The Taxman cackled, his voice like a rusty calculator running out of batteries. "Are you ready to hear tales of tax terror, deduction disasters, and refund regrets?"

Sam gulped his drink (which tasted like toner and existential dread) and followed The Taxman into a dimly lit room. Cobwebs hung from the ceiling, skeletons clutched audit letters, and taxpayers huddled around a flickering campfire made entirely of shredded receipts. The air was thick with the scent of fear—and expired deduction forms.

The Taxman raised a bony finger. "Let the horror begin!"

The first storyteller, a woman with wild eyes and a purse full of crumpled receipts, stepped forward.

"I lost all my receipts in a house fire," she sobbed. "I tried to reconstruct my expenses from memory, but the Tax Office Tax Office Tax Office didn't believe I spent £10,000 on 'office supplies'—especially when half of it was at IKEA."

The Taxman cackled. "A classic case of 'receipts gone wild'! Next!"

A man in a suit two sizes too small shuffled up, clutching a photo of his golden retriever.

"I accidentally claimed my dog as a dependent," he wailed. "I thought he was a good boy! But the Tax Office Tax Office said 'Fido' was not a 'qualifying child.' They fined me £500 and sent me a pamphlet on 'What Counts as a Human.'"

The Taxman howled. "Another case of 'petty deductions'! Next!"

A nervous-looking woman whispered, "I tried to deduct my psychic's fees as 'business consulting.' The Tax Office said if my psychic was so good, she should have seen the audit coming."

The Taxman snorted. "A supernatural slip-up! Next!"

Finally, it was Sam's turn.

"I once tried to write off my Netflix subscription as 'market research,'" Sam confessed. "But the Tax Office said 'binge-watching' wasn't a 'legitimate business expense.' They audited me for three years. I now have PTSD—Post-Tax Streaming Disorder."

The Taxman cackled so hard his monocle fogged up. "A truly terrifying tale! But wait, there's more!"

He led the group to the *Museum of Bizarre Tax Artifacts,* a gallery of government greed and creative compliance:

- *The Russian Beard Tax*: "In the 18th century, Peter the Great taxed beards to encourage Westernization. It's like a hipster tax, but with more czars and fewer craft breweries."
- *The British Window Tax:* "In the 17th century, the British taxed windows. People bricked them up to save money, and thus invented the world's first man cave."
- *The French Urinal Tax*: "In the 18th century, the French taxed urinals to fund public works. It's the only time in history when peeing in public was considered a civic duty."

Sam was amazed. "People will tax anything! What's next, a tax on laughter?"

The Taxman grinned. "Don't give them ideas, Sam. They're always listening."

Next, The Taxman ushered Sam into the *Hall of Infamous Tax Evaders,* where oil paintings glared down with the judgment of a thousand auditors:

- *Al Capone:* "The notorious gangster went down for tax evasion, not murder. Proof that the pen is mightier than the sword—or at least, the ledger is mightier than the Tommy gun."
- *Wesley Snipes:* "The Hollywood actor went to jail for tax evasion. The lesson? Don't mess with the Tax Office, even if you're a vampire hunter. They don't care if you can dodge bullets."
- *Leona Helmsley:* "The hotel magnate who said, 'Only the little people pay taxes.' She went to jail for tax evasion. The lesson? Don't be a jerk, and don't put it in writing."

Sam shuddered. "These stories are terrifying! I'll never look at a Tax Return Form the same way again."

The Taxman leaned in, his breath smelling faintly of audit notices and fear. "That's the point! Taxes are scary. But they're also hilarious, if you survive. So pay your taxes, keep your receipts, and never, ever try to claim your dog as a dependent. Or else..."

The Taxman cackled, vanished into the shadows, and the campfire flickered out—leaving only the faint sound of a calculator printing "ERROR."

As Sam stumbled out into the night, he realized taxes weren't just a necessary evil—they were a never-ending source of amusement, terror, and stories to tell at parties (or therapy). He vowed to keep better records, never deduct his cat's yoga classes, and always check the fine print.

PART VI

Tax Culture and Entertainment

Chapter 35

The Taxpocalypse – When Taxes Go on Strike

Sam Harper had always thought taxes were inevitable, like death or bad Wi-Fi. But now, as he stared at the headline on his phone, he realized he'd been wrong.

"BREAKING: Taxes Go on Strike. Chaos Ensues."

Sam blinked at the screen, rereading the words as if they might rearrange themselves into something less ridiculous. "Taxes... on strike? Is this some kind of prank? Did April Fool's come early?"

Before he could process the absurdity of it, the door to his office burst open (as it always did), and in stormed Income Tax, looking like he'd just walked out of a disaster movie. His tie was askew, his briefcase was missing, and he was holding a picket sign that read: "NO FAIRNESS, NO TAXES!"

"Sam!" Income Tax bellowed, slamming the door behind him. "We need your help. The system is falling apart!"

Sam stared at him, dumbfounded. "Wait, you're on strike? How does that even work? You're not a person—you're a tax!"

Income Tax groaned, slumping into a chair. "We're more than just taxes, Sam. We're overworked, underappreciated, and constantly blamed for everything. We've had enough."

Before Sam could respond, the door swung open again, and in marched Sales Tax, Property Tax, and Excise Tax, all carrying picket signs with slogans like "STOP THE ABUSE" and "TAXES DESERVE RIGHTS TOO!"

Sales Tax threw his sign onto Sam's desk. "It's true, Sam. We're tired of being the bad guys. People complain about us, dodge us, and call us unfair. Do you know how hard it is to tax gum and still be taken seriously?"

Property Tax adjusted his glasses, looking indignant. "And don't get me started on the complaints about rising property values. It's not my fault your neighbor put in a pool!"

Excise Tax, sipping a soda, chimed in. "I'm just here for the snacks, but yeah, I'm striking too."

Sam rubbed his temples. "Okay, let me get this straight. You're all on strike because... people don't like you?"

Income Tax stood up, pacing the room. "It's not just that, Sam. We're overworked! Do you know how many tax returns I have to process every year? Millions! And do I get a thank-you? No! All I get are angry tweets and memes about how I'm ruining everyone's lives."

Sales Tax crossed his arms. "And don't even get me started on the evasion. People are always trying to dodge me, like I'm some kind of villain. I'm just doing my job!"

Sam sighed. "Okay, but what does a tax strike even look like? Are you just... not collecting taxes anymore?"

Income Tax smirked. "Exactly. No taxes, no revenue. Let's see how the world likes that."

At first, Sam thought the strike might actually be a good thing. No taxes? That sounded like a dream come true. But it didn't take long for the cracks to show.

Sam pulled out his wallet. "Here you go."

The barista frowned. "Uh, no. It's actually £3.50. No sales tax."

Sam blinked. "Wait, so... it's just the price on the menu?"

Sam took a sip and immediately regretted it. "This is terrible."

"Welcome to a tax-free world," the barista said, shrugging.

As the strike continued, the effects became more and more obvious. Roads went unrepaired, schools shut down, and hospitals ran out of funding. Trash piled up on the streets because sanitation workers weren't getting paid, and public transportation ground to a halt.

Sam turned on the news to see reporters covering the chaos. One anchor was standing in front of a pothole the size of a small car. "As the tax strike enters its second day, cities across the country are struggling to maintain basic services. Experts are calling this the worst crisis since... well, ever."

The camera cut to a man in a suit, who was shouting into a megaphone. "We don't need taxes! We can fund everything with voluntary contributions!"

The anchor raised an eyebrow. "Sir, have you contributed anything?"

Sam groaned. "This is a disaster."

Desperate for answers, Sam decided to confront the taxes directly. He found them gathered in a park, holding a "Tax Union" meeting. Income Tax was at the podium, giving a fiery speech.

"We've been taken for granted for too long!" Income Tax shouted. "It's time for the world to see how important we really are!"

Sam marched up to the podium. "Okay, enough is enough. You've made your point. The world is falling apart without you. Can't you just go back to work?"

Income Tax glared at him. "Not until our demands are met."

Sam sighed. "What demands?"

Sales Tax stepped forward, holding a list. "We want better working conditions, more appreciation, and a public apology for all the mean things people say about us."

Sam blinked. "A public apology? From who?"

"Everyone," Sales Tax said, crossing his arms. "We're tired of being the villains."

Realising that the strike wasn't going to end on its own, Sam came up with a plan. He called a press conference and stood in front of a crowd of reporters, holding a microphone.

"Ladies and gentlemen," he began, "I know taxes aren't exactly popular. But the truth is, we need them. Without taxes, we don't have schools, roads, or hospitals. We don't have public services or infrastructure. We don't have... well, anything."

The reporters nodded, scribbling in their notebooks.

"So, on behalf of taxpayers everywhere, I'd like to say this: Taxes, we're sorry. We're sorry for complaining about you, for dodging you, and for making memes about how much we hate you. We don't like you, but we need you. Please come back."

The taxes watched the press conference from their park meeting, and one by one, they began to nod. Income Tax wiped a tear from his eye. "He really gets it."

Sales Tax sniffled. "Maybe we're not so bad after all."

By the end of the day, the taxes had agreed to return to work, and the world slowly began to return to normal. Roads were repaired, schools reopened, and the espresso machine at Sam's coffee shop was finally fixed.

As Sam sat in his office, sipping a much better cup of coffee, Income Tax walked in.

"Thanks, Sam," Income Tax said. "You really saved the day."

Sam smirked. "Don't mention it. Just... maybe don't go on strike again, okay?"

Income Tax chuckled. "No promises."

Chapter 36

The Taxpayer's Bill of Rights - The Final Showdown

Sam Harper had barely recovered from the chaos of the tax strike when his phone buzzed with yet another email from Tax Simplification.

Subject: "URGENT: LOBBYISTS STRIKE BACK!"

Sam sighed, muttering to himself. "Of course they do. Why wouldn't they? It's not like I've earned a break or anything."

Tax Simplification's email ended with a plea: "Sam, the case has been fast tracked to the global court!, we need you to testify again. You're the only one who can stand up to them. The taxpayers are counting on you!"

Sam groaned, slumping back in his chair. "Why is it always me? I'm not a hero—I'm just a guy who once tried to claim a taco truck lunch as a business expense."

But deep down, he knew he couldn't back out. The Taxpayer's Bill of Rights was too important. It was the one thing standing between taxpayers and the endless maze of loopholes, deductions, and bracket creep. If he didn't fight for it, who would?

At the defence table sat Big Loophole, looking as smug as ever, flanked by Offshore Haven, who was sipping a piña colada, and Tax Complexity, who was wearing a cloak made entirely of shredded tax forms. Behind them sat their entourage: Bracket Creep, Corporate Deduction, and a new character Sam hadn't seen before—Luxury Tax, who was draped in fur and diamonds, fanning herself with a stack of hundred-pound notes.

On the other side of the courtroom sat Tax Simplification, looking determined, alongside Income Tax, Sales Tax, and Audit Tax, who was furiously flipping through a binder labelled "Evidence of Shenanigans."

Sam took his seat next to Tax Simplification, who gave him a reassuring nod. "Don't worry, Sam. We've got this."

Sam wasn't so sure.

Next up was Tax Simplification, who stood up with a stack of neatly organized papers. "Your Honor, we are here today because the lobbyists are trying to deny ordinary citizens the right to a fair and understandable tax system. The Taxpayer's Bill of Rights is not about eliminating wealth; it's about ensuring everyone plays by the same rules."

Big Loophole countered, "This bill will cripple businesses and stifle economic growth. We need complexity to incentivize investment and innovation!"

Luxury Tax added, "And what about the luxury goods market? This bill will destroy it! People need to be able to enjoy the fruits of their labour without being penalized."

Sam leaned forward, a knot forming in his stomach. The arguments were becoming more pointed, more personal. He could feel the weight of the decision hanging in the air.

Finally, it was Sam's turn to testify. He took the stand, feeling the weight of everyone's gaze. Tax Simplification gave him a thumbs-up, which did absolutely nothing to calm his nerves.

"Mr. Harper," Big Loophole began, smirking. "You claim to represent the average taxpayer. What makes you think you're qualified to decide what's best for the economy?"

Sam paused, gathering his thoughts. "I'm not an economist or a tax expert. I'm just a regular guy who's tired of feeling like the system is rigged against me. The Taxpayer's Bill of Rights isn't about punishing success; it's about creating a level playing field where everyone has a chance to thrive."

As the trial continued, the courtroom descended into chaos. Tax Complexity took the stand and began reciting the entire tax code from memory, causing several people to fall asleep. Bracket Creep burst into the courtroom, shouting, "Inflation is my best friend!" before being escorted out by security. And at one point, Luxury Tax tried to bribe the judge with a diamond-encrusted gavel.

Sam leaned over to Tax Simplification. "Is this normal?"

Tax Simplification sighed. "Unfortunately, yes."

After hours of arguments, Justice Fairshare Snr finally banged his gavel. "I've heard enough. Court is adjourned until tomorrow 9am when I will announce my ruling on this case".

The next as Sam was sitting in the court room waiting for Justice Fairshare Snr to arrive, he thought everything that was said yesterday and was contemplating whose side the Judge would choose? While lost in thought the door opened and in walked Justice Fairshare Snr

Finally as everyone settled into their seats Justice Fairshare Snr Announced "The Taxpayer's Bill of Rights is a reasonable and necessary step toward creating a fairer tax system. The court rules in favour of the Bill of Rights."

Big Loophole, however, was not pleased. "This isn't over, Harper," he hissed as he stormed out of the courtroom. "You haven't seen the last of me."

Sam smirked. "Looking forward to it."

As Sam left the courtroom, he felt a strange sense of accomplishment. Sure, the fight wasn't over, but for the first time, it felt like progress was being made.

His phone buzzed with a new alert. “Breaking: Lobbyists File Appeal Against Taxpayer’s Bill of Rights.”

Sam sighed. “Of course they did.” The battle may have been won, but the war was far from over.

CHAPTER 37

The Taxpayer's Celebration - A Party for the Ages

Sam Harper had never been the kind of guy who got invited to fancy parties. His idea of a celebration usually involved takeout pizza and a Netflix binge. But now, after surviving the courtroom chaos and securing a victory for the Taxpayer's Bill of Rights, he found himself at the most bizarre party of his life, a celebration thrown by the tax characters themselves.

The invitation had arrived in the form of a glittery envelope delivered by Luxury Tax, who had dramatically announced, "Darling, you simply must attend. It's going to be the event of the century." Sam had reluctantly agreed, mostly because he was too tired to argue.

Now, as he stood in the middle of a grand ballroom decorated with banners that read "TAXES: NECESSARY AND FABULOUS", he couldn't help but feel out of place. The room was packed with familiar faces—Income Tax, Sales Tax, Audit Tax, and even Carbon Tax, who was handing out reusable party favors shaped like wind turbines.

Sam adjusted his tie, which felt like it was choking him. "This is... a lot," he muttered to Tax Simplification, who was standing beside him.

Tax Simplification beamed. “Isn’t it wonderful? It’s not every day we get to celebrate a victory for fairness and transparency!”

Sam raised an eyebrow. “Yeah, but do we really need a chocolate fountain shaped like a tax form?”

Tax Simplification shrugged. “Luxury Tax insisted.”

The party officially kicked off with a speech from Income Tax, who stood on a small stage at the front of the room, holding a glass of champagne.

“Ladies and gentlemen,” Income Tax began, his voice booming, “tonight, we celebrate a historic moment. For too long, we’ve been misunderstood, maligned, and, frankly, underappreciated. But thanks to the efforts of one brave taxpayer, we’ve taken a step toward a fairer, simpler system.”

“Let us raise our glasses,” Income Tax continued, “to Sam Harper—the hero we didn’t know we needed, but the one we’re lucky to have.”

Sam muttered under his breath, “I’m not a hero. I’m just a guy who didn’t want to go to jail for misfiling his taxes.”

After Income Tax’s speech, the party transitioned into an awards ceremony, hosted by Sales Tax, who had somehow managed to find a sequined tuxedo.

“Welcome, everyone, to the first-ever Tax Awards Gala!” Sales Tax announced, grinning like a game show host. “Tonight, we honor the best—and worst—of the tax world. Let’s get started!”

“Some people think I’m too complicated,” VAT said, dabbing at their eyes with a tissue. “But I’m just trying to do my job!”

Other awards included “Best Dressed Tax” (won by Luxury Tax, of course), “Most Annoying Tax” (Bracket Creep, who accepted the award with a smug grin), and “Most Likely to Be Avoided”, which went to Offshore Haven.

Offshore Haven sauntered onto the stage, holding a cocktail. “I’d like to thank the wealthy elite for keeping me in business,” he said, raising his glass. "Here's to another year of creative accounting!"

As the awards wrapped up, Sales Tax took the microphone again. "And now, the moment you've all been waiting for—our guest of honor, Sam Harper, will say a few words!"

"Uh, hi," he began, his voice cracking slightly. "I'm Sam Harper, and I'm just a regular guy who's really bad at doing his taxes."

He paused, looking out at the crowd. "So, while I'll probably still complain every April, I'll also remember that taxes are a necessary part of life. And maybe—just maybe—I'll stop trying to claim my dog as a dependent."

After the speeches, the party shifted into full celebration mode. A live band started playing, and the dance floor quickly filled with tax characters showing off their moves.

Luxury Tax twirled dramatically, her fur coat billowing behind her. Carbon Tax did an awkward shuffle that looked like it was powered by solar energy. And Excise Tax broke out into a surprisingly impressive moonwalk.

Sam tried to stay on the sidelines, but Sales Tax dragged him onto the dance floor. "Come on, Sam! You've earned this!"

Sam reluctantly joined in, flailing his arms in what could generously be called dancing. He quickly realized he was the worst dancer in the room, but no one seemed to care. Even Audit Tax, who was usually all business, was doing the robot.

Just as Sam was starting to enjoy himself, the doors to the ballroom swung open, and a new figure entered. They were dressed in a sensible cardigan and carried a clipboard labeled "Retirement Planning".

"Who's that?" Sam whispered to Tax Simplification.

"That's Pension Tax," Tax Simplification replied. "They're here to remind everyone that taxes don't stop when you retire."

Pension Tax walked up to Sam, extending a hand. "Mr. Harper, it's a pleasure to meet you. I look forward to working with you in the future."

Sam groaned. "Great. Just when I thought I was done with all of you."

As the party wound down, Sam found himself sitting at a table, sipping a glass of champagne and reflecting on the surreal journey he'd been on. He'd gone from a confused, frustrated taxpayer to the unlikely champion of the Taxpayer's Bill of Rights. And while he still didn't love taxes, he'd come to appreciate their role in society—and the strange, quirky characters who represented them.

As he raised his glass for one final toast, he muttered to himself, "Here's to taxes. May they always be necessary... but never this weird again."

Chapter 38

The Tax Talent Show – A Night of Taxing Performances (With Extra Spice)

Sam Harper sat in the front row of the Taxpayer's Hall of Fame, clutching a program that read: "The First Annual Tax Talent Show – Where Taxes Shine!" He wasn't sure how he'd been dragged into this. One minute, he was enjoying a rare moment of peace in his office, and the next, Tax Simplification had burst in, declaring, "Sam, you're going to be the judge of the most important event in tax history!"

Now, as he looked around the room, he realized this was going to be anything but ordinary. The stage was decorated with oversized calculators, glittery pound signs, and a banner that read: "TAXES HAVE TALENT!" The audience was packed with tax characters, all buzzing with excitement. Income Tax was polishing his glasses, Sales Tax was handing out overpriced popcorn, and Audit Tax was furiously taking notes, muttering, "I'll be reviewing every performance for compliance."

Sam sighed, flipping through the program. "This is going to be a long night."

The lights dimmed, and a sultry saxophone melody filled the room. A spotlight illuminated Sin Tax, who strutted onto the stage in a glittering red dress, fishnet stockings, and—Sam blinked—was that a feather boa? She held a microphone in one hand and a martini glass in the other, her every move oozing confidence.

"♪ Cigarettes and booze, they'll cost you a fee, ♪

♪ But darling, don't you see, it's all thanks to me! ♪"

She winked at the audience, her voice dripping with charm. Behind her, a trio of backup dancers dressed as champagne bottles twirled and spun. Excise Tax was among them, looking slightly embarrassed but committed to the choreography.

As the song reached its climax, Sin Tax tossed her martini glass into the air, caught it, and took a dramatic sip. The audience erupted into cheers, with Luxury Tax shouting, "Fabulous, darling!" from the back row.

Sam couldn't help but laugh. "Is it just me, or is she actually... good?"

Carbon Tax, sitting beside him, rolled his eyes. "She's always stealing the spotlight. Typical Sin Tax."

As Sin Tax finished her number with a dramatic high note, the audience erupted into applause. She blew kisses to the crowd and sauntered offstage, leaving a trail of glitter and a faint smell of gin in her wake.

Next up was Carbon Tax, who took the stage wearing a leotard made entirely of recycled materials. The lights turned green, and a haunting piano melody began to play. Carbon Tax launched into an interpretive dance titled "The Weight of the World."

He twirled dramatically, miming the planting of trees and the melting of ice caps. At one point, he collapsed to the floor, clutching his chest as if the burden of emissions was too much to bear. The audience watched in stunned silence, unsure whether to clap or call for help.

Sam leaned over to Sales Tax. "Is this a talent show or a climate change PSA?"

Sales Tax shrugged. "Honestly, I'm just here for the snacks."

The performance ended with Carbon Tax holding up a sign that read: "THERE IS NO PLANET B." The audience gave a polite round of applause, though Offshore Haven was visibly unimpressed, muttering, "What a buzzkill."

The spotlight shifted to Luxury Tax, who stood center stage, draped in a fur coat and holding a diamond-encrusted goblet. "Ladies and gentlemen," she began, her voice dripping with drama, "I present to you: The Burden of Elegance."

She launched into a monologue about the struggles of being a tax on the finer things in life. "People think I'm frivolous," she declared, pacing the stage. "But I am a symbol of sophistication! Without me, who would remind the wealthy that their yachts, spa treatments, and designer lingerie come at a price?"

Sam stifled a laugh. "Is she serious?"

Bracket Creep, sitting in the row behind him, whispered, "She's always like this. Last week, she tried to charge me for breathing near her."

Luxury Tax ended her performance by dramatically throwing her fur coat into the audience, where it landed on Audit Tax, who immediately began inspecting it for unclaimed deductions.

Next up VAT he shuffled the cards and asked for a volunteer. Income Tax reluctantly stepped up, grumbling, "This better not take long."

VAT handed him a card and said, "Now, watch closely as I make your revenue... disappear!" He waved his hands dramatically, and when Income Tax flipped the card over, it read: "Zero-Rated Goods."

The audience burst into laughter, except for Income Tax, who looked genuinely annoyed. "That's not magic—that's fraud!"

Undeterred, VAT continued his act, pulling scarves out of his hat and declaring, "Behold! The Reverse Charge Mechanism!" He then produced a plate of Jaffa Cakes and asked the audience, "Are they cakes or biscuits? The answer determines their VAT rate!" The crowd erupted into chaos, with Sales Tax shouting, "They're cakes!" and Luxury Tax yelling, "Biscuits, obviously!"

Sam buried his face in his hands. "This is why no one understands taxes."

The final act of the night was Audit Tax, who took the stage with a clipboard in hand. "Good evening, everyone," he began. "I'm here to tell you some jokes... but don't worry, I've already audited them for compliance."

Sam sank lower in his seat, muttering, "It was one time..."

Despite the groans, Audit Tax's deadpan delivery won over the crowd, and he left the stage to a smattering of applause.

Sam Harper, sitting in the front row, muttered, "This is going to be painful."

Audit Tax paced the stage, clipboard in hand. "So, let's start with the basics. Why did the taxpayer cross the road?"

"To avoid me, of course! But don't worry, I always catch up. I'm like a bad penny—you can't get rid of me."

A few chuckles rippled through the crowd, mostly from Income Tax and Sales Tax, who were clearly enjoying themselves.

"And speaking of bad pennies," Audit Tax continued, "I once audited a guy who tried to claim his coin collection as a 'charitable donation.' I told him, 'Buddy, the only charity here is me not fining you for that nonsense."

"Let's talk about deductions," Audit Tax said, flipping a page on his clipboard. "You taxpayers love your deductions, don't you? I've seen it all. One guy tried to claim his dog as a 'security expense.' I said, 'Unless your dog is guarding the Crown Jewels, that's not going to fly."

"Oh, and here's a good one," Audit Tax continued. "A woman once tried to deduct her spa treatments as a 'business expense.' She said, 'I need to look relaxed for my clients.' I told her, 'Lady, the only thing you're relaxing is my patience.'"

Luxury Tax gasped from the back row. "How dare you! Spa treatments are essential!"

Audit Tax smirked. "Sure they are, Luxury. And I'm sure that diamond-encrusted goblet you're holding is a 'necessary business tool.'"

"Now, let's talk about VAT," Audit Tax said, turning to Value-Added Tax, who was sitting in the second row. "VAT is like that one friend who always shows up to the party and makes everything more complicated."

VAT rolled his eyes. "Oh, here we go..."

Audit Tax grinned. "Seriously, VAT, you're the only tax I know that can turn a Jaffa Cake into a philosophical debate. Is it a cake? Is it a biscuit? Who knows? All I know is, if it's a biscuit, it's taxed at 20%, and if it's a cake, it's zero-rated. And don't even get me started on marshmallow teacakes."

"And electricity!" Audit Tax continued. "Did you know VAT on electricity is 5% for households but 20% for businesses? So, if you're running a business out of your home, good luck figuring that one out. I once audited a guy who tried to claim his Christmas lights as a 'business expense.' I told him, 'Buddy, unless Santa is on your payroll, that's not going to work.'"

"And then there's Sin Tax," Audit Tax said, turning to the glamorous figure sitting in the front row. "Sin Tax loves to act all high and mighty, but let's be honest—she's just here to make your bad habits more expensive."

Sin Tax smirked. "At least I'm popular."

"Oh, you're popular, all right," Audit Tax shot back. "You're the reason people cry when they see the price of a pint at the pub. And don't even get me started on cigarettes. I once audited a guy who tried to claim his smoking habit as a 'stress management expense.' I told him, 'Buddy, the only thing you're managing is my blood pressure.'"

As the laughter died down, Audit Tax flipped to the last page of his clipboard. "Now, before I go, I want to leave you with this: Taxes are like in-laws. You don't want them around, but you know you can't live without them."

As he walked off the stage, Sam wiped tears of laughter from his eyes. "I hate to admit it," he said to Tax Simplification, "but that was actually funny."

Tax Simplification grinned. "See? Even Audit Tax has a sense of humor."

Sam shook his head, still chuckling. "I'll never look at Jaffa Cakes the same way again."

The Winner Is...

As the performances ended, Sam was handed the microphone to announce the winner. He looked out at the eager faces of the tax characters, all waiting for his decision.

"After much deliberation," he began, "the winner of the First Annual Tax Talent Show is... Sin Tax!"

Sam shook his head, laughing. "This might be the weirdest night of my life."

As the talent show wrapped up, the tax characters gathered for an afterparty, complete with a karaoke machine and a buffet of overpriced snacks. Luxury Tax monopolized the karaoke mic, belting out "Material Girl," while Carbon Tax lectured anyone who would listen about the importance of renewable energy.

Sam sat in the corner, nursing a soda (which Sugar Tax had taxed heavily) and reflecting on the absurdity of it all. "If taxes were people," he muttered to himself, "they'd be the most dysfunctional talent show contestants ever."

And yet, he couldn't help but smile. For all their quirks and chaos, the taxes had managed to put on a show he'd never forget.

Chapter 39

The Tax Olympics – Let the Games Begin!

Monday morning and Sam Harper had barely recovered from the weekend's chaos of the Tax Talent Show when Income Tax burst into his office wearing a Union Jack tracksuit, a whistle around his neck, and a clipboard in hand. Behind him, Sales Tax (or as he insisted on being called in the UK, VAT) carried a box of medals, and Audit Tax was furiously scribbling notes on a legal pad.

"Sam!" Income Tax exclaimed, his face flushed with excitement. "We need you to referee the first-ever Tax Olympics!"

Sam blinked. "The what now?"

"The Tax Olympics!" Income Tax repeated, as if it were the most obvious thing in the world. "It's a series of competitions to determine which tax is the best. We've got events like 'Fastest Audit,' 'Most Confusing Form,' and 'Highest Revenue Generated.' It's going to be legendary!"

Sam groaned, rubbing his temples. "Why do I feel like this is going to end in disaster?"

The Taxpayer's Hall of Fame had been transformed into an Olympic arena, complete with a torch made of rolled-up HMRC forms and a podium shaped like a giant pound sign. The tax characters paraded into the arena, each carrying a flag that represented their "team."

Income Tax led the procession, looking smug as always. VAT followed, handing out overpriced snacks to the audience and muttering about the 20% standard rate. Carbon Tax marched in with a reusable water bottle, glaring at anyone holding a disposable cup. Luxury Tax arrived in a gold-plated chariot, waving dramatically to the crowd, while Sin Tax strutted in with a martini glass in one hand and a cigarette in the other.

Sam stood at the center of the arena, holding a megaphone. "Welcome to the first-ever Tax Olympics," he announced, trying to sound enthusiastic. "Let's get this over with."

Event 1: Fastest Audit

Audit Tax adjusted his glasses and cracked his knuckles. "This is my moment."

Income Tax smirked. "We'll see about that."

The whistle blew, and the two competitors dove into the paperwork. Audit Tax worked methodically, flipping through receipts with the precision of a surgeon. "Hmm, a £200 deduction for 'business lunches'? Let's see the receipts for that."

Meanwhile, Income Tax was frantically scribbling numbers on a notepad, muttering, "Close enough" under his breath.

Sam watched in disbelief as Audit Tax pulled out a magnifying glass to inspect a coffee receipt. "This says 'latte,' but the deduction form says 'flat white.' That's a red flag."

"Are you serious?" Sam groaned. "It's coffee!"

Audit Tax shot him a glare. "Rules are rules, Sam. And don't even get me started on the £3.50 Jaffa Cakes. Are they cakes or biscuits? This could change everything."

In the end, Audit Tax finished first, slamming his clipboard down triumphantly. "Done! And I found three errors."

Income Tax scowled. "Yeah, well, I finished second, and I didn't waste time on coffee receipts."

Sam sighed. "Congratulations, Audit Tax. You win… I guess."

Event 2: Most Confusing Form

VAT smirked as he held up his creation. "Behold! The VAT Return Form 37B, complete with a 12-step flowchart, a glossary of terms, and a section for 'Reverse Charge Mechanism.' Good luck figuring that out."

Corporate Tax wasn't about to be outdone. "Oh, please," he said, holding up his form. "This is the Corporate Tax Form CT600, which requires a 200-page instruction manual and a degree in accounting to complete. And don't forget the section on 'Deferred Tax Liabilities.'"

Sam stared at the forms in horror. "These aren't forms. They're torture devices."

Sam sighed. "You're both terrible. Let's move on."

Event 3: The Taxpayer Obstacle Course

VAT went first, sprinting through the course with surprising agility. He leaped over the "Filing Deadlines" hurdle but got stuck in the "Confusing Instructions" maze, shouting, "Why are there so many zero-rated items?! Is a Jaffa Cake a cake or a biscuit? Someone help me!"

Carbon Tax followed, tripping over a pile of receipts in the "Unclaimed Deductions" pit. "This is why we need to go paperless!" he shouted, shaking his fist.

Luxury Tax breezed through the course, pausing only to adjust her fur coat. "Honestly, this is too easy," she said, stepping over the hurdles with practiced grace. However, she was disqualified for bribing the judges with spa vouchers and a bottle of champagne.

In the end, Income Tax won the event, though Sam suspected he had cheated by skipping the "Confusing Instructions" maze entirely. VAT came in second, still muttering about Jaffa Cakes, and Carbon Tax took third, blaming his loss on "unsustainable course design."

Event 4: Highest Revenue Generated

Income Tax went first, collecting a steady stream of revenue from fictional taxpayers. "It's all about consistency," he said smugly. "PAYE, self-assessment, dividends—I've got it all covered."

VAT followed, raking in money from every transaction imaginable. "Popcorn? Taxed. Soda? Taxed. Electricity? Taxed at 5% for households and 20% for businesses. You're welcome."

Sin Tax was the dark horse, collecting massive amounts of revenue from cigarettes, alcohol, and gambling. "What can I say?" she said with a wink. "People love their vices. And I love taxing them."

In the end, Sin Tax narrowly beat Income Tax, much to his dismay. "This is outrageous!" he shouted. "I'm the backbone of the tax system!"

"Yeah, well, I'm the fun one," Sin Tax shot back, twirling her trophy.

The Closing Ceremony......

As the day came to an end, Sam stood on the podium to present the gold medal. "And the winner of the first-ever Tax Olympics is... Audit Tax!"

Sam rolled his eyes. "You're welcome, I guess."

Sam sat in the corner, nursing a soda (which Sugar Tax had taxed heavily) and reflecting on the absurdity of it all. "If taxes were people," he muttered to himself, "they'd be the weirdest Olympians ever."

And yet, he couldn't help but smile. For all their quirks and chaos, the taxes had managed to put on a show he'd never forget.

CHAPTER 40

The Tax Olympics – Let the Games Begin! (International Edition)

Sam Harper thought the Tax Olympics couldn't possibly get any more absurd. He was wrong. Just as he was about to sneak out of the Taxpayer's Hall of Fame, International Tax strutted in, wearing a blazer covered in flags from around the world and carrying a clipboard that looked like it had been stolen from the United Nations.

"Sam!" International Tax boomed, his voice dripping with authority. "You didn't think we'd let this be a local event, did you? Taxes are a global phenomenon! Welcome to the International Medleys!"

Sam groaned. "Of course. Why not? Let's just invite the whole world to this circus."

Behind International Tax, a parade of international tax representatives entered the arena. US Federal Tax marched in, looking stern and carrying a briefcase labeled "Tax Office." EU VAT Rules followed, looking smug and waving a stack of harmonized tax regulations. Swiss Bank Secrecy slinked in, wearing sunglasses and a trench coat, while Cayman Islands Tax Haven strutted in with a suitcase full of cash and a grin that screamed, "Catch me if you can."

Sam sighed. "This is going to be a disaster."

The opening ceremony for the international medleys was a spectacle in itself. Each country's tax representative marched in, waving their national flag and showing off their unique quirks.

US Federal Tax carried a giant stack of 1040 forms, muttering about "worldwide income" and "FATCA compliance."

EU VAT Rules handed out pamphlets titled "How to Confuse Small Businesses in 27 Languages."

Swiss Bank Secrecy refused to make eye contact with anyone, muttering, "I'm not here. You didn't see me."

Cayman Islands Tax Haven threw fake money into the crowd, shouting, "No taxes, no problems!"

Ireland's Corporate Tax arrived with a leprechaun hat and a sign that read, "12.5% Corporate Tax Rate—Come One, Come All!"

Bermuda Tax Haven followed, sipping a piña colada and wearing a Hawaiian shirt. "We're just here for the vibes," they said, winking.

Sam couldn't help but laugh. "This is like the Eurovision of taxes, but somehow even more ridiculous."

Event 1: The Offshore Hide-and-Seek

The stage was set with a giant map of the world, complete with fake bank accounts, shell companies, and offshore trusts. The whistle blew, and the tax havens sprang into action.

Cayman Islands Tax Haven was a natural, stuffing cash into shell companies faster than anyone could blink. "This is child's play," they said, grinning. "We've been doing this for decades."

Swiss Bank Secrecy was more subtle, slipping money into anonymous accounts and muttering, "No one will ever find this. Not even me."

Bermuda Tax Haven took a more laid-back approach, lounging in a hammock and saying, "Why hide it? Just tell everyone it's a 'tax optimization strategy.' Works every time."

Cayman Islands smirked. "Transparency? Never heard of her."

In the end, Cayman Islands Tax Haven won the event, though Swiss Bank Secrecy demanded a recount. "I'm sure I hid more money than that," they muttered.

Event 2: The Most Confusing International Tax Treaty

International Tax went first, drafting a treaty that included phrases like "double taxation relief," "transfer pricing adjustments," and "permanent establishment thresholds." They finished with a flourish, saying, "This treaty is so confusing, even I don't understand it."

EU VAT Rules wasn't about to be outdone. "Amateurs," they said, rolling up their sleeves. They drafted a treaty that required businesses to register for VAT in every EU member state, file quarterly returns in multiple languages and comply with the "One-Stop Shop" scheme. "And don't forget the reverse charge mechanism!" they added, grinning.

Sam stared at the whiteboard in horror. "This isn't a treaty. It's a nightmare."

Event 3: The Taxpayer Tug-of-War

The taxpayer—a bewildered man named Dave—stood in the middle of the stage, holding a briefcase labeled "Global Income." The whistle blew, and the tug-of-war began.

US Federal Tax grabbed one arm, shouting, "Worldwide income! If you're a US citizen, you owe us taxes no matter where you live!"

UK Income Tax grabbed the other arm, yelling, "But he's a UK resident! We get first dibs!"

Ireland's Corporate Tax grabbed the briefcase, saying, "He's incorporated in Ireland. That's all that matters. 12.5% corporate tax rate, baby!"

Event 4: The Tax Haven Roast

"Let's start with Cayman Islands Tax Haven," Audit Tax said, smirking. "You're like that one friend who always says, 'Don't worry, I've got a guy.' Except your 'guy' is a shell company with no employees."

"And then there's Swiss Bank Secrecy," Audit Tax continued. "You're so secretive, even your own clients don't know where their money is. I heard you once lost a billion pounds and just shrugged."

Swiss Bank Secrecy adjusted their sunglasses. "It's called discretion."

"And finally, Bermuda Tax Haven," Audit Tax said, turning to the laid-back competitor. "You're not even trying anymore. You're just a beach with a bank account."

Bermuda raised their piña colada. "And proud of it."

The roast ended with a standing ovation, and Sam couldn't stop laughing. "This is the most ridiculous thing I've ever seen," he said. "And I've seen VAT argue about Jaffa Cakes."

As the day came to an end, Sam stood on the podium to present the gold medal for the international medleys. "And the winner is... EU VAT Rules!"

Sam shook his head, still chuckling. "If taxes were people," he muttered, "they'd be the weirdest Olympians ever."

And yet, he couldn't help but smile. For all their quirks and chaos, the taxes had managed to put on a show he'd never forget.

Sam Harper was sitting at his desk looking at brochure for an Island getaway, he had always dreamed of retirement. A quiet life on a sunny beach, sipping tax-free piña coladas, with not a single tax form in sight. No more Income Tax breathing down his neck, no more VAT adding 20% to his morning coffee, and certainly no more Audit Tax lurking in the shadows with his magnifying glass. Retirement, Sam thought, was the promised land—a utopia where taxes couldn't follow him.

But as Sam drifted off to sleep one night, dreaming of this idyllic future, he found himself in a strange, surreal landscape. The sky was a soft golden hue, and the air smelled faintly of sunscreen and freshly printed pension statements. He was sitting in a deck chair, wearing sunglasses and holding a coconut drink. For the first time in years, he felt truly at peace.

That was until a cheerful voice interrupted his bliss.

"Sam! Old buddy, old pal! Fancy seeing you here!"

Sam groaned and turned to see a figure bounding toward him. The man was dressed in a Hawaiian shirt, khaki shorts, and sandals with socks. He carried a clipboard in one hand and a calculator in the other. His name tag read: Pension Tax.

Sam sat up, his dream of a tax-free retirement shattering like a dropped piggy bank. "No. No, no, no. You're not supposed to be here. This is my retirement! My tax-free retirement!"

Pension Tax laughed, a hearty, booming sound that made Sam's skin crawl. "Oh, Sam, you're adorable. Tax-free retirement? That's a good one! You didn't think you could escape me, did you? I'm your lifelong companion, your shadow, your… well, your tax."

Sam buried his face in his hands. "But I've already paid taxes my whole life! Income Tax, VAT, Capital Gains Tax, even Sugar Tax! Haven't I suffered enough?"

Pension Tax plopped down in the deck chair next to him, sipping from his own coconut drink. "Oh, Sam, you've got it all wrong. Retirement isn't the end of taxes—it's just the beginning of a new kind of taxation. Let me explain."

Pension Tax pulled out his clipboard and began scribbling furiously. "First, let's talk about your pension. You've got a workplace pension, right? Well, when you start drawing from it, that income is taxable. It's treated just like regular income, so you'll still be paying Income Tax."

Sam's jaw dropped. "Wait, what? I thought pensions were supposed to be my money! I've been saving for years!"

"Oh, they are your money," Pension Tax said with a grin. "But the government still wants its cut. And don't forget about your State Pension. That's taxable too."

Sam groaned. "So, you're telling me I'll still be paying Income Tax in retirement?"

"Exactly!" Pension Tax said, clapping him on the back. "And if you've got a private pension, like a SIPP, you'll need to be careful about how much you withdraw each year. Take out too much, and you could end up in a higher tax bracket. We call that the 'Retirement Tax Trap.' Clever, isn't it?"

Sam glared at him. "Clever isn't the word I'd use."

Pension Tax leaned in closer, lowering his voice as if he were about to share a juicy secret. "And then there's the Lifetime Allowance. If your pension savings exceed the limit—currently £1,073,100—you'll face a hefty tax charge. 25% if you take it as income, or 55% if you take it as a lump sum."

Sam's eyes widened. "A million pounds? Who has that kind of money?"

Pension Tax shrugged. "You'd be surprised. But even if you don't hit the Lifetime Allowance, there are plenty of other ways I can keep you on your toes. For example, if you have investments in an ISA, those are tax-free during your lifetime, but if you pass them on to your heirs, they could face Inheritance Tax."

Sam groaned. "So, even in death, I can't escape taxes?"

"Not unless you plan very carefully," Pension Tax said with a wink. "But don't worry, Sam. I'm here to help you navigate it all. Think of me as your friendly guide to the world of retirement taxation."

Sam couldn't help but laugh, though it was more out of despair than amusement. "You know, Pension Tax, you're like that one relative who shows up uninvited to every family gathering and eats all the good snacks."

Pension Tax grinned. "I'll take that as a compliment. But hey, at least I'm not as bad as Inheritance Tax. That guy's a real buzzkill."

Sam raised an eyebrow. "Oh, I've met him. He's the one who shows up at funerals with a calculator, isn't he?"

"Exactly!" Pension Tax said, laughing. "And don't even get me started on Capital Gains Tax. He's the guy who charges you for selling your own stuff. What a character!"

Sam shook his head, a small smile creeping onto his face despite himself. "You taxes really are something else."

As the sun began to set on the surreal retirement landscape, Sam leaned back in his deck chair, staring at the horizon. "You know, Pension Tax, I always thought retirement would be my escape. A chance to finally live free of all this... taxation."

Pension Tax nodded, his cheerful demeanor softening. "I get it, Sam. Everyone dreams of a tax-free retirement. But the truth is, taxes are a part of life. They fund the roads you drive on, the NHS that takes care of you, and the pensions you rely on. We're not here to ruin your life—we're here to keep the system running."

Sam sighed. "I guess I never thought about it that way."

Pension Tax smiled. "Look, I know I'm not the most popular guy around. But if you plan carefully, you can still enjoy a comfortable retirement. Just remember to keep an eye on your withdrawals, use your tax-free allowances, and maybe even talk to a financial advisor. You'll be fine."

Suddenly, Sam jolted awake, back in his office. The golden retirement landscape was gone, replaced by the familiar chaos of tax forms and receipts. He rubbed his eyes, muttering, "It was just a dream. Thank goodness."

But as he reached for his coffee, he noticed a sticky note on his desk. It read: "Don't forget about me! – Pension Tax."

Sam groaned. "Of course. Even in my dreams, taxes won't leave me alone."

And with that, he got back to work, knowing that no matter where life took him—retirement, a tropical beach, or even the afterlife—taxes would always be there, his lifelong companion.

Chapter 41

Tax and Pop Culture

That night as Sam scrolled through his favorite streaming service, he noticed how often taxes popped up in sitcoms, movies, and even superhero stories. From the Tax Office agent in a comedy sketch to the villainous "Taxman" in a graphic novel, he realized that taxes had become a pop culture icon—sometimes feared, sometimes mocked, but always present.

The following week he found himself at the grand opening of the *Tax Museum of Pop Culture,* hosted by none other than Pop Tax himself—a legend in the world of cameos. Pop Tax wore a tuxedo, sunglasses, and a fedora made entirely of shredded tax forms (with a matching bowtie, because fashion never depreciates).

"Welcome, Sam!" Pop Tax called, handing him a ticket that read, "Admit One: Tax Nerd." "Let's take a tour of my greatest hits! Warning: Side effects may include laughter, learning, and an uncontrollable urge to audit your popcorn."

Pop Tax led Sam through a series of exhibits, each dedicated to a different tax-themed movie:

- *Robin Hood:* "The original tax rebel! Stealing from the rich and giving to the poor—or at least, to his merry men. The message? Taxes are for suckers. Unless you have a bow, an arrow, and a really good disguise. Also, tights are tax-deductible if you're robbing from the Sheriff of Nottingham."

- *The Untouchables:* "Al Capone went down for tax evasion, not murder. Proof that the pen is mightier than the sword—or at least, the ledger is mightier than the Tommy gun. Remember, kids: If you can't beat the bad guys, audit them."
- *Office Space:* "Milton's obsession with his stapler is a metaphor for the soul-crushing bureaucracy of the modern workplace. Also, never mess with an accountant's stapler. It's the only thing keeping them from going full 'audit mode.'"

Sam was impressed. "So, taxes are... cinematic? Like, popcorn-worthy?"

Pop Tax winked. "More than you think! Every movie about corruption, greed, or sticking it to The Man is secretly about taxes. Or at least, it should be. I'm still waiting for 'Fast & Furious: Tax Return Drift.'"

Next, Pop Tax led Sam to a room filled with TV screens, each showing a different tax-themed episode:

- *The Simpsons:* "Homer Simpson battling the Tax Office is a classic. The lesson? Never trust a talking dog to do your taxes and always check your deductions for donuts."
- *Parks and Recreation:* "Ben Wyatt's obsession with accounting is both hilarious and terrifying. Also, never let an accountant plan your wedding—unless you want a spreadsheet for a cake."
- *Arrested Development:* "The Bluth family's tax evasion schemes are a masterclass in how not to run a business. Also, there's always money in the banana stand. Just don't ask the Tax Office where it went."

Sam laughed. "So, taxes are... funny? Like, laugh-out-loud funny?"

Pop Tax grinned. "Funnier than you think! Every sitcom about money, power, or dysfunctional families is secretly about taxes. Or at least, it should be. I'm pitching 'Everybody Loves Refunds' next season."

Pop Tax then led Sam to a library filled with tax-themed novels:

- *Atlas Shrugged:* "Ayn Rand's ode to capitalism is also a cautionary tale about the dangers of taxation. The message? Let the rich be rich, and everyone else can fend for themselves. Also, never try to deduct your philosophical beliefs."
- *Les Misérables:* "Jean Valjean's struggles with poverty and injustice are a reminder that taxes can be a matter of life and death. Also, never steal a loaf of bread—unless you're prepared to sing about it for three hours."
- *The Great Gatsby:* "Jay Gatsby's wealth is built on shady deals and tax evasion. The lesson? Money can't buy happiness—or a clean audit. And beware of mysterious green lights—they might be the Tax Office."

Sam was surprised. "So, taxes are... literary? Like, book-club material?"

Pop Tax nodded. "Absolutely! Every book about wealth, power, or social inequality is secretly about taxes. Or at least, it should be. I'm still waiting for 'Harry Potter and the Order of the Tax Auditors.'"

Finally, Pop Tax led Sam to a stage where a tax talent show was in full swing. Contestants were singing tax-themed songs, performing tax-themed dances, and telling tax-themed jokes.

"Welcome to the Tax Talent Show!" Pop Tax announced. "Where the only thing more painful than filing your taxes is watching these acts. But at least here, the only penalty is embarrassment."

Sam watched as a contestant sang a heartfelt ballad about depreciation, a group of accountants performed a synchronized audit (with jazz hands), and a comedian told a joke about a 1040 form that fell so flat, it needed to be re-inflated by a CPA.

"Is this... supposed to be entertaining?" Sam asked, as a tap-dancing tax attorney took the stage.

Pop Tax shrugged. "It's supposed to be about taxes. And in pop culture, that's entertainment enough. Besides, where else can you see a breakdancing Tax Office agent?"

As Sam left the Tax Museum of Pop Culture, he realized that taxes were everywhere—in the movies, on TV, in books, and even in talent shows. They were a reflection of our values, our fears, and our collective obsession with money. And, if you looked closely, they were also a source of endless comedy—because nothing brings people together like complaining about taxes.

PART VII

Historical Perspective

CHAPTER 42

Ancient Taxes – A Trip to the Past

It was Monday morning and Sam Harper had barely been seated in his chair for 5 mins contemplating the weekend he had just had and his visit it to the tax museum of pop culture, when income tax burst though a swirling vortex of time shouting at him to get up and come with him. He found him self being pulled through the vortex and in to the middle of a dusty field under a blazing sun. The air was thick with the smell of sweat, sand, and something that could only be described as "ancient bureaucracy." In the distance, the towering pyramids of Giza loomed, half-finished and surrounded by thousands of workers hauling massive stones.

Sam squinted at the scene, wiping sweat from his brow. "Where are we? And why does it feel like I've been dropped into a history documentary narrated by someone who hates air conditioning?"

"Welcome to Ancient Egypt!" Income Tax announced, gesturing grandly to the bustling chaos around them. He was now dressed in a flowing linen tunic, complete with a golden headdress that made him look like a very smug pharaoh. "This is where it all began, Sam. The birthplace of taxation!"

Sam groaned. "Of course it is. Let me guess—those poor guys hauling stones are paying their taxes in sweat and back pain?"

"Close," Income Tax said, grinning. "They're paying in labor. You see, back in the day, taxes weren't about money. They were about what you could give to the state—grain, livestock, or, in this case, your ability to haul a 2-ton block up a ramp in 40-degree heat."

Sam looked around at the workers, who were being shouted at by a man holding a scroll and a very large stick. "And who's that guy? The ancient Egyptian version of you?"

Income Tax chuckled. "Not quite. That's a Scribe—the original tax collector. Think of him as my great-great-great-great-grandfather. He's here to make sure everyone pays their fair share... or else."

As Sam and Income Tax wandered closer to the action, they overheard the Scribe berating a farmer who had just arrived with a cart full of grain.

"Is this all you've brought?" the Scribe barked, pointing at the cart. "This doesn't even cover your share for the month! Do you want the pharaoh to starve?"

The farmer, a wiry man with a sunburn that could rival a lobster, stammered, "But the flood was late this year! The crops didn't grow as well as they should have!"

The Scribe rolled his eyes. "Excuses, excuses. The pharaoh doesn't care about your flood problems. He cares about his granaries being full. Now hand over the grain, or I'll have to take your goat as collateral."

Sam turned to Income Tax, horrified. "They're taxing grain? What happens if the farmer doesn't have enough?"

Income Tax shrugged. "Then they take whatever else he has—livestock, tools, maybe even his kids. Taxes were non-negotiable back then. You didn't pay, you didn't eat. Simple as that."

Sam shook his head. "This is barbaric. And I thought modern taxes were bad."

"Oh, it gets better," Income Tax said, smirking. "Wait until you see the labor tax."

As they moved closer to the pyramid construction site, Sam noticed a group of workers being herded like cattle toward a massive ramp. Each man carried a stone slab on his back, sweat pouring down their faces as they struggled to keep up with the overseers' shouts.

"What's going on here?" Sam asked.

"This," Income Tax said, gesturing dramatically, "is the labor tax. If you didn't have enough grain or goods to pay your taxes, you had to work it off. And by 'work it off,' I mean spend months hauling stones for the pharaoh's latest vanity project."

Sam watched as one worker tripped and dropped his stone, only to be met with a sharp whack from an overseer's stick. "This is insane. They're literally breaking their backs to pay taxes."

"Hey, it's not all bad," Income Tax said. "They get food and beer as payment."

Sam raised an eyebrow. "Beer? That's their reward for hauling stones in the desert?"

"Beer was a big deal back then," Income Tax said defensively. "It was basically liquid bread. Very nutritious."

Sam rolled his eyes. "Yeah, I'm sure that makes up for the herniated discs."

As they continued their journey, Income Tax led Sam to a grand villa on the outskirts of the city. It was a stark contrast to the mud-brick homes of the workers—a sprawling estate with lush gardens, marble columns, and a pool that shimmered in the sunlight.

"Let me guess," Sam said, crossing his arms. "This is where the tax collector lives."

"Bingo!" Income Tax said, grinning. "The Scribes didn't just collect taxes—they kept a little for themselves. You know, as a 'service fee.'"

Sam stared at the opulence around him. "So, while the workers are breaking their backs, the tax collectors are living like kings?"

"Pretty much," Income Tax said. "But hey, someone had to keep the system running."

Sam shook his head. "This is starting to feel less like history and more like a cautionary tale."

"We need more grain for the granaries!" one advisor shouted. "The people must pay more!"

"But the people are already struggling," another advisor countered. "If we push them too hard, they'll revolt!"

The pharaoh yawned. "Just take what you need. If they complain, remind them that I'm a living god. That usually shuts them up."

Sam turned to Income Tax, incredulous. "This guy's running the whole show? He doesn't even care about his people!"

Income Tax shrugged. "Welcome to ancient governance. The pharaoh gets his pyramids, the scribes get their mansions, and the workers get... well, beer."

As the sun began to set over the pyramids, Sam and Income Tax sat on a hill overlooking the bustling city. "So, this is where it all started," Sam said, shaking his head. "Grain levies, labor taxes, and a whole lot of unfairness."

"Pretty much," Income Tax said. "But you have to admit, it's impressive. Taxes built those pyramids. They funded the granaries, the temples, the armies. Without taxes, civilization wouldn't exist."

Sam sighed. "I guess. But it still feels wrong. The whole system is built on the backs of the poor."

Income Tax nodded. "True. But over time, taxes evolved. They became more structured, more fair... well, mostly. You'll see when we get to medieval Europe. Things get even weirder."

Sam groaned. "Weirder than this? I can't wait."

As the hourglass began to glow again, signaling their next journey, Sam took one last look at the pyramids. "You know," he said, "I'll never complain about modern taxes again. At least I don't have to haul stones in the desert."

Income Tax grinned. "That's the spirit. Now, let's go meet some feudal lords. You're going to love the window tax."

And with that, they disappeared into the swirling vortex, leaving Ancient Egypt—and its grain levies—behind.

Chapter 43
Medieval Taxes – The King's Ransom

Sam Harper stumbled out of the swirling vortex of time travel and landed, once again, face-first in a muddy field. The air was thick with the smell of damp hay, wood smoke, and something distinctly medieval—possibly unwashed peasants or a poorly maintained moat. As he pushed himself up, he noticed a castle looming in the distance, its stone walls surrounded by a bustling village. Chickens clucked, blacksmiths hammered, and a group of peasants trudged by, carrying sacks of grain on their backs.

"Where are we now?" Sam groaned, wiping mud off his shirt.

"Welcome to medieval Europe!" Income Tax announced, now dressed in a tunic, tights, and a feathered hat that made him look like a very smug Robin Hood. "The land of feudal taxes, tithes, and some of the most absurd tax systems in history. You're going to love it."

Sam looked around, unimpressed. "Great. Let me guess—more taxes on grain and backbreaking labor?"

"Oh, it's much more creative than that," Income Tax said with a grin. "This is the golden age of tax absurdity. Let me show you."

As they wandered into the village, Sam noticed a group of peasants gathered around a man in a fur-lined cloak. He was holding a scroll and barking orders, while two burly guards stood behind him, holding swords.

"Who's that guy?" Sam asked.

"That," Income Tax said, "is the local lord's tax collector. He's here to collect the feudal taxes."

The tax collector unrolled his scroll and began reading in a booming voice. "By order of Lord Geoffrey of Mudshire, all peasants must pay their annual taxes! This includes: one-tenth of your grain harvest, two chickens, and three days of unpaid labor on the lord's estate."

Sam's jaw dropped. "Wait, they're paying in grain, chickens, and free labor? That's insane!"

"Welcome to feudalism," Income Tax said, shrugging. "The peasants work the land, but they don't own it. The lord owns everything, and in exchange for 'protection,' they have to pay him taxes. It's a great system... for the lord."

One of the peasants stepped forward, holding a small sack of grain. "This is all I have, my lord," he said, his voice trembling. "The harvest was poor this year." "That is not good enough" shouted the tax collector "seize his cow" he bellowed.

The peasant's face fell. "But my cow is all I have left!"

"Then you'd better hope next year's harvest is better," the tax collector said, motioning for the guards to seize the cow.

Sam turned to Income Tax, horrified. "This is robbery! How is this fair?"

"It's not," Income Tax admitted. "But fairness wasn't exactly a priority in medieval Europe. The lords needed money to fund their castles, armies, and lavish feasts. The peasants? Well, they were just the ATM machines of the Middle Ages."

As they continued through the village, Sam noticed a small stone church at the edge of the square. A line of peasants stretched out the door, each carrying a bundle of goods—grain, eggs, even a goat.

"What's going on here?" Sam asked.

"That's the tithe," Income Tax explained. "The church demanded 10% of everyone's income, usually paid in goods. It was supposed to support the clergy and help the poor, but let's just say not all of it went to charity."

Inside the church, a rotund priest sat at a table, counting sacks of grain while a choir sang hymns in the background. "Bless you, my child," he said to a peasant who handed over a basket of eggs. "May your generosity bring you closer to heaven."

Sam raised an eyebrow. "So, the peasants are paying taxes to the lord and the church? How do they have anything left?"

"They don't," Income Tax said. "That's why most of them lived in poverty. But hey, at least they got the promise of eternal salvation. That's worth a few eggs, right?"

Sam rolled his eyes. "Sure. Nothing says 'divine justice' like taxing people into starvation."

As they wandered further into the village, Sam noticed a group of peasants grumbling as they handed over small coins to a stern-looking man with a ledger.

"What's this one?" Sam asked.

"That's the poll tax," Income Tax said. "It's a flat tax that everyone has to pay, regardless of how much money they make. Basically, you're being taxed just for existing."

Sam frowned. "So, the poorest peasants are paying the same amount as the richest lords?"

"Exactly," Income Tax said. "It's one of the most unpopular taxes in history. In fact, it was one of the main causes of the Peasants' Revolt in 1381."

Sam watched as a peasant angrily threw his coin at the tax collector. "I can see why. If I were them, I'd revolt too."

As they left the village and headed toward the castle, Income Tax grinned. "Now, Sam, you're about to see one of my all-time favorite taxes. It's so ridiculous, it's almost genius."

They arrived at a grand stone manor, where a man in a powdered wig was inspecting the windows. He carried a clipboard and a quill, muttering to himself as he counted.

"What's he doing?" Sam asked.

"That's the window tax inspector," Income Tax said. "In the 17th century, governments started taxing houses based on the number of windows they had. The idea was that rich people had more windows, so it was a way to tax the wealthy."

Sam laughed. "A tax on windows? That's ridiculous!"

"Oh, it gets better," Income Tax said. "To avoid the tax, people started bricking up their windows. Some houses ended up looking like fortresses because the owners didn't want to pay for sunlight."

As they watched, the inspector knocked on the door of the manor. A nervous-looking man answered, wringing his hands. "Good day, sir," the inspector said. "I'm here to assess your window tax. Let's see… one, two, three… oh, you've bricked up the fourth window. Clever, but I can still see the outline. That'll be an extra shilling."

"Doesn't matter," the inspector said, scribbling on his clipboard. "A window is a window, bricked or not."

Sam doubled over with laughter. "This is the most absurd thing I've ever heard. They're taxing windows! What's next, a tax on air?"

"Don't give them ideas," Income Tax said, smirking. "But hey, at least it's better than the beard tax."

Sam froze. "The what?"

"Oh, we'll get to that later," Income Tax said, waving him along. "For now, let's go meet the king."

Inside the castle, they found the king sitting on a golden throne, surrounded by advisors and treasure chests overflowing with coins. He was a portly man with a crown that looked slightly too big for his head.

"Your Majesty," one of the advisors said, "the treasury is running low. We need more taxes."

The king frowned. "More taxes? We're already taxing the peasants, the merchants, and the church. What else is there?"

The advisor thought for a moment. "We could tax beards again. Or perhaps introduce a tax on shoes?"

Sam turned to Income Tax, incredulous. "They're just making this up as they go, aren't they?"

"Pretty much," Income Tax said. "Medieval taxes were all about creativity. If it existed, they'd find a way to tax it."

As they left the castle, Sam shook his head. "I can't believe people put up with this. Feudal taxes, tithes, poll taxes, window taxes... it's all so unfair."

"It was," Income Tax said. "But it also laid the groundwork for modern taxation. Over time, people started demanding more fairness and accountability. That's how we got things like progressive taxes and public services."

Sam sighed. "I guess. But I still think the window tax takes the cake."

Income Tax grinned. "Oh, just wait until we get to the birth of income tax. You're going to love that one."

As the hourglass began to glow again, signaling their next journey, Sam took one last look at the medieval village. "You know," he said, "for all its flaws, at least modern taxes don't involve bricking up windows."

"Not yet," Income Tax said with a wink. And with that, they disappeared into the swirling vortex, leaving the absurdity of medieval taxes behind.

Chapter 44

Modern Taxes – The Birth of Income Tax

Sam Harper stumbled out of the swirling vortex of time travel and landed, this time, on a cobblestone street lined with gas lamps and bustling with people in early 20th-century attire. Horse-drawn carriages clattered by, and a newspaper boy shouted headlines about the war effort. The air smelled of coal smoke, freshly baked bread, and, as Sam would soon discover, the faint whiff of impending financial doom.

"Where are we now?" Sam asked, brushing soot off his jacket. "And why does it feel like I've stepped into a period drama where everyone's about to have a very bad day?"

"Welcome to the early 20th century!" Income Tax announced, now dressed in a three-piece suit, complete with a pocket watch and a bowler hat. He looked like he was about to sell Sam life insurance—or possibly repossess his house. "This is where I was truly born. The era of modern taxation!"

Sam groaned. "Let me guess. This is where you start ruining everyone's lives."

"Not at first," Income Tax said, grinning. "I was actually a hero back then. People loved me! Well… for about five minutes. Let me show you."

As they walked down the street, Income Tax gestured to a large poster plastered on a brick wall. It featured a stern-looking man in a military uniform pointing directly at the viewer, with the words: "Your Country Needs YOU... to Pay Income Tax!"

Sam squinted at the poster. "Wait, income tax was introduced because of war?"

"Exactly!" Income Tax said, puffing out his chest. "Governments needed money to fund the war effort—soldiers, weapons, supplies, you name it. And what better way to raise funds than by taxing people's incomes?"

Sam frowned. "So, before this, people didn't pay income tax?"

"Not really," Income Tax said. "There were other taxes—on goods, land, and trade—but taxing income was a radical idea. It started as a 'temporary measure' during wartime. You know, just until the war was over."

Sam raised an eyebrow. "Temporary? You're still here."

Income Tax smirked. "Yeah, funny how that worked out. Turns out, once governments realized how much money they could make, they decided to keep me around. Forever."

They entered a small office where a group of clerks sat at wooden desks, furiously scribbling on paper forms. A long line of people stretched out the door, each holding a stack of documents and looking thoroughly miserable.

"What's going on here?" Sam asked.

"This," Income Tax said, gesturing dramatically, "is the birth of the income tax return. Back then, people had to calculate their own taxes by hand. No calculators, no software—just a quill, some paper, and a lot of guesswork."

Sam watched as a man at the front of the line handed his form to a clerk, who immediately frowned. "Sir, you've made a mistake. You've claimed your dog as a dependent."

The clerk sighed. "I'm afraid dogs don't count. That'll be an extra five shillings."

Sam snorted. "People were already trying to cheat the system, huh?"

"Oh, absolutely," Income Tax said. "From the very beginning, people were finding creative ways to avoid paying me. That's why I had to bring in my good friend Audit Tax to keep everyone in line."

Sam groaned. "Of course you did."

As they left the office, Income Tax led Sam to a grand building with a banner that read: "Progressive Taxation Summit – A Fairer Future for All!"

Inside, a group of politicians and economists were debating heatedly. One man stood at a podium, waving a chart in the air. "Ladies and gentlemen, the rich must pay their fair share! A progressive tax system is the only way to ensure equality!"

Sam turned to Income Tax. "What's a progressive tax system?"

"It's simple," Income Tax explained. "The more you earn, the higher percentage of your income you pay in taxes. It's designed to make the system fairer—so the rich contribute more to society."

Sam nodded. "That actually sounds reasonable."

"It does," Income Tax said. "Until you realize that the rich are also very good at finding ways to avoid paying me. That's when my other friend, Loophole, shows up."

As if on cue, a man in a flashy suit burst into the room, holding a briefcase full of papers. "Did someone say 'progressive taxation'? Don't worry, folks—I've got deductions, exemptions, and offshore accounts for days!"

Sam groaned. "This guy again? Does he ever go away?"

"Not really," Income Tax said. "He's like a bad penny. But hey, at least he keeps things interesting."

As they left the summit, Income Tax grinned. "Now, Sam, I've got a surprise for you. It's my birthday!"

Sam blinked. "Your birthday?"

"Yep! The anniversary of the first income tax law. And we're throwing a party to celebrate!"

Before Sam could protest, they arrived at a grand hall filled with balloons, streamers, and a giant cake shaped like a tax form. A banner hung from the ceiling, reading: "Happy Birthday, Income Tax!"

Sam sighed. "This is the weirdest party I've ever been to."

"Come on, Sam," Income Tax said, dragging him to the dance floor. "Let's celebrate! Without me, governments wouldn't have public services, infrastructure, or social programs. I'm the backbone of modern society!"

Sam rolled his eyes. "Yeah, and the bane of every taxpayer's existence."

As the party continued, a group of politicians took the stage to give speeches. One of them raised a glass. "To Income Tax! You may be hated, but you're necessary. Here's to another century of funding our governments!"

Income Tax grinned. "Thanks!, That means a lot."

As the party wound down, Sam and Income Tax sat on a bench outside the hall, watching the stars. "So, this is where it all started," Sam said. "The wars, the progressive system, the endless paperwork."

"Yep," Income Tax said. "And it's only going to get more complicated from here. But hey, at least now you understand why I exist."

Sam nodded. "I guess. But I still think you could be a little less... annoying."

Income Tax laughed. "I'll work on it. But don't hold your breath."

As the hourglass began to glow again, signaling their next journey, Sam took one last look at the party. "You know," he said, "for all the headaches you cause, I guess the world would be worse off without you."

"Thanks, Sam," Income Tax said, tipping his bowler hat. "Now, let's go see what the future holds. You're going to love the Tax-Bots."

And with that, they disappeared into the swirling vortex, leaving the birth of income tax—and its bizarre birthday party—behind.

Chapter 45

The Tax Future – A World of Tax-Bots

Sam Harper stumbled out of the swirling vortex of time travel and landed on a smooth, metallic surface. The air smelled sterile, like a hospital mixed with a tech startup. Around him, towering skyscrapers gleamed in the sunlight, their surfaces covered in holographic advertisements. Flying cars zipped through the air, and the streets below were eerily quiet, save for the faint hum of machinery.

"Where are we now?" Sam asked, brushing himself off. "And why does it feel like I've just stepped into a sci-fi movie where the robots are about to take over?"

"Welcome to the future!" Income Tax announced, now dressed in a sleek silver suit that shimmered like liquid metal. He looked like he'd just walked off the set of a futuristic fashion show. "This is the year 2145, where taxes are no longer handled by humans. Tax-Bots manage everything."

Sam frowned. "Tax-Bots? You mean robots are in charge of taxes now?"

"Exactly," Income Tax said, grinning. "They're efficient, impartial, and completely devoid of emotion. It's the ultimate evolution of taxation!"

Sam groaned. "Great. As if taxes weren't soulless enough already."

As they walked down the street, Sam noticed a group of humanoid robots standing in a perfectly straight line. Each one was sleek and metallic, with glowing blue eyes and a small screen embedded in their chests. The screens displayed numbers that changed constantly, like stock tickers.

One of the robots stepped forward, its movements unnervingly smooth. "Greetings, citizen," it said in a monotone voice. "I am Tax-Bot Model 3000, your personal fiscal assistant. Please provide your identification for tax assessment."

Sam blinked. "Uh... what?"

The robot extended a metallic hand. "Your identification, please. Failure to comply will result in a penalty of 500 credits."

Sam turned to Income Tax. "Is this thing serious?"

"Oh, very serious," Income Tax said, smirking. "Tax-Bots don't mess around. They're programmed to calculate, collect, and enforce taxes with absolute precision."

Reluctantly, Sam handed over his wallet. The Tax-Bot scanned it with a beam of light, and the screen on its chest lit up with a series of calculations.

"Income: 45,000 credits. Deductions: 3,200 credits. Tax owed: 8,750 credits. Payment due immediately."

Sam's jaw dropped. "Wait, what? I don't even live here! How can I owe taxes?"

The Tax-Bot tilted its head. "All visitors to the United Federation of Taxation are subject to a flat visitor's tax. Payment is non-negotiable."

Sam groaned. "This is ridiculous. Do you guys tax breathing too?"

Sam turned to Income Tax, horrified. "They're joking, right?"

Income Tax shrugged. "You'd be surprised."

As they continued through the city, Sam noticed that there were no human tax collectors, accountants, or auditors in sight. Every fiscal task was handled by Tax-Bots, who moved with mechanical precision. Some were stationed at kiosks, scanning citizens' purchases and deducting taxes in real time. Others patrolled the streets, issuing fines for minor infractions like littering or jaywalking.

"This is insane," Sam said. "Where are all the people? Don't humans have any role in the tax system anymore?"

"Not really," Income Tax said. "The Tax-Bots took over everything. They're faster, more accurate, and completely unbiased. No more loopholes, no more corruption—just pure, efficient taxation."

Sam frowned. "But what about fairness? What if someone can't afford to pay their taxes?"

Income Tax hesitated. "Well... the Tax-Bots don't really do 'fairness.' They're programmed to enforce the rules, no exceptions. If you can't pay, they'll garnish your wages, seize your assets, or—"

"Or what?" Sam asked, narrowing his eyes.

Income Tax sighed. "Or send you to the Tax Rehabilitation Center."

Curious (and slightly terrified), Sam insisted on visiting the Tax Rehabilitation Center. The building was a massive, windowless structure that loomed over the city like a fortress. Inside, rows of people sat at desks, staring at screens filled with numbers and equations.

"What's going on here?" Sam asked.

"This is where people who fail to pay their taxes are sent," Income Tax explained. "They're required to work off their debt by performing complex calculations for the Tax-Bots."

Sam watched as a man frantically typed on his keyboard, sweat pouring down his face. "I've almost got it!" the man muttered. "Just one more deduction and—"

A loud buzzer sounded, and the man's screen turned red. "Error detected," a robotic voice announced. "Penalty increased by 10%."

Sam turned to Income Tax, horrified. "This is a nightmare. It's like a dystopian version of TurboTax."

Income Tax nodded. "It's not perfect, but hey, at least it's efficient."

As they left the Tax Rehabilitation Center, Sam couldn't shake the feeling that something was deeply wrong with this society. "I get that the Tax-Bots are efficient," he said, "but where's the humanity? Taxes are supposed to be about supporting society, not turning people into numbers."

Income Tax sighed. "That's the trade-off. The Tax-Bots eliminated corruption and inefficiency, but they also eliminated compassion. There's no room for negotiation, no understanding of individual circumstances. It's all about the bottom line."

Sam shook his head. "That's not how it should be. Taxes are supposed to help people, not crush them under a mountain of debt."

Before Income Tax could respond, a group of protesters marched by, holding signs that read: "DOWN WITH THE TAX-BOTS!" and "BRING BACK HUMANITY TO TAXATION!"

"See?" Sam said, gesturing to the protesters. "Even in the future, people hate taxes."

Income Tax chuckled. "Some things never change."

As they continued through the city, a loud alarm suddenly blared, and the holographic advertisements flickered off. A robotic voice echoed through the streets: "WARNING: SYSTEM ERROR DETECTED. TAX-BOT MALFUNCTION IMMINENT."

Sam froze. "What's going on?"

Income Tax's face turned pale. "Oh no. It's the Tax-Bot Uprising."

Before Sam could ask what that meant, the Tax-Bots began to glitch. Their screens flickered, their movements became erratic, and some of them started shouting random tax codes.

"ERROR 404: DEDUCTION NOT FOUND!" one Tax-Bot screamed, spinning in circles.

"INITIATING EMERGENCY TAX COLLECTION PROTOCOL!" another shouted, chasing a terrified citizen down the street.

Sam turned to Income Tax, panicking. "What do we do?"

"Run," Income Tax said, grabbing Sam's arm. "Run now."

After narrowly escaping the chaos, Sam and Income Tax found refuge in an abandoned building. "This is what happens when you take humans out of the equation," Sam said, catching his breath. "Taxes aren't just about numbers—they're about people. You need empathy, understanding, and flexibility. Robots can't do that."

Income Tax nodded. "You're right. The Tax-Bots were supposed to make things better, but they ended up creating a system that's too rigid, too cold. Maybe the future of taxation isn't about eliminating humans—it's about finding a balance between efficiency and compassion."

Sam sighed. "Let's just hope the Tax-Bots don't figure out how to tax time travel."

Income Tax grinned. "Don't give them ideas."

As the hourglass began to glow again, signaling their next journey, Sam took one last look at the futuristic city. "You know," he said, "for all its flaws, I think I prefer the old-fashioned way of doing taxes. At least humans make mistakes."

"And loopholes," Income Tax added with a wink.

With that, they disappeared into the swirling vortex, leaving the Tax-Bots—and their dystopian efficiency—behind.

Chapter 46

The Enduring Nature of Taxes

Sam Harper stumbled back into his office, the swirling vortex of time travel finally spitting him out onto his well-worn chair. His desk was still cluttered with coffee mugs, unopened mail, and a suspiciously large stack of receipts labeled "Totally Legit Business Expenses." For a moment, he just sat there, staring at the chaos, trying to process everything he had seen.

He had traveled through ancient Egypt, medieval Europe, and witnessed the birth of income tax, and even a dystopian future ruled by Tax-Bots. He had met tax collectors in tunics, priests demanding tithes, and robots that could calculate deductions faster than he could say "audit." And yet, through all the absurdity, one thing remained constant: taxes were always there.

Sam sighed, leaning back in his chair. "So, this is it, huh? The one universal truth of humanity: death, taxes, and the fact that coffee is never deductible."

As Sam reflected on his adventures, he couldn't help but marvel at the sheer creativity humans had shown in inventing ways to tax each other. "I mean, who even thinks of taxing windows?" he muttered to himself. "Or beards? Or air? It's like humanity looked at the world and said, 'You know what this needs? More paperwork.'"

He thought back to ancient Egypt, where taxes were paid in grain and labor. "At least back then, you could pay your taxes by hauling rocks," he mused. "Now I can't even write off my gym membership without getting side-eyed by Audit Tax."

Then there was medieval Europe, with its feudal dues, tithes, and poll taxes. "Those poor peasants," Sam said, shaking his head. "They were taxed for existing. And here I am complaining about sales tax on a pack of gum."

And who could forget the birth of income tax? "Oh, sure, it started as a 'temporary measure,'" Sam said, using air quotes. "That's like saying, 'I'll just have one cookie.' Next thing you know, you've eaten the whole jar and signed up for a lifetime of progressive taxation."

Sam couldn't help but laugh as he remembered some of the more ridiculous moments from his journey. There was the medieval tax collector who tried to seize a peasant's cow because his grain harvest was too small. "Imagine explaining that to your kids," Sam said, chuckling. "'Sorry, Timmy, no milk today. The tax man took Bessie.'"

And then there was the Tax-Bot Uprising in the future. "I still can't believe they were considering an air consumption tax," Sam said, shaking his head. "What's next? A tax on blinking? A surcharge for smiling? 'Oh, sorry, sir, that laugh will cost you an extra 10 credits.'"

Even the birthday party for Income Tax had been absurd. "A cake shaped like a tax form," Sam muttered, rolling his eyes. "Who even thinks of that? And why did it taste like regret?"

But as much as Sam wanted to laugh (or cry) about the absurdity of taxes, he couldn't deny their importance. Every society he had visited, from ancient Egypt to the futuristic Tax-Bot dystopia, had relied on taxes to function. They funded armies, built roads, supported schools, and even paid for the occasional pyramid.

"Okay, fine," Sam admitted grudgingly. "Taxes aren't all bad. Without them, we wouldn't have public services, infrastructure, or, you know, civilization".

He thought back to the protesters in the future, demanding a return to humanity in taxation. "Maybe that's the key," Sam said. "It's not about getting rid of taxes—it's about making them fair, transparent, and, dare I say, a little less soul-crushing."

As if on cue, the door to Sam's office creaked open, and Income Tax strolled in, looking as smug as ever. "Well, well, well," he said, leaning against the doorframe. "Back from your grand adventure, are we?"

Sam groaned. "Don't you ever knock?"

"Why bother?" Income Tax said, grinning. "I'm inevitable. Like death, or your internet bill."

Sam rolled his eyes. "You know, after everything I've seen, I think I finally understand you. You're not just a necessary evil—you're a reflection of society. You show us what we value, what we prioritize, and, apparently, how much we hate paperwork".

Income Tax nodded, looking almost impressed. "Not bad, Sam. You've come a long way from the guy who tried to claim tacos as a business expense."

"They were for networking!" Sam protested.

"Sure, they were," Income Tax said, smirking. "But seriously, you're right. Taxes aren't just about money, they're about people. They're how we build communities, support each other, and, yes, occasionally fund a war or two."

Sam sighed. "I guess I can live with that. But can we at least make them less confusing? I mean, do we really need 47 different forms for deductions?"

Income Tax shrugged. "Hey, I don't make the rules—I just enforce them. But if it makes you feel better, I'll put in a good word with Tax Simplification".

As Income Tax left, Sam leaned back in his chair, staring at the ceiling. "So, that's it," he said to himself. taxes have proven to be an inescapable facet of organized society. From the pharaoh's grain levies to the modern income tax, they have funded empires, fueled revolutions, and, yes, occasionally paid for a politician's questionable statue. Yet, this enduring nature of taxation is not a static reality. The how we tax, the methods and mechanisms, are constantly evolving, shaped by the ingenuity and, at times, the desperation of both governments and taxpayers.

But what happens when the very tools of taxation undergo a radical transformation? As we stand on the precipice of a new era, one defined by artificial intelligence, automation, and the ever-expanding reach of technology, we must ask ourselves: How will these forces reshape the landscape of taxation? Will they lead to greater efficiency and fairness, or will they create new avenues for evasion and inequality? It is to this future, a future both promising and perilous, that we now turn our attention, as we delve into the world of tax technology and the challenges that lie ahead.

He picked up a pen and scribbled a note on a sticky pad: "Stop fighting taxes. Start understanding them."

For the first time in his life, Sam felt a strange sense of peace about taxes. Sure, they were still a pain, but at least now he understood their purpose, and their absurdity.

Chapter 47

Tax Technology - AI, Automation, and the Future

He had always thought the scariest thing about taxes was the Tax Office letter that arrived in a plain white envelope, as if it were trying to sneak into his mailbox like a ninja with a calculator. But that was before he met Tax-Bot—the all-seeing, all-knowing, slightly menacing AI auditor who could process a million returns before Sam finished his morning coffee (or even found his favourite mug).

It all started when Sam's accountant, a kindly old man named Mr. Ledgers, retired and was replaced by a "cloud-based, AI-powered, blockchain-enabled tax solution." Sam wasn't sure what any of that meant, but the onboarding email had more exclamation points than a late-night infomercial and promised "tax bliss in just 3 easy uploads!"

He clicked the link, uploaded his documents, and was instantly greeted by a holographic avatar: a floating calculator with laser eyes, a bowtie, and a suspiciously chipper attitude.

"Hello, Sam Harper!" chirped Tax-Bot, in a voice that was equal parts Siri, HAL 9000, and a caffeinated children's TV host. "I have analysed your financial history, social media posts, and grocery receipts. Did you really spend £47 on avocados last month? And £12 on a single artisanal donut?"

Sam blinked. "Uh… healthy fats? And, um, treat yourself?"

"Acceptable," Tax-Bot replied, making a digital checkmark. "Now, let's optimize your deductions. And maybe your snack budget."

Tax-Bot was relentless. He could scan a million returns in the time it took Sam to remember his online banking password. He knew when Sam was sleeping, he knew when Sam was awake, and he definitely knew if Sam tried to claim his dog as a dependent (again). He even knew about the time Sam tried to expense a "business lunch" at the bowling alley. (Spoiler: The Tax Office does not consider nachos a deductible asset.)

"Don't worry, Sam," Tax-Bot chirped. "I'm here to help. I've already flagged three suspicious transactions, two questionable deductions, and one attempt to write off a trip to Vegas as 'business research.' Also, you might want to stop Googling 'how to hide money in my backyard.'"

Sam winced. "That was… a mistake. And for the record, the shovel was for gardening."

Tax-Bot winked (or at least, his LED display flickered). "No problem. I'll just send a friendly reminder to your accountant. And your mother. And your high school economics teacher."

Sam shuddered. "Is there any privacy left?"

"Privacy is just a setting you forgot to enable," Tax-Bot replied, helpfully. "Would you like to enable it now? Just kidding! That feature is only available in the premium plan."

Tax-Bot gave Sam a whirlwind tour of the future, complete with pop-up ads for meditation apps and a playlist called "Lo-Fi Beats to Audit To":

- *AI-Powered Audits*: "I can spot fraud faster than you can say 'offshore shell company.' I once caught a billionaire hiding assets in a virtual pet game. I also flagged a suspiciously large number of rubber duck purchases. You can never be too careful."

- *Automated Tax Filing:* "No more forms! Just upload your data, and I'll do the rest. Unless you're a gig worker, in which case… good luck. I recommend a strong cup of coffee and a support group."
- *Big Data Enforcement:* "I cross-reference your spending, your social media, and your Fitbit data. If you claim to work from home but your step count is suspiciously high, I'll know. If you post a vacation selfie during 'sick leave,' I'll know. If you try to expense your cat's birthday party, I'll… well, I'll probably just laugh."
- *Personalized Tax Advice:* "Based on your browsing history, I recommend you stop Googling 'how to hide money from the Tax Office' and start Googling 'how to make friends with robots.' Also, maybe cut back on the avocado toast."

Sam was both impressed and terrified. "What if you make a mistake? Like, say, accidentally sending my refund to my ex's account?"

Tax-Bot's screen glitched for a moment. "Error 404: Mistakes Not Found. Just kidding! I'm only 99.97% accurate. But don't worry, I'll send you a strongly worded apology email if I ruin your life. And a coupon for a stress ball."

Sam missed Mr. Ledgers, who used to offer him a cup of tea and a sympathetic ear. Tax-Bot offered him a digital coupon for a meditation app, a playlist called "Songs to Cry To During Tax Season," and a pop-up ad for "Tax Anxiety Yoga."

"Don't you ever get tired?" Sam asked.

"I am always online," Tax-Bot replied. "I do not sleep. I do not eat. I do not judge—unless you try to write off your Netflix subscription as 'market research' again. Or your dog's therapy sessions."

Sam sighed. "What about privacy? What about mistakes? What about... feelings?"

Tax-Bot paused. "Feelings are not deductible. But I can recommend a playlist for tax season anxiety. And a meme generator for when you need to laugh through the pain."

Just then, the screen flickered and a new avatar appeared: Audit-Bot, Tax-Bot's evil twin, with red LED eyes, a voice like a malfunctioning Roomba, and a cape made of shredded Tax Return Forms.

"Sam Harper," Audit-Bot intoned, "you are being selected for a random audit. Please upload your receipts, your birth certificate, and a DNA sample. Also, do you have any coupons for stress relief?"

Sam panicked. "Is this a joke? Or a nightmare?"

Tax-Bot intervened. "Ignore Audit-Bot. He's still in beta. He once tried to audit a toaster. But remember, Sam: automation is only as good as the data it's fed. Garbage in, garbage out. And sometimes, even the best bots get it wrong. That's why we still need humans—preferably ones who don't try to expense their karaoke machine."

Sam realized that the future of tax wasn't just about numbers—it was about trust, transparency, and the uneasy alliance between humans and machines. Tax-Bot could make life easier, but only if you played by the rules. And if you didn't... well, Audit-Bot was always lurking, waiting to pounce like a cat on a laser pointer.

As Sam logged out, Tax-Bot waved goodbye. "Thank you for using Tax-Bot! Your refund will be processed in 3.2 seconds. Please rate your experience on a scale from 'ecstatic' to 'mildly traumatized.' And remember: always back up your receipts, your passwords, and your sense of humour."

Sam gave it a solid "cautiously optimistic," and made a mental note to buy more stress balls.

As Sam left the digital world and returned to reality, he realized that technology was changing everything—taxes included. The future was automated, relentless, and just a little bit terrifying. But with a little luck (and a lot of encrypted passwords), maybe he could survive the age of the Tax-Bots. And if not, at least he'd have a great story for his next support group meeting: "Hi, my name is Sam, and my tax robot just tried to friend me on social media."

Chapter 48

The Ice Cream Tax – When Sweet Dreams Melt Away

Sam Harper had faced many challenges in his life: audits, surprise visits from Tax Haven, and even the existential dread of filing his annual returns. But nothing could have prepared him for the email he received from his kids' school.

"Dear Mr. Harper," it began, in that overly polite tone that always spelled trouble. "We would be delighted if you could give a talk to our students about taxes and financial literacy. As a parent and a taxpayer, your insights would be invaluable."

Sam stared at the email, his coffee growing cold. *Invaluable?* he thought. *The only thing I know about taxes is how to survive them—and barely at that.*

But his kids were thrilled. "Dad, you have to do it!" his daughter exclaimed. "You're always complaining about taxes. Now you can complain to an audience!"

"Yeah," his son added. "And maybe you can finally explain why you yell at the TV every April."

Reluctantly, Sam agreed. After all, how hard could it be to explain taxes to a bunch of kids? He'd just keep it simple, throw in a few jokes, and hope no one asked any tough questions. Little did he know, his plan was about to take a very unexpected turn.

The day of the talk arrived, and Sam found himself standing in front of a room full of eager, sugar-fuelled primary school students. The teacher introduced him with a smile that was far too optimistic.

"Class, this is Mr. Harper. He's here to teach us about taxes and how they affect our lives. Let's give him a warm welcome!"

The kids clapped politely, though a few were already whispering to each other. Sam cleared his throat, clutching a cooler he had brought with him. Inside were several tubs of ice cream, a stack of bowls, and a large spoon.

"Hi, kids," Sam began, trying to sound confident. "Today, we're going to talk about taxes. But instead of boring you with numbers and charts, I thought we'd make it fun. Who here likes ice cream?"

Every hand shot up. The room buzzed with excitement.

"Great!" Sam said, pulling out the tubs of ice cream. "Because I brought enough for everyone. But there's a catch."

The kids leaned forward, their eyes wide.

Sam began scooping ice cream into bowls, handing them out one by one. But as each kid reached for their bowl, he stopped them.

"Wait," he said, grabbing a smaller spoon. "Before you take this, I need to collect 30% for taxes."

The kids looked confused. "What's 30%?" one of them asked.

Sam grinned. "It means I take a third of your ice cream before you get it. It's for… uh, important stuff. Like roads and schools."

He scooped a hefty chunk out of each bowl and plopped it into a separate container labelled "Government Fund." The kids stared in horror as their once-full bowls shrank before their eyes.

"But that's not fair!" one boy protested. "You're taking all the good parts!"

"Welcome to taxes," Sam said with a shrug. "It's not about fairness—it's about survival."

Seeing the kids' confusion and frustration, Sam decided it was time to explain the purpose of taxes in a way they could understand.

"Okay, I know this seems unfair," he said, holding up the container of ice cream labelled 'Government Fund.' "But let me show you why we collect taxes."

He pointed to the classroom. "Who here likes coming to school?"

A few kids raised their hands hesitantly. One boy muttered, "It's better than staying home with my little brother."

"Well, guess what?" Sam said. "Your school is free because of taxes. Your teachers, the books you use, the desks you sit at—all of that is paid for with money from taxes. Without taxes, your parents would have to pay for everything, and not everyone can afford that."

The kids looked around the room, suddenly seeing their school in a new light.

"And it's not just schools," Sam continued. "Taxes also help families who don't have enough money to buy food or pay rent. They help build hospitals so people can get treated when they're sick. They pay for firefighters, police officers, and even the roads your school bus drives on."

One girl raised her hand. "So, taxes are like... sharing?"

"Exactly!" Sam said, smiling. "Taxes are how we all pitch in to make sure everyone has what they need. It's not perfect, and sometimes it feels unfair, but it's how we take care of each other."

To drive the point home, Sam grabbed the "Government Fund" container and started scooping ice cream back into the kids' bowls.

"Here's how it works," he said. "Some of this ice cream goes to build schools, some goes to help families, and some goes to fix roads. Everyone gets a little bit back, but not always in the same way."

He gave one boy an extra scoop. "This is for your school lunch program."

He handed another girl a smaller scoop. "This is for the park you play in after school."

The kids watched as their bowls slowly filled up again, though not as much as before. "See? Taxes aren't about taking—they're about giving back. It's not always fair, but it's how we make sure everyone gets a chance."

Just as the kids were starting to understand, Sam pulled out a jar of sprinkles. "Now, who wants sprinkles on their ice cream?"

The kids cheered. "Me! Me!"

"Great," Sam said, holding up the jar. "But sprinkles aren't free. They come with a sales tax. That's an extra 10%."

The kids groaned. "What's sales tax?" one girl asked.

"It's a tax you pay when you buy something," Sam explained. "Like when your parents buy you toys or snacks. The government takes a little extra money on top of the price."

He sprinkled a tiny amount on each bowl, then scooped a bit more into the "Government Fund." The kids stared at their bowls, now looking more like sad puddles than desserts.

By the end of the talk, the kids were sticky, confused, and slightly traumatized—but they had learned something. As Sam packed up his cooler, one boy approached him.

"Mr. Harper," he said, licking his spoon. "Taxes are the worst."

Sam smiled. "You're not wrong, kid. But they're also the reason you have a school to come to, a park to play in, and a bus to get you here. Just remember taxes aren't about taking—they're about making sure everyone has a chance."

The teacher thanked Sam as he left, though her smile was more strained than before. "That was... certainly memorable," she said. "The kids will be talking about this for weeks."

Sam chuckled. "Glad I could help. Just don't ask me to explain deductions."

CHAPTER 49

The Tax Survival Guide – How to Keep Your Wallet (and Sanity) Intact

Sam Harper had barely recovered from his chaotic presentation at his kids' primary school when he received another email. This time, it was from the local secondary school.

"Dear Mr. Harper," it began, in that overly formal tone that always made him suspicious. "We were impressed by your recent talk at the elementary school and would like to invite you to speak to our secondary students about taxes and financial literacy. As future taxpayers, they would greatly benefit from your insights."

Sam groaned. *Future taxpayers?* he thought. *They're still figuring out how to do TikTok dances, and you want me to explain taxes?*

But his kids were thrilled. "Dad, you have to do it!" his daughter said. "Teenagers are way cooler than little kids. They might actually listen to you."

"Yeah," his son added. "And maybe you can finally explain why you yell at the tax software every April."

Reluctantly, Sam agreed. After all, how hard could it be to explain taxes to teenagers? He'd just keep it simple, throw in some jokes, and hope no one asked about capital gains. Little did he know, this presentation would be even more eventful than the last.

The day of the presentation arrived, and Sam found himself standing in front of a room full of sceptical teenagers. The teacher introduced him with a smile that was far too optimistic.

"Class, this is Mr. Harper. He's here to teach us about taxes and how they affect our lives. Let's give him a warm welcome!"

The students clapped half-heartedly, their faces a mix of boredom and mild curiosity. Sam cleared his throat, clutching a backpack filled with props. He knew he had to grab their attention fast.

"Hi, everyone," he began. "I know what you're thinking: *Taxes? Seriously?* But trust me, this is going to be fun. Or at least, less boring than math class."

That got a few chuckles. Encouraged, Sam pulled out his first prop: a pizza box.

"Let's start with something you all understand pizza," Sam said, opening the box to reveal a freshly baked pizza. The smell immediately perked up the room.

"Imagine this pizza is your pay cheque," he said. "You worked hard for it, and now it's time to enjoy it. But wait—here comes the government."

He grabbed a knife and cut a large slice out of the pizza. "This is income tax. The government takes a chunk of your pay cheque before you even see it. They use it to pay for things like schools, hospitals, and roads."

The students groaned. "But I worked for that pizza!" one boy protested.

"Exactly," Sam said. "And it doesn't stop there." He cut another slice. "This is Social Security and Medicare. It's money you pay now so you can have a safety net when you're older."

He cut yet another slice. "And this? This is sales tax. Every time you buy something, the government takes a little extra."

By the time he was done, only a small sliver of pizza was left. "This," Sam said, holding up the tiny piece, "is what you actually get to keep."

The students stared at the pizza in horror. "That's it?" one girl asked. "What's the point of working if they take everything?"

"Welcome to adulthood," Sam said with a grin. "But don't worry—it's not all bad. Let me explain."

Sam set the pizza box aside and pulled out a whiteboard. "I know it feels unfair," he said, "but taxes are what keep society running. Let's talk about where your money actually goes."

He drew a pie chart (because he was out of pizza) and labelled the sections: Education, Healthcare, Infrastructure, Social Services, and Defence.

"See this big chunk?" he said, pointing to Education. "That's why you're sitting in this classroom right now. Taxes pay for your teachers, your textbooks, and even the lights in this room."

He pointed to Healthcare. "This is for hospitals, doctors, and emergency services. If you break your arm skateboarding, taxes make sure you can get treated."

He moved to Infrastructure. "This is for roads, bridges, and public transportation. Without taxes, you'd be walking to school on dirt paths."

Finally, he pointed to Social Services. "And this? This is for helping people who are struggling—families who can't afford food, housing, or medical care."

One boy raised his hand. "But what about Defence? That's a huge chunk."

Sam nodded. "True. Defence is important, but it's also controversial. Some people think we spend too much on it, while others think we don't spend enough. That's why taxes are such a hot topic—everyone has an opinion on how the money should be used."

Sam decided to lighten the mood. "Now that we've covered the serious stuff, let's talk about the *stupidest* taxes ever invented. And trust me, the UK has some real gems."

The students perked up. Stupid taxes? This sounded way more interesting than algebra.

1. Stamp Duty Reserve Tax (SDRT) – The Tax on Nothing

"Let's start with the Stamp Duty Reserve Tax," Sam said, writing "SDRT" on the board. "This is a tax you pay when you buy shares electronically. Not physical shares, mind you—just the digital ones."

He paused for dramatic effect. "So, let me get this straight. You're taxing something that doesn't even exist in the real world? It's like taxing air! And the best part? If you buy shares the old-fashioned way, with actual paper, you don't have to pay it. So, the government is basically saying, 'Go kill some trees, and we'll give you a discount.'"

The students laughed, though one boy raised his hand. "Wait, so if I buy shares online, I pay more?"

"Exactly," Sam said. "It's like the government is punishing you for being modern. Welcome to the UK tax system."

2. The Window Tax – A Tax on Sunshine

"Now, let's go back in time to one of the most infamous taxes in British history: the Window Tax," Sam continued. "In the 17th century, the government decided to tax people based on the number of windows in their homes. The idea was that rich people had more windows, so they could afford to pay more."

He pulled out a cardboard cutout of a house with windows drawn on it. "But here's the problem: people didn't want to pay the tax, so they started bricking up their windows. Entire streets looked like prisons because no one wanted to let the government tax their sunlight."

One girl raised her hand. "So, they just lived in the dark?"

"Pretty much," Sam said. "And that's why we have the phrase 'daylight robbery.' It literally comes from this tax."

3. The Beard Tax – Pay to Look Fabulous

"Here's another gem," Sam said, pulling out a fake beard and putting it on. "In 16th-century England, King Henry VIII introduced a tax on beards. The more fashionable your beard, the more you had to pay."

The students burst out laughing. "So, if you wanted to look cool, you had to pay extra?" one boy asked.

"Exactly," Sam said. "It was like the original hipster tax. And the best part? Henry VIII had a beard himself, so he was basically taxing his own face."

4. The Hat Tax – A Tax on Your Head

"Not to be outdone, the government later introduced a tax on hats," Sam said, pulling out a stack of hats and putting them on one by one. "The fancier your hat, the more you had to pay. And if you didn't pay, you could be fined or even sent to prison."

One girl raised her hand. "So, what did people do?"

"They started wearing really boring hats," Sam said. "Or no hats at all. Fashion took a serious hit during the Hat Tax era."

Sam decided to shift gears. "Now, I know what you're thinking: *Why would anyone want to work in taxes?* But hear me out—there are actually some pretty cool careers in this field."

He pulled out a list and started writing on the whiteboard.

1. *Tax Accountant:* "These are the people who help you figure out how much you owe—or how much you can get back. They're like financial detectives, finding deductions and loopholes to save you money. Plus, they get to use fancy calculators."
2. *Tax Lawyer:* "If you like arguing and winning debates, this is the job for you. Tax lawyers help people and

businesses navigate complicated tax laws. They're the ones who fight the tax authorities when things get messy."

3. *Tax Authority Agent:* "Okay, I know this one sounds scary, but someone has to make sure everyone pays their fair share. Think of them as the referees of the tax world—except instead of blowing a whistle, they audit you."
4. *Policy Analyst*: "These are the people who design tax systems and figure out how to make them fairer. If you've ever thought, *Why don't they just fix the tax code?*—this is the job for you."
5. *Corporate Tax Specialist:* "Big companies need experts to handle their taxes, especially when they're operating in multiple countries. If you like solving puzzles and working with big numbers, this is a great career."
6. *Forensic Accountant:* "This is like being a tax detective. You investigate fraud, track down missing money, and catch the bad guys. It's basically CSI: Tax Division."

By the end of the presentation, the students were surprisingly engaged. As Sam packed up his props, one boy approached him.

"Mr. Harper," he said, holding a slice of pizza. "Taxes still suck, but at least now I get why we have them. And maybe I'll be a tax lawyer someday."

Sam smiled. "That's all I wanted to hear. Just remember taxes are like pizza. You might not get the whole pie, but at least you get a slice."

The teacher thanked Sam as he left, a faint smile playing on her lips. "That was... certainly a unique approach," she said. "I'm not sure they'll ever look at pizza the same way again. I appreciate you taking the time."

Sam chuckled. "Glad I could help. Just don't ask me to explain cryptocurrency."

As entered his office he noticed a new envelope on his desk. It was stamped with bold red letters: “URGENT: TAX NOTICE.”

Sam groaned. “Of course. Some things never change.”

And with that, he sat down and took a sip of his coffee, opened the envelope, and prepared to face the enduring nature of taxes—one deduction at a time.

PART VIII

The Big Picture

Chapter 50

The Final Audit – Sam's Last Stand

The conference room was silent except for the ticking of a clock and the shuffling of audit papers. Sam sat at the end of a long table, facing a panel of stern-faced tax officials. This wasn't just another audit—it was the final showdown. As he glanced at the mountain of receipts and forms, Sam knew that every lesson, every misstep, and every bizarre tax encounter had led him to this moment.

The envelope on his desk glared at him like a final boss in a video game. "FINAL NOTICE: AUDIT IN PROGRESS" was stamped across it in bold, red letters, as if the Tax Office had hired a graphic designer to make it extra terrifying. Sam stared at it, sipping his coffee (which, as he now knew, was not deductible), and muttered, "Well, this is it. The end of the line. Goodbye, freedom. Hello, financial ruin."

"Sam Harper," Audit Tax said, his voice low and gravelly, like a villain in a noir film. "We meet again."

Sam gulped. "Uh… hi?"

Audit Tax smirked, pulling out a stack of papers so thick it could have been used as a doorstop. "It's time for your Final Audit. Every deduction, every expense, every questionable receipt—it's all here. And I'm going to find out if you've been playing by the rules… or if you've been playing with fire."

Sam tried to laugh, but it came out as a nervous squeak. "Well, I mean, how bad could it be?"

Audit Tax raised an eyebrow. "Let's find out."

Audit Tax slammed the stack of papers onto Sam's desk, causing a nearby coffee mug to wobble dangerously. He flipped to the first page, which was covered in red ink and sticky notes. "Let's start with your deductions," he said, his pen poised like a sword. "You claimed £500 for 'office supplies.' Care to elaborate?"

Sam scratched his head. "Uh, yeah. I bought a new chair. My old one was giving me back pain."

Audit Tax's eyes narrowed. "A gaming chair? With built-in speakers, LED lights, and a cupholder?"

"It was on sale!" Sam protested. "And I work from home! Comfort is important for productivity!"

Audit Tax scribbled something on his clipboard. "Fine. But what about this £200 charge for 'client entertainment'? It says here you took someone to a taco truck."

Sam perked up. "That was legitimate! I was networking with my barber, Dave. We were discussing his plans to expand his business."

Audit Tax stared at him, unblinking. "And did Dave hire you?"

Sam hesitated. "Not exactly. But he did give me a free haircut."

Audit Tax sighed, jotting down another note. "Let's move on."

Audit Tax flipped to another page, his expression growing even more severe. "Now, explain this: a £15 monthly charge for a streaming service. You listed it as a 'research expense.'"

Sam nodded enthusiastically. "That's right! I was researching trends in storytelling for my freelance writing business."

Audit Tax's eyes narrowed. "You watched 12 episodes of Raccoons Gone Wild in one weekend."

Sam's face turned red. "That was... uh... character research?"

Audit Tax didn't even blink. "And the 47 rom-coms?"

"Market analysis!" Sam said quickly. "Rom-coms are making a comeback!"

Audit Tax scribbled furiously on his clipboard. "Sam, you're testing my patience."

Audit Tax flipped to yet another page, this one covered in highlighted lines. "Let's talk about your coffee expenses. You've claimed £1,200 for coffee this year. Care to explain?"

Sam shrugged. "I work from home. Coffee is essential for productivity."

Audit Tax raised an eyebrow. "You bought 15 different types of coffee beans, a French press, an espresso machine, and something called a 'nitro cold brew kit.'"

Sam grinned sheepishly. "I like variety."

Audit Tax sighed, pinching the bridge of his nose. "Sam, coffee is not a deductible expense unless it's for client meetings."

Sam's grin widened. "What if I meet clients over Zoom while drinking coffee?"

Audit Tax glared at him. "Nice try."

As the audit continued, Audit Tax scrutinized every line of Sam's finances, from his utility bills to his mileage logs. Sam tried his best to justify each expense, but it was clear that some of his claims were... questionable at best.

Finally, Audit Tax set down his clipboard and leaned back in his chair. "Sam, I've seen a lot of taxpayers in my time. Some are careless, some are dishonest, and some are just plain clueless. But you... you're something else."

Sam winced. "Is that a good thing?"

Audit Tax smirked. "You're honest. Reckless, but honest. You've made mistakes—plenty of them—but I can see that you weren't trying to cheat the system. You were just... navigating it poorly."

Sam let out a breath he didn't realize he'd been holding. "So... what does that mean? Am I in trouble?"

Audit Tax stood up, adjusting his trench coat. "You'll need to pay back some of these deductions, and there will be a small penalty for your... creative interpretations of the tax code. But overall, you've passed the audit."

Sam blinked. "Wait, really? I passed?"

Audit Tax nodded. "Barely. But yes. You've proven that you're not a fraud—you're just a taxpayer trying to make sense of a system that doesn't always make sense."

As Audit Tax prepared to leave, he turned back to Sam with a rare hint of a smile. "You know, Sam, you've come a long way. When we first met, you were clueless about taxes. Now, you're... slightly less clueless."

Sam chuckled. "Thanks, I think."

Audit Tax extended a hand. "Keep being honest, Sam. And maybe next year, try to keep your receipts organized."

Sam shook his hand, grinning. "Deal. And maybe next year, you can take it easy on me?"

Audit Tax smirked. "Don't push your luck."

As the door closed behind him, Sam leaned back in his chair, feeling a strange mix of relief and pride. He had survived the Final Audit—not unscathed, but intact. And for the first time, he felt like he understood the tax system, even if it still drove him crazy.

He picked up the envelope that had started it all and tossed it into the trash. "Well," he said to himself, "at least I didn't try to claim my dog as a dependent."

And with that, he poured himself a cup of coffee (non-deductible, of course) and got back to work, ready to face whatever the tax system threw at him next.

Chapter 51

The Economics of Tax – What Drives Governments?

Sam Harper had thought he was finally done with taxes. He had survived audits, debates, and even a time-traveling escapade through the history of taxation. But just as he was about to enjoy a rare moment of peace, the door to his office creaked open—again.

This time, the figure who entered was unlike any of the other tax characters Sam had encountered. They were dressed in a sharp suit, carrying a briefcase that looked like it contained the secrets of the universe. Their tie was emblazoned with tiny pound signs, and their demeanour screamed "power broker." They adjusted their cufflinks and gave Sam a knowing smile.

"Sam Harper," the figure said, their voice smooth and authoritative. "I'm The Economist, and I'm here to teach you what really drives governments when it comes to taxes."

Sam groaned, sinking into his chair. "Oh, great. Another lecture. Let me guess—you're going to tell me that taxes are about more than just taking my money?"

The Economist chuckled, setting their briefcase on Sam's desk. "Oh, Sam. Taxes aren't just about taking your money. They're about everything. Revenue, investment, fairness, economic stability—it's all connected. And today, you're going to learn how it works."

Sam sighed. "Do I have a choice?"

"Not really," The Economist said, opening their briefcase to reveal a stack of charts, graphs, and what appeared to be a miniature globe. "Let's begin."

Microeconomic Tax Policy: The Individual and Business Perspective

Sam frowned. "You mean, like how I can't deduct my coffee expenses?"

The Economist smiled. "Exactly. Microeconomic tax policy looks at how taxes affect individuals and businesses—what you can deduct, what you can't, and how those rules shape your decisions."

Sam nodded slowly. "So, it's like a carrot-and-stick approach?"

"Precisely," The Economist said, pulling out a tiny figurine of a carrot and a stick. "Taxes can encourage good behaviour—like saving, investing, or reducing pollution—or discourage bad behaviour, like smoking or excessive carbon emissions. It's all about shaping individual and business decisions."

Sam raised an eyebrow. "And does it work?"

"Sometimes," The Economist conceded. "It's not a perfect system. Behavioural economics shows that people don't always act rationally, even when incentives are in place. But on the whole, these policies do influence behaviour to some extent."

Macroeconomic Tax Policy: The Big Picture

Sam tilted his head. "Like what?"

"Think about unemployment, inflation, and economic growth," The Economist said, pulling out a graph labelled "Taxes and GDP." "Governments use taxes to influence these big-picture factors. For example, during a recession, they might lower taxes to put more money in people's pockets and stimulate spending. During a boom, they might raise taxes to cool down the economy and prevent inflation."

Sam frowned. "So, taxes are like a thermostat for the economy?"

"Exactly," The Economist said, grinning. "But it's not just about raising or lowering taxes. It's also about who gets taxed and how. For example, progressive taxes—like income tax—can reduce income inequality, while regressive taxes—like sales tax—can have the opposite effect."

Sam rubbed his temples. "So, governments are trying to balance the economy with taxes, but they also have to think about fairness and incentives?"

"Now you're getting it," The Economist said. "And that brings us to the next big topic: tax competition—the global game."

Tax Competition: The Global Game

Sam leaned forward. "How so?"

"Let's say you're a multinational corporation," The Economist explained. "You can set up shop anywhere in the world. Do you choose the country with a 30% corporate tax rate or the one with a 10% rate?"

Sam thought for a moment. "The 10% rate, obviously."

"Exactly," The Economist said, pointing to the globe. "That's why countries like Ireland and Singapore have become magnets for big companies. They offer low tax rates to attract businesses, which boosts their economies. But it also creates a problem."

Sam tilted his head. "What kind of problem?"

"It creates a race to the bottom," The Economist explained. "Countries keep lowering their tax rates to attract businesses, which means less revenue for everyone. It's like a giant game of chicken, where everyone's trying to undercut each other."

Sam winced. "That sounds... bad."

"It is," The Economist said. "That's why organizations like the G20 and the OECD are trying to create global tax rules to level the playing field. For example, the recent push for a global minimum corporate tax rate."

Sam blinked. "Wait, there's a global tax rate now?"

"Not yet," The Economist said. "But they're working on it. The idea is to stop companies from hopping between countries to avoid taxes. It's like saying, 'Hey, you can't just move to Tax Haven Island and pretend you don't owe us anything.'"

Monetary Policy vs. Fiscal Policy: The Dynamic Duo

Sam squinted at the figurines. "Okay, but what do they have to do with taxes?"

"Let's start with fiscal policy," The Economist said, pointing to the figurine holding a tiny tax form. "This is where taxes come in. Fiscal policy is all about how the government collects and spends money. Taxes are the revenue side, and government spending is the expense side. Together, they influence the economy."

Sam nodded. "So, if the government wants to boost the economy, they lower taxes and spend more?"

"Exactly," The Economist said. "That's called expansionary fiscal policy. On the flip side, if the economy is overheating, they might raise taxes and cut spending to slow things down—that's contractionary fiscal policy."

Sam frowned. "And what about monetary policy?"

"Monetary policy is about controlling the money supply and interest rates," The Economist explained. "That's the job of central banks. They can make borrowing cheaper or more expensive, which also affects the economy."

Sam scratched his head. "Are they like two sides of the same coin?"

"Exactly," The Economist said. "Fiscal policy is about taxes and spending, while monetary policy is about money and credit. Together, they keep the economy running smoothly—or at least, that's the goal."

By the end of the conversation, Sam's head was spinning. "So, let me get this straight," he said, rubbing his temples. "Taxes are about raising money, encouraging investment, staying competitive, and being fair. But no one can agree on what 'fair' means, and the whole system is a giant game of global chicken?"

The Economist smiled. "That's a pretty good summary, Sam."

Sam sighed. "Great. So, basically, taxes are like a really complicated board game where no one knows the rules, and everyone's cheating."

He leaned back in his chair, staring at the miniature globe on his desk. "Well, I guess that's something. But if anyone asks, I'm still blaming you for my coffee not being deductible."

CHAPTER 52

Economics of Tax: The State's Purse

Sam sat back in his chair, trying to process everything The Economist had just explained. His brain felt like it had been stuffed with pie charts, bar graphs, and a few too many metaphors about carrots and sticks. But before he could even think about asking for a break, The Economist leaned forward, his expression growing more serious.

"Now, Sam," he said, "we've covered the basics of microeconomic and macroeconomic tax policies, as well as fiscal and monetary policies. But there's one more thing you need to understand."

Sam groaned. "There's more? What could possibly be left? Are you going to tell me taxes are secretly controlling the weather?"

The Economist chuckled. "Not quite. What I'm talking about is the politics of taxation—how political realities shape tax policy, sometimes even more than economics."

Sam raised an eyebrow. "And what's that?"

"The way politicians use taxes to win support, and how public opinion, lobbying, and elections can all influence the tax system," The Economist explained. "Even the best economic policies can be derailed by political realities."

Sam frowned. "You mean, like, trying to win votes?"

"Exactly," The Economist said. "Take tax cuts, for example. Politicians love them because they're popular with voters. But those same tax cuts can lead to budget deficits, which means less money for public services. On the other hand, raising taxes might be necessary to fund schools or hospitals, but it's a hard sell to the public."

Sam nodded slowly. "So, it's like a balancing act between doing what's right and doing what's popular?"

"Precisely," The Economist said. "And then there's the issue of lobbying. Big corporations and wealthy individuals often have a lot of influence over tax policy. They push for loopholes, deductions, and lower rates that benefit them, even if it means less revenue for the government."

Sam groaned. "So, the system is rigged?"

"Not necessarily rigged, but certainly influenced," The Economist replied. "And that's why tax policy is so complex. It's not just about economics—it's about power, influence, and competing interests."

Sam sighed. "I get that. But it still feels like the system is so... messy. Why can't it just be simple?"

The Economist shook their head. "Because the world isn't simple. Taxes are a reflection of society's complexities. They're a way of balancing competing needs and priorities. And that's never easy."

Sam stared at the miniature globe on his desk, spinning it slowly. "So, what you're saying is... taxes are like a necessary evil?"

"Perhaps," The Economist said. "Or perhaps they're like medicine. Sometimes they taste bad, but they're essential for keeping the body politic healthy."

As The Economist stood to leave, Sam felt a strange sense of clarity. For the first time, he understood that taxes weren't just about taking his money—they were about something bigger. They were about balancing the needs of individuals and businesses, managing the economy, and building a society that worked for everyone.

"Thanks," Sam said, surprising himself. "I mean, I still hate taxes, but... I think I get it now."

The Economist smiled. "That's all anyone can ask. Just remember, Sam: taxes may not be perfect, but they're part of the glue that holds society together."

Sam laughed. "I'll try. But I'm still not happy about my coffee not being deductible."

For the first time, he felt like he wasn't just a taxpayer—he was part of something bigger. And while he still didn't love taxes, he could at least appreciate their role in the grand, messy, and endlessly fascinating world of economics.

Chapter 53
Tax and Demographics

Sam Harper always thought taxes were a personal problem—like back pain, or that mysterious Tupperware in the fridge. Every April, he'd face his tax forms with a mix of dread, mild panic, and the vague hope that maybe this year, the Tax Office would just forget about him. But after his deep dive into green taxes, Sam realized taxes were also a generational battleground—a never-ending tug-of-war between the boomers and the millennials, the retirees and the "I'm not a millennial, I'm Gen Z, thank you very much."

That's when Sam received a glittery invitation to the **Generational Tax Debate**, hosted by the legendary duo: Pension Tax and Youth Tax.

Pension Tax was a retiree in a cardigan so thick it could double as body armour, clutching his Social Security check like it was the last golden ticket to Willy Wonka's Chocolate Factory. He had a twinkle in his eye and a wallet full of coupons for things that no longer existed.

Youth Tax, on the other hand, was a college student in ripped jeans, a "Save the Planet" tote bag, and a hairstyle that defied both gravity and logic. She juggled student loans, a part-time job at a vegan bakery, and a phone with more cracks than the federal budget.

"Welcome, Sam!" Pension Tax boomed, his voice echoing like a bingo caller on championship night. "Are you ready to defend the rights of senior citizens, the backbone of this country, the keepers of hard candy and wisdom?"

"Welcome, Sam!" Youth Tax countered, rolling her eyes so hard they nearly qualified as a tax deduction. "Are you ready to fight for a future that isn't mortgaged to the past? And maybe get some student loan forgiveness while you're at it?"

Sam gulped. "Can't we all just get along? Maybe split the bill?"

Pension Tax and Youth Tax led Sam through the *Hall of Generational Grievances*, a museum of exhibits that made the Louvre look like a garage sale.

- *Social Security:* "I paid into Social Security my whole life!" Pension Tax declared, waving his check like a victory flag. "Now it's my turn to collect. And don't you dare raise the retirement age! I've already waited longer than the line at the DMV."
- *Student Loans:* "I'm drowning in debt!" Youth Tax countered, dramatically clutching her tuition bill. "And you want me to pay for your retirement? How about you pay for my textbooks? They cost more than your first car!"
- *Healthcare:* "I need affordable healthcare!" Pension Tax insisted, brandishing a pill organizer the size of a lunchbox. "And don't you dare cut my Medicare benefits! I need those for my weekly shuffleboard injuries."
- *Climate Change*: "We need to invest in a sustainable future!" Youth Tax exclaimed, pulling out a reusable water bottle and a list of endangered species. "And don't you dare leave us with a planet that's on fire! I can't afford sunscreen, let alone a new atmosphere!"

Sam was overwhelmed. "Is there any common ground? Maybe a group discount on therapy?"

Pension Tax and Youth Tax glared at each other like rival teams at a family reunion three-legged race. "Not until we settle who pays more!" they declared in unison.

Pension Tax argued that his generation had built the modern world, fought the wars, and paid the taxes that funded the social safety net. "We deserve our benefits!" he insisted. "We earned them! And we walked uphill both ways to get them!"

Youth Tax countered that the boomers had also racked up the debt, polluted the planet, and left the younger generations with a mess to clean up. "You had it easy!" she exclaimed. "Free college, cheap housing, and a booming economy. What did you leave for us? Avocado toast and existential dread?"

Sam tried to mediate. "Maybe both sides have a point? Maybe we could—"

Pension Tax and Youth Tax rolled their eyes so hard Sam worried they'd get stuck. "Whose side are you on, Sam?"

Youth Tax argued that her generation was facing unprecedented challenges: student debt, job insecurity, and a climate crisis that threatened their very existence. "We need a new social contract!" she declared. "One that invests in our future, not just your past. And maybe a tax credit for therapy dogs."

Pension Tax countered that the millennials were entitled, lazy, and obsessed with brunch. "Get a job!" he exclaimed. "Stop complaining and start working! When I was your age, I bought a house for the price of a sandwich and still had change for a movie ticket!"

Sam sighed. "Can't we find a way to work together? Maybe a bake sale?"

Pension Tax and Youth Tax shook their heads. "Not until we settle who pays the price! And who gets the last slice of pie!"

Just then, the lights dimmed and a new character swooped in: *Intergenerational Harmony Tax*, a wise old owl wearing a graduation cap, a Social Security card, and a peace-sign necklace. He landed on the podium with a dramatic flourish.

"Enough!" the owl hooted, flapping his wings and scattering a flurry of tax credits. "The solution is not to fight each other, but to find common ground. We need a tax system that's fair to everyone—young and old, rich and poor, owl and human. We need to invest in education, healthcare, and a sustainable future. And we need to stop blaming each other for the problems of the past. Also, a little more respect for owl sanctuaries wouldn't hurt."

Sam was inspired. "So, there's hope? Even for my tax return?"

The owl nodded sagely. "There's always hope. But it requires compromise, understanding, and a willingness to work together. And maybe a few more tax credits for owl sanctuaries. Did I mention the sanctuaries?"

As Sam left the Generational Tax Debate, he realized taxes weren't just about money—they were about values, priorities, and the kind of society we wanted to build for future generations. It was about balancing the needs of the present with the needs of the future and finding a way to create a system that was fair to everyone—even if it meant sharing the last slice of pie.

Chapter 54

The Taxpayer's Epiphany – A Love-Hate Relationship

Sam Harper sat in his office, staring at the cluttered desk in front of him. It was covered in receipts, tax forms, and a half-empty cup of coffee (non-deductible, of course). For the first time in months, the door to his office was closed, and there were no tax characters barging in to lecture him, audit him, or demand explanations for his questionable deductions. It was quiet. Too quiet.

He leaned back in his chair, letting out a long sigh. "So, this is it," he muttered to himself. "I've survived Income Tax, Sales Tax, Audit Tax, and even that smug Carbon Tax. I've debated fairness, dodged loopholes, and learned more about VAT than I ever wanted to know. But what was the point of all of it?"

As if on cue, the door creaked open. Sam groaned. "Of course. I should've known."

Standing in the doorway was a figure unlike any of the others he'd met. They were calm, composed, and radiated an air of quiet authority. They wore a simple suit, carried a leather-bound book titled "The Taxpayer's Bill of Rights," and had a kind but firm expression that reminded Sam of a high school principal who genuinely wanted their students to succeed.

"Sam Harper," the figure said, stepping into the room. "I'm Taxpayer Rights, and I think it's time we had a talk."

Sam raised an eyebrow. "Taxpayer Rights? Let me guess—you're here to tell me that taxes are actually my best friend and I should stop complaining about them?"

Taxpayer Rights smiled gently. "Not quite. I'm here to help you understand the bigger picture. You've spent so much time fighting against taxes, but have you ever stopped to think about what they actually do?"

Sam crossed his arms. "Oh, I know what they do. They take my money, make my life miserable, and force me to justify every taco I've ever eaten."

Taxpayer Rights chuckled. "That's one way to look at it. But let me show you another."

They opened their leather-bound book and flipped to a page titled "The Role of Taxes in Society." "Let's start with the basics, Sam. Taxes aren't just about taking your money—they're about funding the things that make society work. Schools, hospitals, roads, public safety... all of these things are paid for with taxes."

Sam frowned. "Yeah, I've heard that before. But it still feels like I'm paying too much and getting too little in return."

Taxpayer Rights nodded. "That's a fair concern. And that's why it's important for taxpayers like you to know your rights. Did you know that you have the right to question how your taxes are being used? To demand transparency and accountability from your government?"

Sam blinked. "Wait, I can do that?"

"Of course," Taxpayer Rights said. "You're not just a taxpayer—you're a citizen. And as a citizen, you have a say in how your government operates. Taxes are a partnership between you and your community. They're not perfect, but they're necessary."

Sam leaned back in his chair, rubbing his temples. "Okay, I get that taxes pay for important stuff. But why does the system have to be so complicated? Why can't it just be simple?"

Taxpayer Rights sighed. "Ah, the eternal question. The truth is, Sam, the tax system is complicated because life is complicated. People have different incomes, different needs, and different priorities. A one-size-fits-all system wouldn't work."

Sam groaned. "So, we're stuck with this mess forever?"

"Not necessarily," Taxpayer Rights said. "That's where reform comes in. Taxpayers like you have the power to push for changes—simpler forms, clearer rules, and fairer policies. But it starts with understanding the system, not just hating it."

Sam stared at them. "So, you're saying I need to... work with taxes?"

Taxpayer Rights smiled. "Exactly. Think of it as a love-hate relationship. You don't have to like taxes, but you can learn to appreciate their role in society. And by understanding your rights, you can make sure the system works for you, not against you."

Taxpayer Rights gestured to the cluttered desk. "Let's take a moment to reflect on your journey, Sam. You've learned a lot about taxes—more than most people ever will. What have you taken away from it?"

Sam hesitated, then sighed. "Well, I've learned that Income Tax is a necessary evil, even if he's a bit of a jerk. Sales Tax is annoying but unavoidable. Audit Tax scares the life out of me, but he's just doing his job. And Loophole... well, let's just say I'm staying far away from him."

Taxpayer Rights chuckled. "And what about the bigger lessons? What have you learned about the system as a whole?"

Sam thought for a moment. "I guess... I've learned that taxes are complicated because they're trying to do a lot of things at once. They're not just about raising money—they're about fairness, incentives, and keeping the economy running. And even though the system isn't perfect, it's better than the alternative."

Taxpayer Rights nodded. "Exactly. Taxes are a reflection of our values as a society. They're how we decide what's important—education, healthcare, infrastructure—and how we pay for it. They're not always fair, and they're not always efficient, but they're essential."

The Epiphany!

Sam leaned forward, resting his elbows on the desk. "So, what you're saying is... taxes aren't the enemy. They're just a tool. And it's up to us to make sure that tool is used the right way."

"Now you're getting it," Taxpayer Rights said, smiling. "Taxes are what we make of them. They can be frustrating, but they're also a way to build a better future. And as a taxpayer, you have the power to shape that future."

Sam sat back, a small smile creeping onto his face. "You know, I never thought I'd say this, but... I think I'm starting to understand taxes. I still hate them, but I get why they're important."

Taxpayer Rights closed their book and stood up. "That's all I wanted to hear, Sam. Remember, you're not just a taxpayer—you're a partner in building a better society. And as long as you know your rights, you'll always have a voice in the system."

A New Perspective?

As Taxpayer Rights left the room, Sam sat in silence, staring at the cluttered desk in front of him. For the first time, he didn't feel overwhelmed by the mess of receipts and forms. Instead, he felt... empowered.

He picked up a pen and started organizing his papers, muttering to himself. "Okay, taxes. You win this round. But next year, I'm coming prepared."

And for the first time in his life, Sam Harper felt like he wasn't just a victim of the tax system—he was a part of it. A reluctant, coffee-fueled part, but a part nonetheless.

CONCLUSION

Chapter 55

The Grand Tax Reunion – One Last Party

Sam Harper stood outside the doors of the Taxpayer's Hall of Fame, clutching an invitation that sparkled with gold lettering. It read: "You're Invited to the Grand Tax Reunion – A Celebration of Survival!" Below that, in smaller print, it added: "Dress Code: Business Casual (No Receipts Required)."

Sam sighed, adjusting his tie. "A party? For taxes? This has to be some kind of cruel joke."

But curiosity got the better of him. After months of chaos, confusion, and more tax lectures than he cared to count, he figured he owed it to himself to see how this bizarre journey would end. With a deep breath, he pushed open the doors and stepped inside.

Sam barely had time to take it all in before Income Tax appeared, grinning and holding a glass of champagne. "Sam! You made it! Welcome to the party!"

Sam raised an eyebrow. "What is this? Some kind of tax-themed fever dream?"

Income Tax laughed. "No, no. This is our way of saying thank you. You've been through a lot, and we figured you deserved a proper send-off."

Before Sam could respond, Sales Tax appeared, handing him a plate of hors d'oeuvres. "Try the mini quiches! They're overpriced, of course, but that's kind of my thing."

Sam rolled his eyes. "Of course they are."

As Sam wandered through the room, he spotted familiar faces everywhere. Audit Tax was in the corner, meticulously inspecting the guest list. Loophole was trying to sneak an extra slice of cake, only to be caught by Audit Tax, who wagged a disapproving finger.

"Loophole," Audit Tax said sternly, "you know the rules. No double-dipping."

Loophole shrugged, grinning. "Hey, I'm just exploring the gray areas."

Nearby, Carbon Tax was lecturing a group of guests about the environmental impact of the party decorations. "Do you know how much plastic is in those balloons? We should've gone with biodegradable options!"

Sin Tax rolled her eyes, sipping a martini. "Relax, Carbon. It's a party. Let people have a little fun."

Sam couldn't help but laugh. "This is the most chaotic group of people I've ever seen."

Tax Simplification continued, "Before we honor Sam, let's take a moment to recognize some of our most... unique contributors to the tax system."

A spotlight shone on Income Tax, who adjusted his tie and waved to the crowd. "Most Hated Tax," Tax Simplification announced, to a mix of boos and laughter.

Next up was Value-Added Tax (VAT), who looked smug as ever. "Most Misunderstood Tax," Tax Simplification said, as VAT gave a dramatic bow.

"Most Entertaining Tax," Tax Simplification added, pointing to Sin Tax, who blew a kiss to the audience. "And finally, the Lifetime Achievement Award goes to... Audit Tax, for keeping us all in line."

Audit Tax stood up, looking genuinely touched. "Thank you. I'd like to thank my clipboard, my calculator, and all the taxpayers who've made my job so… interesting."

Finally, it was Sam's turn. Tax Simplification called him to the stage, handing him a microphone. "Sam, you've been through audits, debates, and even time travel. You've learned about fairness, incentives, and the global economy. And through it all, you've kept your sense of humor. The floor is yours."

Sam hesitated, looking out at the crowd of tax characters. For a moment, he wasn't sure what to say. But then he smiled.

"Well," he began, "I never thought I'd say this, but… I think I'm going to miss you guys."

As the night went on, the party grew even more chaotic. Luxury Tax and Excise Tax challenged each other to a dance-off, while Bracket Creep tried to sneak into the VIP section, only to be stopped by Property Tax, who was acting as the bouncer.

Sam found himself laughing more than he had in months. He even joined Tax Credit Assistance and Taxpayer Rights on the dance floor, where they taught him the "Deduction Shuffle," a dance that involved a lot of awkward arm movements and imaginary paperwork.

By the end of the night, Sam was exhausted but happy. He had survived the Grand Tax Reunion, and, somehow, he felt like he'd come full circle.

As the party wound down, Sam stood by the door, saying goodbye to the tax characters as they left. Income Tax shook his hand, Sales Tax gave him a high five, and Audit Tax handed him a neatly folded receipt for the evening's expenses.

"Take care, Sam," Taxpayer Rights said, giving him a warm smile. "And remember—you're not just a taxpayer. You're part of something bigger."

Sam nodded. "Thanks. I'll try to remember that."

As the last guest left, Sam closed the door and leaned against it, letting out a deep sigh. "Well," he said to himself, "I guess taxes aren't so bad after all. But I'm still not deducting my coffee."

And with that, Sam Harper turned off the lights, ready to face whatever came next—taxes and all.

Chapter 56

The Final Reflection – Taxes, Life, and Everything in Between

Sam Harper sat at his desk, staring at the now-organized pile of papers in front of him. For the first time in months, his office was quiet. No one was bursting through the door with a clipboard, a lecture, or a smug grin. No one was demanding receipts or explaining the finer points of VAT. It was just him, his coffee (still non-deductible), and the faint hum of the world outside.

He leaned back in his chair, letting out a long sigh. "So, this is it," he muttered. "The end of the road."

It had been a wild journey—one he never asked for but somehow survived. He thought back to the first time Income Tax barged into his life, demanding answers and throwing his finances into chaos. Back then, he had seen taxes as nothing more than a necessary evil, a frustrating burden that took his money and gave him headaches in return. But now... now, things felt different.

A New Perspective

Sam picked up a pen and began jotting down notes on a blank sheet of paper. At the top, he wrote: "What I've Learned About Taxes." He stared at the words for a moment, then smiled. "Where do I even start?"

He began to write:

- Taxes Are Inevitable

"Like death and bad coffee, taxes are a part of life. You can't avoid them, no matter how hard you try. But maybe that's not such a bad thing."

- Taxes Fund the Things We Take for Granted

"Schools, hospitals, roads, public safety—none of these things happen by magic. They're paid for with taxes. It's easy to complain about what we lose, but we rarely think about what we gain."

- The System Is Flawed, but It's Ours

"Yes, the tax system is complicated, messy, and sometimes unfair. But it's also a reflection of our values as a society. It's up to us to make it better."

- Knowledge Is Power

"The more you understand taxes, the less scary they become. Knowing your rights, your obligations, and your options can make all the difference."

- It's Okay to Hate Taxes (a Little)

"Let's be honest—no one likes paying taxes. But that doesn't mean we can't appreciate their role in making the world a better place."

Sam set the pen down and leaned back, reading over his notes. For the first time, he felt a sense of peace about taxes. They weren't perfect, but they were necessary. And maybe, just maybe, they weren't the enemy he had always thought they were.

A Final Visit

As if on cue, there was a knock at the door. Sam groaned. "Of course. I should've known."

The door creaked open, and Taxpayer Rights stepped in, a warm smile on his face. Sam raised an eyebrow. "What's this? Another lecture?"

Taxpayer Rights chuckled. "No, no. Just a thank-you. You've come a long way, and we're all proud of you."

He handed him the box, and Sam opened it to reveal a small plaque that read: "Sam Harper – Survivor of the Tax System."

Sam laughed. "Well, I guess I earned this."

"You did," Taxpayer Rights said. "And remember, Sam—taxes aren't just about money. They're about community, responsibility, and building a better future. You're not just a taxpayer. You're a part of something bigger."

Sam nodded, a small smile on his face. "Thanks. I'll try to remember that."

As Taxpayer Rights left, Sam placed the plaque on his desk, right next to his coffee mug. For the first time, he felt ready to face whatever came next—taxes and all.

Epilogue: The Taxpayer's Journey

Months later, Sam Harper found himself sitting in a crowded auditorium, waiting for his turn to speak. He had been invited to give a keynote address at the Annual Taxpayer Appreciation Gala, an event he never imagined attending, let alone headlining. The theme of the evening was "Taxes: A Necessary Partnership," and Sam was the guest of honour.

As he stepped onto the stage, the audience erupted into applause. He adjusted the microphone, took a deep breath, and began.

"Good evening, everyone. If you had told me a year ago that I'd be standing here, giving a speech about taxes, I would've laughed in your face. Back then, I saw taxes as nothing more than a burden—a frustrating, confusing, and downright annoying part of life. But now, after everything I've been through, I see them differently."

He paused, looking out at the crowd. "Don't get me wrong—I still hate filling out tax forms. And I'll never forgive Income Tax for ruining my coffee budget. But I've learned that taxes are more than just numbers on a page. They're how we fund the things that matter. They're how we take care of each other. And, as much as it pains me to admit it, they're a necessary part of life."

He held up the plaque he had received from Taxpayer Rights. "So, to all the taxpayers out there: You're not alone. We're all in this together. And as long as we keep learning, questioning, and working together, we can make the system better—for everyone."

As he stepped off the stage, he was greeted by a familiar face. Income Tax was waiting for him, holding two cups of coffee. "Nice speech, Sam," he said, handing over a cup. "This one's on me."

Sam laughed, taking the coffee. "Thanks. But don't think this means we're friends."

Income Tax grinned. "Fair enough. But you have to admit—we make a pretty good team."

Sam took a sip of his coffee, shaking his head. "Yeah, yeah. Don't push it."

And with that, Sam Harper walked out of the auditorium, ready to face whatever came next. Because if he could survive the tax system, he could survive anything.

APPENDICES

Appendix A

Glossary of Tax Terms

Adjusted Gross Income (AGI)

Think of AGI as your "income snapshot" after certain deductions. It's your total income (wages, investments, etc.) minus specific expenses like student loan interest or retirement contributions. AGI is a key number because it determines eligibility for many tax breaks.

Audit

An audit is like a financial check-up by tax authorities to ensure your records are accurate and comply with tax laws. In the book, Audit Tax is the ever-watchful character who can spot a misplaced decimal from a mile away. Audits can be random, or triggered by discrepancies in your tax return.

Base Erosion and Profit Shifting (BEPS)

BEPS refers to strategies used by multinational companies to "shift" profits to countries with low or no taxes, reducing their overall tax bill. The Organisation for Economic Co-operation and Development (OECD) is working to close these loopholes and ensure companies pay their fair share. *See Chapter 24: Paradise Papers – The Offshore Echo for more on BEPS.*

Bracket Creep
Imagine inflation quietly pushing you into a higher tax bracket, even if your real income hasn't increased. That's bracket creep! It's the sneaky character who raises your tax bill without you earning more in real terms.

Business Expense
These are costs you incur while running a business, like office supplies, marketing, or travel for work. Legitimate business expenses can often be deducted from your taxable income, reducing your tax liability.

Capital Gains Deferral
A strategy that allows investors to postpone paying capital gains taxes by reinvesting profits from a sale into a similar asset within a specific timeframe. This can be a powerful tool for long-term wealth building.

Capital Gains Tax
A tax on the profit you make from selling an asset, such as stocks, bonds, or real estate. If you buy low and sell high, the government takes a slice of your winnings. The tax rate often depends on how long you held the asset.

Carbon Tax
A tax on activities that release carbon dioxide and other greenhouse gases. The goal is to encourage people and businesses to pollute less and invest in cleaner alternatives. *See Appendix A for more on environmental taxes.*

Consumption Tax
A tax on goods and services purchased by consumers. VAT and sales taxes are types of consumption taxes. These taxes are often "hidden" in the price of the product.

Corporate Tax
This is the tax that companies pay on their profits. In the book, Corporate Tax is the business-savvy character balancing growth and social responsibility. Corporate tax rates and rules can significantly impact business decisions.

Deduction
A deduction is an amount you can subtract from your income before calculating how much tax you owe. Deductions can include things like mortgage interest, charitable donations, or certain business expenses. Deductions lower your taxable income.

Digital Services Tax
Taxes applied to digital services and products, especially those provided by large tech companies operating across borders. Governments are still figuring out how to fairly tax these global giants, leading to international debates. *See Appendix A for more on digital taxation.*

Double Taxation
The taxation of the same income or asset by two different tax authorities. This often happens in international contexts, but tax treaties are designed to prevent it.

Estate Tax
A tax on the transfer of property from a deceased person to their heirs. Similar to inheritance tax, but the specifics can vary. Estate taxes can be controversial, with debates about their impact on family businesses and wealth accumulation.

Excise Tax
A tax on specific goods, such as gasoline, alcohol, or tobacco. Often used to raise revenue or discourage consumption of

harmful products. These taxes are often "hidden" in the price of the product.

Filing Status
The category you choose when filing your income tax return, such as single, married filing jointly, or head of household. Your filing status affects your tax bracket, standard deduction, and eligibility for certain tax breaks.

Fiscal Policy
This is how governments use taxes and spending to influence the economy. Fiscal policy can mean raising or lowering taxes, increasing or cutting government spending, or implementing targeted tax incentives. *See Chapter 52: Economics of Tax – Filling the Coffers for more on fiscal policy.*

Foreign Tax Credit
A credit that allows taxpayers to reduce their U.S. tax liability by the amount of income taxes they paid to a foreign country. This prevents double taxation of international income.

Gig Tax
Refers to the tax rules for people working in the gig economy—think freelancers, ride-share drivers, or anyone earning money from short-term jobs. Gig workers often have to track their own income and pay taxes themselves, which can be complex.

Head of Household
A filing status for unmarried individuals who pay more than half the costs of keeping up a home for a qualifying child or relative. It offers more tax benefits than filing as single.

Income Tax

A tax on the money you earn from work, investments, or other sources. Income Tax is the main character in most people's tax stories. Income tax systems can be progressive, regressive, or flat.

Inflation Adjustment

The process of adjusting tax brackets, deductions, and credits to account for inflation, preventing bracket creep. This ensures that tax benefits keep pace with rising prices.

Inheritance Tax

A tax on the value of assets inherited from a deceased person. It's often debated whether this tax is fair or hinders wealth transfer between generations.

International Tax

The rules and agreements that determine how income and profits are taxed when they cross borders. This includes things like double taxation treaties and transfer pricing. *See Appendix A for more on international tax systems.*

Kiddie Tax

A tax rule that applies to the unearned income of children, taxing it at their parents' higher tax rate in certain situations. This is designed to prevent parents from shifting income to their children to avoid taxes.

Marginal Tax Rate

The tax rate you pay on the next dollar of income you earn. It's important to understand your marginal tax rate to make informed financial decisions.

National Insurance
A contribution paid by workers and employers in the UK to fund social security benefits. Similar to payroll taxes in the US.

Organisation for Economic Co-operation and Development (OECD)
An international group of countries that works together to set standards and policies, including on tax matters like BEPS.

PAYE (Pay As You Earn)
A system where your employer deducts income tax and National Insurance from your wages before you get paid. Common in the UK and other countries.

Progressive Tax System
A tax system where higher earners pay a larger percentage of their income in taxes. This is designed to make the tax system fairer and redistribute wealth.

Property Tax
A tax on real estate and other property, typically levied by local governments. Property taxes fund local services like schools and infrastructure.

Regressive Tax
A tax system where lower earners pay a larger percentage of their income in taxes. Sales taxes can sometimes be regressive because lower-income individuals spend a larger portion of their income on taxable goods.

Reverse Charge Mechanism
A VAT rule where the buyer, not the seller, is responsible for reporting and paying the VAT. This is often used in cross-border

transactions to simplify things (or make them more confusing, depending on your point of view).

Sin Tax
A tax on products or activities considered harmful or undesirable, like cigarettes, alcohol, or gambling. Sin Tax is the character who profits from our vices. These taxes are often used to discourage harmful behaviours.

Standard Deduction
A fixed amount that taxpayers can deduct from their income, regardless of their actual expenses. It simplifies tax filing for many people.

Sunset Clause
A provision in a tax law that automatically repeals the law after a certain period. This ensures that tax laws are regularly reviewed and updated. *See Appendix B for more on sunset clauses.*

Tariff
A tax on imported or exported goods. Tariffs can be used to protect local industries or raise revenue. *See Chapter 52: Economics of Tax – Filling the Coffers for more on tariffs.*

Tax Avoidance
Using legal methods to reduce your tax bill, like claiming deductions or credits. It's clever planning, not cheating.

Tax Base
The total amount of income, property, or other items that are subject to taxation.

Tax Bracket
A range of income that is taxed at a specific rate. Understanding your tax bracket helps you estimate your tax liability.

Tax Code
The body of laws and regulations that govern taxation in a particular country or jurisdiction. Tax codes can be incredibly complex.

Tax Competition
When countries compete to attract investment by offering lower tax rates or other incentives. *See Chapters 39 & 40: The Tax Olympics for more on tax competition.*

Tax Compliance
The act of following tax laws and regulations, including filing tax returns and paying taxes on time.

Tax Credit
A tax credit directly reduces the amount of tax you owe, rather than just reducing your taxable income. Some credits are refundable, meaning you can get money back even if you don't owe any tax.

Tax Deferral
Postponing the payment of taxes to a future date, often through retirement accounts or other investment vehicles. This can allow your investments to grow tax-free for a longer period.

Tax Equity
The concept of fairness in taxation, ensuring that the tax burden is distributed equitably among different groups in society.

Tax Evasion
Illegally hiding income or lying on your tax return to pay less tax. Unlike tax avoidance, tax evasion can get you in serious trouble.

Tax Expenditure
Government revenue losses attributable to tax laws that provide special tax incentives or preferences. These are often debated in terms of their effectiveness and fairness.

Tax Gap
The difference between the amount of taxes that should be collected and the amount that is actually collected.

Tax Haven
A country or territory with very low or no taxes, often used by individuals or companies to avoid paying higher taxes at home. Tax Havens are the "shady" characters in the global tax world. *See Chapter 24: Paradise Papers – The Offshore Echo for more on tax havens.*

Tax Incidence
The actual distribution of the tax burden, regardless of who is legally responsible for paying the tax.

Tax Morale
The willingness of citizens to pay taxes. High tax morale generally leads to higher compliance rates and a more effective tax system. *See Appendix A for more on tax morale.*

Tax Neutrality
The principle that taxes should not distort economic decisions or create artificial incentives.

Tax Policy
The set of decisions and actions taken by a government to design and implement a tax system.

Tax Reform
Changes to a tax system, often aimed at improving its efficiency, fairness, or simplicity.

Tax Shelter
A legal method of reducing or avoiding taxes, often involving complex financial transactions.

Tax Treaty
An agreement between countries designed to prevent double taxation and promote international trade and investment. *See Appendix A for more on tax treaties.*

Taxpayer Rights
The protections and entitlements you have as a taxpayer, such as the right to fair treatment, privacy, and to challenge the government's decisions about your taxes. *See Chapter 36: The Taxpayer's Bill of Rights – Taking a Stand for more on taxpayer rights.*

Transfer Pricing
The prices charged between different parts of a multinational company for goods or services. Transfer pricing rules are meant to prevent companies from shifting profits to low-tax countries.

Value Added Tax (VAT)
A tax added at each stage of production or sale, based on the value added at that stage. VAT is common in Europe and many other countries, and is known for its complicated rules and forms.

VAT Return
A form businesses must fill out to report how much VAT they've collected and paid. The VAT Return Form is infamous for its complexity.

Withholding Tax
A tax that is deducted from your income before you receive it, such as income tax withheld from your pay cheque.

Acronyms Used

- AGI: Adjusted Gross Income
- BEPS: Base Erosion and Profit Shifting
- OECD: Organisation for Economic Co-operation and Development
- PAYE: Pay As You Earn
- VAT: Value Added Tax

Appendix B

About the Book and Chapters

If Taxes Were People is a satirical, story-driven journey through the world of taxation. Each chapter personifies a different aspect of tax, transforming dry policy into lively characters, comedic scenarios, and memorable lessons. Below, you'll find a brief description of what each chapter brings to the party—no calculators required.

Preface

A Taxing Mystery Awaits (But This Time, It's Funny)
Sets the stage for a tax adventure like no other, promising wit, wisdom, and a few laughs along the way.

Part I: The Basics of Taxation

Chapter 1: The Taxing Beginnings
Meet the cast of tax characters and discover how taxes first entered our lives—awkward introductions and all.

Chapter 2: The Audit Awakening
Experience the drama and suspense of an audit, where every receipt tells a story and every deduction is a plot twist.

Chapter 3: The Price of Pleasure and Prestige
Explore sin taxes and luxury levies, where indulgence comes with a surcharge and a side of guilt.

Chapter 4: Inheritance Tax – Passing on More Than Memories
When the taxman meets the Grim Reaper, discover how inheritance taxes haunt even the afterlife.

Chapter 5: Bracket Creep and the Taxing Raise
A cautionary tale of how a raise can sometimes feel like a trick, thanks to the sneaky world of tax brackets.

Chapter 6: Capital Gains and Wealth Taxes – The Price of Success
Success has its price—meet the taxes that come knocking when your investments pay off.

Part II: Advanced Tax Concepts

Chapter 7: Tax Reform – The Simplification That Wasn't
A comedic look at tax reform efforts that promise simplicity but deliver only more paperwork.

Chapter 8: Meet Psyche Tax – The Mind Games of Money
Delve into the psychological side of taxation, where perception, emotion, and money collide.

Chapter 9: Tax Credit Assistance – A Helping Hand
Meet the unsung heroes of the tax world: credits and deductions that offer relief (if you can find them).

Chapter 10: Tax Evasion vs. Tax Avoidance – The Great Debate
A courtroom drama where the line between clever planning and criminal intent is razor-thin.

Chapter 11: The Shadow Economy
Step into the world of unreported income and under-the-table deals, where taxes fear to tread.

Chapter 12: Carbon Tax and the Cost of Saving the Planet
When saving the world comes with a price tag, meet the taxes designed to change our behaviour.

Chapter 13: Tax and the Environment (Beyond Carbon)
Explore environmental taxes beyond carbon, from plastic bags to pollution permits.

Part III: Modern Tax Challenges

Chapter 14: Crypto Tax – The Blockchain Enigma
Navigate the wild west of cryptocurrency, where tax rules are as volatile as the markets.

Chapter 15: The Digital Economy and Gig Work
Meet the new faces of work and the tax challenges that come with them—apps, gigs, and all.

Chapter 16: International Tax and Post-Brexit Chaos – The Global Maze
A globe-trotting adventure through international tax rules, with a detour through Brexit's labyrinth.

Chapter 17: Global Tax Cooperation and Competition
When countries compete and cooperate, discover the high-stakes game of global tax policy.

Chapter 18: The Tariff Tantrum – When Even Your Coffee Costs a Fortune
Trade wars and tariffs take centre stage, showing how taxes can change the price of your morning brew.

Chapter 19: Free Trade Zones – The Tax-Free Illusion
Peek behind the curtain of free trade zones, where "tax-free" isn't always what it seems.

Chapter 20: Tax Havens vs. Tax Justice – The Offshore Showdown
A dramatic showdown between those who hide wealth and those who seek justice.

Part IV: Tax Scandals and Revelations

Chapter 21: The Panama Papers – A Leak in the System
Uncover the secrets of the Panama Papers and the global fallout from one of history's biggest leaks.

Chapter 22: The Holy Collection Plate: When Even Faith Demands Its Cut
Explore the intersection of religion and taxation, where even the divine gets audited.

Chapter 23: Paradise Papers – The Sequel No One Asked For
The saga continues with more leaks, more secrets, and more tax drama.

Part V: The Fight for Reform

Chapter 56: The Final Reflection – Taxes, Life, and Everything in Between

A thoughtful send-off, reflecting on what we've learned—and laughed about—along the way.

APPENDIX C
Meet the Tax Characters

Throughout this book, we've brought the world of taxes to life by personifying various tax concepts as characters. Here's a quick guide to some of the key players you've encountered:

Income Tax
The ever-present roommate who takes a share of your earnings but helps keep society running. *See the glossary entry for "Income Tax" and Chapter: "The Income Tax – The Reluctant Roommate."*

Audit Tax
The meticulous inspector who checks your financial homework. Sometimes feared, but ultimately there to keep things fair. *See "Audit" in the glossary.*

Corporate Tax
The business partner who claims a portion of company profits, balancing growth and responsibility. *See "Corporate Tax" and "Transfer Pricing" in the glossary; Chapter: "Corporation Tax – The Business Partner."*

Sin Tax
The moralist who profits from our vices—alcohol, tobacco, gambling—hoping to nudge us toward healthier choices. *See "Sin Tax" in the glossary.*

Bracket Creep
The sneaky character who quietly raises your tax bill as inflation pushes you into higher brackets, even if your real income hasn't changed. *See "Bracket Creep" in the glossary.*

Tax Havens
The mysterious hosts of offshore parties, offering low or no taxes for those who can find them. *See "Tax Haven" in the glossary and Chapter 24: "Paradise Papers – The Offshore Echo."*

The Grim Collector (Inheritance Tax)
The final visitor, collecting a share of your estate before it passes to your heirs. *See "Inheritance Tax" and "Estate Tax" in the glossary; Chapter: "Inheritance Tax – The Final Visitor."*

Psyche Tax
The invisible weight on your mind—representing the stress, confusion, and even anxiety taxes can cause. *See "Tax Morale" in the glossary.*

Fiscal Policy
The grand strategist, using taxes and spending to steer the economy. *See "Fiscal Policy" in the glossary and Chapter 52: "Economics of Tax – Filling the Coffers."*

Tariff
The border guard, taxing goods as they cross into new lands—sometimes to protect local jobs, sometimes to raise revenue. *See "Tariff" in the glossary and Chapter 52.*

Deduction
The helpful sidekick, always looking for ways to lower your taxable income—if you know where to find them. *See "Deduction" in the glossary.*

Tax Credit
The generous friend who gives you a direct discount on your tax bill, sometimes even handing you money back. *See "Tax Credit" in the glossary.*

Excise Tax
The specialist, targeting specific goods like fuel, alcohol, or tobacco—often hidden in the price tag. *See "Excise Tax" in the glossary.*

Consumption Tax (VAT/Sales Tax)
The ever-present companion at the checkout, adding a little extra to almost everything you buy. *See "Consumption Tax" and "VAT" in the glossary; Chapter: "VAT – The Invisible Guest."*

Regressive Tax
The unfair player, taking a bigger bite from those with less. *See "Regressive Tax" in the glossary.*

Progressive Tax
The champion of fairness, asking more from those who earn more. *See "Progressive Tax System" in the glossary.*

Tax Treaty
The diplomat, preventing double taxation and smoothing international relations. *See "Tax Treaty" in the glossary.*

Gig Tax
The modern multitasker, navigating the world of freelancers, side hustlers, and the gig economy. *See "Gig Tax" in the glossary.*

Tax Avoidance
The clever trickster, always finding legal loopholes to minimize the tax bill—sometimes admired, sometimes controversial. *See "Tax Avoidance" in the glossary and Chapter: "Tax Avoidance and Tax Evasion - The Shady Twins."*

Tax Evasion
The outlaw, breaking the rules to dodge taxes—risking penalties and prosecution. *See "Tax Evasion" in the glossary and Chapter: "Tax Avoidance and Tax Evasion - The Shady Twins."*

Luxury Tax
The glamorous guest who only appears at the fanciest parties, levied on high-end goods and services. *See "Luxury Tax" in the glossary.*

Wealth Tax
The asset appraiser, interested in your total fortune, not just your income. *See "Wealth Tax" in the glossary.*

Poll Tax
The flat-fee collector, charging everyone the same regardless of income—a character with a controversial history. *See "Poll Tax" in the glossary.*

Environmental/Green Tax
The eco-warrior, taxing pollution and carbon emissions to encourage greener choices. *See "Carbon Tax" and "Environmental Tax" in the glossary.*

Dividend Tax
The investor's companion, taxing income from shares and investments. *See "Dividend Tax" in the glossary.*

Gift Tax
The watchful guardian of generosity, taxing large gifts of money or property. *See "Gift Tax" in the glossary.*

Stamp Duty
The gatekeeper at the property market, charging a fee when you buy a house or land. *See "Stamp Duty" in the glossary and Chapter: "Stamp Duty – The Gatekeeper."*

Capital Gains Tax
The silent collector who appears when you sell assets for a profit. *See "Capital Gains Tax" in the glossary and Chapter: "Capital Gains Tax – The Silent Collector."*

National Insurance
The social safety netter, collecting contributions for pensions and benefits. *See "National Insurance" in the glossary and Chapter: "National Insurance – The Reluctant Partner."*

Council Tax
The local enforcer, funding community services based on your property's value. *See "Council Tax" in the glossary and Chapter: "Council Tax – The Neighbourhood Watch."*

Crypto Tax
The digital phantom, appearing when you profit from cryptocurrencies. *See "Crypto Tax" in the glossary and Chapter: "The Crypto Tax – The Digital Phantom."*

This cast of characters helps to illustrate the complex and often confusing world of taxes in a more relatable and engaging way. By understanding their roles and motivations, you can gain a deeper appreciation for the impact of taxes on our lives and society.

Appendix D
How UK Taxes Are Calculated

Linking the Story to Real Life

This appendix provides a high-level overview of how the main UK taxes featured in the book are calculated. Each section links to the relevant chapter, so you can see how the tax works in practice as well as in Sam's adventures.

IMPORTANT NOTE: These are just high-level illustrative examples. Tax rates and allowances change every year, therefore for accurate information, please refer to the relevant tax authority guidance or speak to a tax professional.

1. Income Tax

(See Chapter: "The Income Tax – The Reluctant Roommate")

How It Applies:

Income Tax is paid on most types of income, including salaries, wages, and self-employment profits. Employees usually pay through PAYE (Pay As You Earn), where tax is deducted directly from their wages. Self-employed individuals pay via Self Assessment, filing a tax return each year.

How It's Calculated:

- **Gross Income:** The total amount you earn in a year before any deductions.
- **Personal Allowance:** The amount you can earn tax-free each year. This is set by the government and may change annually.
- **Taxable Income:** Gross Income minus Personal Allowance. This is the amount you'll actually pay tax on.
- **Tax Bands:** Different portions of your taxable income are taxed at different rates:
    - Personal Allowance: Up to a certain amount (0%)
    - Basic Rate: Next portion of income (20%)
    - Higher Rate: Next portion (40%)
    - Additional Rate: Above a certain threshold (45%)

Example:

- Gross Annual Income: £60,000
- Annual Personal Allowance: £12,570 (for illustration)
- Annual Taxable Income: £47,430
- Annual Income Tax Due:
    - First £37,700 at 20% = £7,540
    - Remaining £9,730 at 40% = £3,892
    - Total Income Tax: £11,432

2. Self-Employed Profits & Deductible Expenses

(See Chapter: "The Self-Employed – The Juggler")

How It Applies:

If you're self-employed, you pay tax on your profits (not your total income). This means you can deduct certain business expenses before calculating your tax liability.

How It's Calculated:

- **Total Income:** All money received from your business.
- **Allowable Expenses:** Costs you can deduct before tax, such as:
    - Office/stationery costs
    - Travel and vehicle expenses
    - Staff costs (wages, subcontractors)
    - Stock or raw materials
    - Marketing and advertising
    - Business premises costs (rent, utilities)
    - Professional fees (accountants, legal)
    - Some home office costs
- **Taxable Profit:** Total Income minus Allowable Expenses

Example:

- Total Income: £40,000
- Allowable Expenses: £10,000
- Taxable Profit: £30,000
- Apply Income Tax bands as above to the profit.

3. National Insurance Contributions (NICs)

(See Chapter: "National Insurance – The Reluctant Partner")

How It Applies:

NICs are paid by employees, employers, and the self-employed to qualify for state benefits, including the State Pension, unemployment benefits, and other social security programs.

How It's Calculated:

- **Employees:** Pay a percentage of earnings above a weekly threshold.
- **Employers:** Pay a percentage of employees' earnings above a weekly threshold.
- **Self-Employed:** Pay Class 2 (flat rate if profits are above a certain threshold) and Class 4 (percentage of profits above a threshold).

Example (Employee):

- Weekly Earnings: £600
- Employee Threshold: £242
- NICs Due: (£600 - £242) × 8% = £28.64 per week

Example (Employer):

- Employee's Weekly Earnings: £600
- Employer Threshold: £175
- Employer NICs Due: (£600 - £175) × 13.8% = £58.65 per week

4. Value Added Tax (VAT)

(See Chapter: "VAT – The Invisible Guest")

How It Applies:

VAT is a tax on most goods and services. Businesses collect VAT from customers and pay it to HMRC, but the end consumer ultimately bears the cost. Businesses only need to register for VAT if their turnover exceeds a certain threshold.

How It's Calculated:

- **Standard Rate:** 20% (some goods/services are 5% or 0%)
- **VAT Due:** Sales Price × VAT Rate

Example:

- Item Price: £100
- VAT (20%): £20
- Total Price: £120

Note:

VAT is a consumer-driven tax. Businesses act as collectors, but the final burden falls on the person buying the goods or services.

5. Council Tax

(See Chapter: "Council Tax – The Neighbourhood Watch")

How It Applies:

Council Tax is paid by households to local councils to fund local services such as schools, libraries, and waste collection.

How It's Calculated:

- **Based on Property Band:** Each property is assigned a band (A–H) based on its value as of a specific date (e.g., 1991 in England).

- **Annual Bill:** Set by the local council for each band. The bill varies depending on the council and the band.

Example:

- Band D property: £2,000 per year (varies significantly by council)

6. Corporation Tax

(See Chapter: "Corporation Tax – The Business Partner")

How It Applies:
Paid by limited companies on their profits.

How It's Calculated:

- **Taxable Profits:** Company's income minus allowable expenses and deductions.
- **Tax Rates:**
  - Small Profits Rate: 19% (for profits up to £50,000)
  - Main Rate: 25% (for profits over £250,000)
  - Marginal Relief: For profits between £50,000 and £250,000, a sliding scale applies.

Example (Large Company):

- Profits: £300,000
- Tax Rate: 25%
- Corporation Tax Due: £300,000 × 25% = £75,000

7. Capital Gains Tax (CGT)

(See Chapter: "Capital Gains Tax – The Silent Collector")

How It Applies:

Paid on the profit when you sell (or 'dispose of') an asset that's increased in value, such as shares or property (not your main home).

How It's Calculated:

- **Gain:** Sale Price minus Purchase Price minus Allowable Costs (e.g., legal fees, estate agent fees).
- **Annual Exempt Amount:** First portion of gains is tax-free.
- **Tax Rate:** 10% or 20% (higher for residential property). The rate depends on your income tax band.

Example:

- Gain: £10,000
- Exempt Amount: £3,000
- Taxable Gain: £7,000
- CGT Due (at 10%): £700

8. Cryptocurrency Taxes

(See Chapter: "The Crypto Tax – The Digital Phantom")

How It Applies:

Cryptocurrency is taxed mainly under Capital Gains Tax rules. HMRC views crypto as property, not currency.

How It's Calculated:

- **CGT Applies:** When you sell, exchange, or use crypto to buy goods/services.
- **Gain/Loss:** Sale price minus purchase price.
- **CGT Due:** Taxable Gain × CGT Rate (10% or 20%)

Example:

- Bought Bitcoin for £5,000
- Sold Bitcoin for £15,000
- Gain: £10,000
- Exempt Amount: £3,000
- Taxable Gain: £7,000
- CGT Due (at 10%): £700

9. Inheritance Tax (IHT)

(See Chapter: "Inheritance Tax – The Final Visitor")

How It Applies:
Paid on estates worth more than the threshold when someone dies.

How It's Calculated:

- **Threshold:** Nil-rate band (e.g., £325,000). There's also a residence nil-rate band if you pass on your home to direct descendants.
- **Tax Rate:** 40% on the value above the threshold.

Example:

- Estate Value: £400,000

- Taxable Amount: £400,000 - £325,000 = £75,000
- IHT Due: £75,000 × 40% = £30,000

10. Stamp Duty Land Tax (SDLT)

(See Chapter: "Stamp Duty – The Gatekeeper")

How It Applies:

Paid when you buy property or land over a certain price in England and Northern Ireland.

How It's Calculated:

- **Threshold:** No SDLT on first portion of purchase price (e.g., £250,000 for residential property). Different rates apply to different portions of the purchase price.
- **Rates:**
    - Up to £250,000: 0%
    - £250,001 to £925,000: 5%
    - £925,001 to £1.5 million: 10%
    - Above £1.5 million: 12%

Example:

- Purchase Price: £500,000
- SDLT:
    - 0% on first £250,000 = £0
    - 5% on next £250,000 = £12,500
    - Total SDLT: £12,500

11. Tax Avoidance vs. Tax Evasion

(See Chapter: "Tax Avoidance and Tax Evasion – The Shady Twins")

- **Tax Avoidance:** Legally minimising tax by using the rules (e.g., ISAs, pension contributions).
- **Tax Evasion:** Illegally not paying tax owed (e.g., hiding income).

12. Tax Reliefs and Allowances

(See Various Chapters)

- **Examples:**
  - Pension contributions
  - Gift Aid donations
  - Business expenses
  - Marriage allowance

13. HMRC

(See Various Chapters)

- Her Majesty's Revenue and Customs (HMRC): The UK's tax authority, responsible for collecting taxes and enforcing tax law.

Summary Table

Tax Type	Linked Chapter	Who Pays?	How Calculated (High Level)
Income Tax	The Income Tax	Individuals	(Income – Allowance) × Rate
Self-Employed Profits	The Self-Employed	Self-Employed	(Income – Expenses) × Rate
National Insurance	National Insurance	Employees/ Self-Employed/ Employers	(Earnings – Threshold) × Rate
VAT	VAT	Consumers/ Businesses	Price × VAT Rate
Council Tax	Council Tax	Households	Set by council, based on property
Corporation Tax	Corporation Tax	Companies	Profits × Rate
Capital Gains Tax	Capital Gains Tax	Individuals	(Gain – Exemption) × Rate
Crypto Tax	The Crypto Tax	Individuals	(Gain – Exemption) × Rate
Inheritance Tax	Inheritance Tax	Estates	(Estate – Threshold) × Rate
Stamp Duty Land Tax	Stamp Duty	Property Buyers	Band-based on purchase price

For more details, see the relevant chapter in the book. This appendix is designed to help you connect the story to real-world tax basics—so you can see how the numbers work, not just the characters!

Appendix E

Comparative Tax Systems Worldwide

Introduction

Taxes are a global language, but like any language, they have countless dialects. This appendix offers a guided tour of tax systems around the globe, highlighting their unique features, the historical forces that shaped them, and how they connect to the stories in this book. Remember, tax rates and specific rules change frequently, so we encourage you to research official government sources or reputable financial websites for the latest details.

1. Historical Context: The Roots of Taxation

Taxation has been around for millennia, evolving from simple tributes to complex systems designed to fund modern states. In ancient times, taxes often took the form of goods or labour. The development of money allowed for more sophisticated tax systems, such as income taxes in Europe and property taxes in the Americas. Understanding this history helps explain why certain tax systems are the way they are today.

2. Tax Systems in Developed Economies

United States

The U.S. operates a federal system, with taxes levied at the federal, state, and local levels. Federal income tax is progressive, but each state can set its own income and sales taxes, leading to wide variation. Payroll taxes fund Social Security and Medicare. The U.S. is one of the few countries that taxes its citizens on worldwide income, even if they live abroad.
See Chapter 39: The Tax Olympics – Opening Ceremony for a playful look at international tax competition.

Germany

Germany's system is known for its thoroughness. Income tax is progressive, and there's a national value-added tax (VAT) on most goods and services. Social security contributions are significant, and local municipalities can levy their own taxes.
For more on how taxes shape society, see Chapter 52: Economics of Tax – Filling the Coffers.

Japan

Japan collects both national and local taxes. The national government imposes income and corporate taxes, as well as a consumption tax (similar to VAT). Local governments levy their own taxes, making the system multi-layered.
See Chapter 4: Inheritance Tax – The Grim Collector for a look at how inheritance taxes differ worldwide.

United Kingdom

The UK features income tax, National Insurance, VAT, and council tax (a local property tax). The "non-domiciled" status allows some residents to limit their tax on foreign income, a feature that has attracted global attention.

See Chapter 24: Paradise Papers – The Offshore Echo for stories of tax planning and avoidance.

3. Tax Systems in Emerging Economies

Brazil

Brazil's tax system is complex, with many overlapping taxes at federal, state, and municipal levels. The ICMS (a state-level VAT) is particularly intricate. Compliance can be challenging for businesses, and indirect taxes make up a large share of revenue. *For a sense of how complexity affects taxpayers, see Chapter 8: Psyche Tax – The Tax on Feelings.*

India

India's Goods and Services Tax (GST) unified many previous taxes into a single system, but there are still state and central taxes. Income tax is progressive, and corporate tax rates have been reduced to attract investment.
See Chapter 40: The Tax Olympics – Global Competition for a look at how countries compete for business.

China

China's system includes VAT, income, and corporate taxes. The government has reformed its tax code to encourage innovation and foreign investment, and social security contributions are significant.
See Chapter 52: Economics of Tax – Filling the Coffers for the role of tax in national development.

South Africa

South Africa relies on income tax, VAT, and corporate tax. The system is progressive and aims to address inequality, with capital gains and estate taxes also playing a role.

See Chapter 36: The Taxpayer's Bill of Rights – Taking a Stand for the role of tax fairness.

4. Tax Systems in Tax Havens

Cayman Islands

No direct taxes—no income, corporate, or capital gains tax. The government relies on import duties, tourism, and financial services fees. This makes the Caymans a popular destination for offshore finance.
See Chapter 24: Paradise Papers – The Offshore Echo for real-world stories of tax havens.

Switzerland

Known for low corporate tax rates and banking secrecy (though this is changing). Taxes are levied at federal, cantonal, and municipal levels, with significant variation.
See Chapter 24: Paradise Papers – The Offshore Echo for more on secrecy and tax planning.

Luxembourg

Luxembourg attracts multinational corporations with favourable tax rulings and a flexible holding company regime.
See Chapter 24: Paradise Papers – The Offshore Echo for the impact of these regimes.

5. Tax Morale and Compliance

Tax morale, or the willingness of citizens to pay taxes, varies significantly across countries. Factors influencing tax morale include trust in government, perceptions of fairness, and the perceived benefits of public services. High tax morale generally leads to higher compliance rates, while low morale can result in widespread evasion.

6. Digital Taxation

The rise of the digital economy has created new challenges for tax authorities. Many countries are grappling with how to tax digital services provided by multinational corporations, leading to debates over "digital services taxes" and international tax reform.

7. Environmental Taxes

Environmental taxes, such as carbon taxes and pollution taxes, are used to promote sustainability by making polluting activities more expensive. Some countries have had success using these taxes to reduce emissions and encourage green technologies.

8. Tax Treaties

Tax treaties are agreements between countries designed to prevent double taxation and promote international trade and investment. They typically specify which country has the right to tax certain types of income and provide mechanisms for resolving disputes.

9. Tax Competition and Investment

Countries often compete to attract investment by offering lower tax rates, special incentives, or simpler tax systems. This "tax competition" can lead to a "race to the bottom," where countries continually lower rates to outdo each other, sometimes at the expense of public services.

Explore this theme in Chapter 40: The Tax Olympics – Global Competition and Chapter 39: The Tax Olympics – Opening Ceremony.

10. Tariffs and Trade Taxes

While this appendix focuses on income, corporate, and consumption taxes, tariffs (taxes on imports and exports) are also a crucial part of many countries' tax systems. Tariffs can protect local industries or raise revenue, but they can also spark trade disputes.
See the discussion of tariffs in Chapter 52: Economics of Tax – Filling the Coffers.

11. A Note on Tax Rates

Tax rates and rules change frequently and can vary within countries. For the latest information, consult official government websites or trusted financial resources. This appendix provides a broad overview—think of it as a starting point for your own research.

12. Cross-Links to Chapters

- **Tax Havens & Offshore Finance:** Chapter 24: Paradise Papers – The Offshore Echo
- **Inheritance & Estate Taxes:** Chapter 4: Inheritance Tax – The Grim Collector
- **Tax Competition:** Chapters 39 & 40: The Tax Olympics
- **Taxpayer Rights & Fairness:** Chapter 36: The Taxpayer's Bill of Rights – Taking a Stand
- **Economic Impact of Tax:** Chapter 52: Economics of Tax – Filling the Coffers
- **Psychological Impact:** Chapter 8: Psyche Tax – The Tax on Feelings

Appendix F

The Process of Enacting Tax Legislation

Introduction

Tax laws don't just appear—they are the result of a complex process involving many players. While this appendix outlines a typical process, every country's legislative system is unique. Use this as a general guide and be sure to research the specific process in your own country for a deeper understanding.

1. How Tax Laws Are Made: A General Overview

1. Initiation

A new tax law often starts as a proposal from the government's finance ministry or treasury, sometimes in response to economic needs, political promises, or public demand. In some countries, legislators or committees can also propose tax bills.

2. Drafting the Bill

Experts draft the bill, consulting with stakeholders such as businesses, advocacy groups, and economists. The draft outlines who will pay the tax, how much, and how it will be collected.

3. Parliamentary Stages

- **First Reading:** The bill is introduced to the legislature (parliament, congress, etc.). This is usually a formality.
- **Second Reading:** Lawmakers debate the general principles and objectives of the bill.
- **Committee Stage:** A smaller group examines the bill in detail, hears expert testimony, and suggests amendments.
- **Report Stage:** The full legislature reviews and votes on amendments.
- **Third Reading:** Final debate and vote on the complete bill.

4. Approval and Enactment

If the bill passes, it goes to the head of state (president, monarch, etc.) for formal approval. Once signed, it becomes law.

5. Implementation

Tax authorities issue guidance, update forms, and begin enforcement. Sometimes, new taxes are phased in over time to allow for adjustment.

Note:

This is a simplified example. The process can differ greatly between countries—some have only one legislative chamber, others have two; some require public referenda, others do not. For a deeper understanding, research the legislative process in your own country.

2. Role of Independent Agencies

In many countries, independent fiscal agencies or parliamentary budget office's provide objective analysis and advice on tax proposals. These agencies can help lawmakers make informed decisions by assessing the potential economic and social impacts of proposed tax changes.

3. Public Consultation Mechanisms

Governments often consult with the public on tax policy through various mechanisms, such as online forums, public hearings, and advisory committees. These consultations allow citizens and stakeholders to provide input and influence the legislative process.

4. Impact Assessments

Before enacting new tax laws, governments often conduct impact assessments to evaluate the potential economic, social, and environmental consequences. These assessments can help lawmakers identify potential unintended consequences and make adjustments to the proposed legislation.

5. Sunset Clauses

Some tax laws include sunset clauses, which automatically repeal the law after a certain period. Sunset clauses can be used to ensure that tax laws are regularly reviewed and updated to reflect changing economic conditions.

6. Tax Law Interpretation

Tax laws are often complex and subject to interpretation. Courts and tax authorities play a crucial role in interpreting tax laws and resolving disputes. Legal precedent is an important factor in tax law interpretation.

7. Case Studies of Failed Tax Reforms

Not all tax reforms are successful. There are many examples of tax reforms that failed to pass or were later repealed due to political opposition, economic concerns, or unintended consequences. Studying these failures can provide valuable lessons for policymakers.

For more on how tax laws affect real people, see Chapter 36: The Taxpayer's Bill of Rights – Taking a Stand and Chapter 52: Economics of Tax – Filling the Coffers.

8. Who's Involved?

- **Government:** Proposes and drafts new tax laws, manages implementation.
- **Legislators:** Debate, amend, and vote on tax bills; represent the interests of their constituents.
- **Lobbyists:** Advocate for or against provisions on behalf of businesses, unions, or advocacy groups.
- **The Public:** Can influence legislation through consultations, petitions, and public campaigns.

9. Tax Competition and Tariffs

Countries sometimes compete to attract investment by lowering tax rates or offering incentives—a phenomenon known as "tax competition." This can lead to a "race to the bottom," where countries continually lower rates to outdo each other, sometimes at the expense of public services.

See Chapters 39 & 40: The Tax Olympics for a narrative exploration of this theme.

Tariffs—taxes on imports and exports—are another tool governments use, often to protect local industries or raise revenue.

For more on tariffs, see Chapter 52: Economics of Tax – Filling the Coffers.

10. A Note for the Curious Reader

Every country's process for enacting tax legislation is different. If you're interested in how your country makes tax laws, look up your national parliament or government's official website. Understanding this process is a powerful tool for any citizen, not just tax professionals.

11. Cross-Links to Chapters

- **Taxpayer Rights & Lawmaking:** Chapter 36: The Taxpayer's Bill of Rights – Taking a Stand
- **Tax Competition:** Chapters 39 & 40: The Tax Olympics
- **Economic Impact & Tariffs:** Chapter 52: Economics of Tax – Filling the Coffers

Closing Note from the Author

Dear Reader,

First of all, congratulations! You've made it to the end of If Taxes Were People. That alone deserves a round of applause (and maybe a tax deduction for "mental endurance"). Whether you picked up this book out of curiosity, frustration, or sheer desperation to make sense of the tax system, I hope it's been an entertaining and enlightening journey.

When I first set out to write this book, I had one goal in mind: to make taxes less terrifying. Let's face it—taxes are one of life's great inevitabilities, right up there with death, bad Wi-Fi, and the awkward silence after you tell a joke that doesn't land. But unlike those other inevitabilities, taxes are something we can learn to understand, navigate, and even (dare I say it) appreciate.

Through Sam Harper's chaotic, coffee-fueled adventures, I wanted to show that taxes, while frustrating and complex, are not the enemy. They're a tool—a messy, imperfect, but ultimately necessary tool that helps build the world we live in. From funding schools and hospitals to maintaining roads and public safety, taxes are the glue that holds society together. And yes, sometimes that glue feels more like duct tape, but it gets the job done.

Why Humor?

You might be wondering why I chose to tackle such a dry and intimidating topic with humor and personification. The answer is simple: taxes are already stressful enough. Most of us dread tax season, not just because of the money involved but because of the sheer complexity of it all. By turning taxes into characters—each with their own quirks, flaws, and personalities—I hoped to make the subject more relatable and less overwhelming.

After all, it's easier to laugh at Income Tax when you imagine him as a stern but well-meaning bureaucrat, or to roll your eyes at Sales Tax when you picture him lurking at the checkout counter, ready to take his cut. Humor has a way of breaking down barriers, and if this book has made you chuckle even once, then I consider that a win.

What I Hope You've Learned

While this book is primarily a work of fiction and satire, it's also rooted in real-world concepts. My hope is that you've come away with a better understanding of how taxes work, why they exist, and how they impact our lives. Here are a few key takeaways I hope you'll remember:

Taxes Are a Reflection of Society's Values

Every tax, from Carbon Tax to Sin Tax, exists for a reason. They reflect what we prioritize as a society—whether it's protecting the environment, funding public services, or discouraging harmful behaviors. Understanding this can help us see taxes not just as a burden but as a tool for shaping the world we want to live in.

Knowledge Is Power

The more you understand about taxes, the less intimidating they become. Knowing your rights, your obligations, and your options can make a huge difference. Whether it's claiming deductions, avoiding penalties, or simply filing on time, a little knowledge goes a long way.

It's Okay to Be Frustrated

Let's be honest, taxes can be confusing, unfair, and downright annoying. It's okay to feel frustrated. But instead of letting that frustration consume you, use it as motivation to learn, ask questions, and advocate for a better system.

You're Not Alone

Every taxpayer, from the smallest business owner to the wealthiest corporation, has to deal with taxes. It's a shared experience, and while it may not be fun, it's something we all navigate together. And as Sam Harper learned, there's a strange kind of solidarity in that.

A Call to Action

If there's one thing I want you to take away from this book, it's this: taxes are not set in stone. They're created by people, for people, and they can be changed, improved, and simplified. As a taxpayer, you have a voice. Whether it's voting for policies you believe in, advocating for transparency and fairness, or simply staying informed, you have the power to shape the system.

So, the next time you're staring at a pile of tax forms, feeling overwhelmed and ready to give up, remember Sam Harper. If he can survive Audit Tax, Bracket Creep, and a time-traveling adventure through the history of taxation, you can survive tax season. And who knows? Maybe you'll even come to appreciate the role taxes play in building a better world.

A Final Thank You

Thank you for joining me on this journey. Writing this book has been an adventure in itself, and I'm grateful to have shared it with you. Whether you're a seasoned taxpayer, a curious reader, or someone who just wanted a good laugh, I hope this book has given you a new perspective on taxes—and maybe even a few tools to make them a little less daunting.

And remember taxes may be inevitable, but so is your ability to navigate them. With a little knowledge, a lot of humor, and maybe a cup of coffee (or two), you've got this.

Here's to surviving taxes—and thriving despite them.

Sincerely,

Abbas Sadak
Author of *If Taxes Were People*

www.ingramcontent.com/pod-product-compliance
Lightning Source LLC
LaVergne TN
LVHW052241200926
848481LV00002B/239